Decision Making for Technology Executives:
Using Multiple Perspectives to Improve Performance

For a complete listing of the *Artech House Technology Management and Professional Development Library*, turn to the back of this book.

Decision Making for Technology Executives:
Using Multiple Perspectives to Improve Performance

Harold A. Linstone

Artech House
Boston • London

Library of Congress Cataloging-in-Publication Data
Linstone, Harold A.
   Decision making for technology excutives : using multiple
perspectives to improve performance / Harold A. Linstone
      p.   cm. — (Artech House technology management and
professional development library)
   Includes bibliographical references and index.
   ISBN 0-89006-403-2 (alk. paper)
   1. Decision making   2. Technology-- Management.   I. Title.
II. Series: Artech House professional developement and technology
management library
T57.95. L55   1999
658.4 '03—DC21   99-19222
                                                           CIP

British Library Cataloguing in Publication Data
Linstone, Harold A.
Decision making for technology excutives : using multiple
perspectives to improve performance. -   (Artech House
 technology management and professional developement library)
   1. Decision making 2. Performance
   I. Title
   658.4 ' 03

   ISBN 0-89006-403-2

Cover design by Lynda Fishbourne

International Standard Book Number: 658.4 ' 03
Library of Congress Catalog Card Number: 99-19222

10 9 8 7 6 5 4 3 2 1

In memory of my parents,
who opened my mind to many perspectives.

Contents

Foreword

The toys with which we play tell us a lot about ourselves. Good toys, especially of the puzzle or game variety, are fun for several reasons. First, they are challenging. The correct solution is usually not readily apparent or easily attainable. A good puzzle or game demands some skill, knowledge, or dexterity. Second, unlike life, puzzles and games generally produce clear-cut winners or losers, experts versus novices. Generally one and only one correct solution exists. Furthermore, it is generally very clear when one has either solved the puzzle or not. It is also rather easy to distinguish between expert and novice play. Thus, there is little, if any, doubt regarding good versus bad performance. As a result, puzzles afford an immense degree of satisfaction to one who is able to work through them. In fact, such satisfaction is often in direct proportion to the degree of frustration inherent in getting to the correct solution. Third, and this aspect is generally least mentioned of all, a good game or puzzle is aesthetic. Either the pieces themselves or the puzzle as a whole has a nice shape. In other cases, the solution itself is elegant or aesthetically pleasing. Fourth, the means or process of arriving at the correct answer must itself be interesting or intrinsically rewarding. In other words, it must be fun or rewarding to "spend" one's time on playing the game. Fifth, one generally must be able to share one's skill or excellence with others. Even the most solitary of games has some social or sharing aspect, even if it is only to brag to others how good one is.

One of the reasons for the enormous popularity of Rubik's Cube was that it possessed all of these qualities to a high degree. Certainly, its aesthetic appeal was extremely high, not to mention its great portability. No one who ever saw it could fail to be attracted to it; its shape and colors alone exerted a magnetic appeal.

And yet, for all the endearing and fascinating qualities of games and puzzles, problems involving human beings are infinitely more intriguing and, by the same token, infinitely more frustrating. It is absolutely vital to appreciate the differences between the two because too many people assume that the way we solve puzzles should be the standard against which we measure success in solving society's problems. The plain fact of the matter is that such problems are radically different from puzzles of the Rubik's Cube variety in at least one very crucial respect. Unlike puzzles, society's problems do not have a single, correct solution that is recognized and accepted as such by all the contending parties who are affected by the problem or who have a strong opinion on it. Problems like beauty and ugliness reside in the eye and, ultimately, in the mind of the beholder. People have such different values and start from completely different ideas as to what society should be, that what is a problem and a good solution for one person is often an irrelevant, stupid, silly, or even evil idea for another. If these problems bear any resemblance to Rubik's Cube, it is only because each person has his or her own unique cube. No two cubes are exactly alike. If your cube has six sides, then mine has eight (a very strange "cube" indeed). If the colored sides of your cube are red, blue, green, white, orange, and black, for example, then mine are light gray, dark gray, a mixture of black and blue and brown. Even stranger, what is a nicely ordered shape to you, like a cube, may be a phantom object to me that changes its shape over time and in different parts of the country—a condition that is certainly true of social problems.

Why belabor all of this? For several reasons. Virtually all significant problems involve human beings, either singly or collectively. Business and military decisions, economic and health care planning, the diffusion of technology, the administration of justice, even the Apollo lunar and space shuttle programs cannot be adequately understood on a purely technical level. If sociotechnical and social systems are fundamentally not like Rubik's Cube, then we are seriously remiss in how we prepare people for working on a vast array of important problems and in the institutions we have designed for managing them in our society at large. Except for the humanities, education in the social and technical professions and sciences largely prepares people for tackling problems of the Rubik's Cube variety. Unless a problem is clearly stated and accepted by all parties as the "same," it is likely to be rejected as a "problem." Students from the humanities really fare no better. While they are certainly exposed to issues that have no single, widely agreed on solution, let alone formulation, only the most brilliant, to put it mildly, can translate this "exposure" from the great issues of the past to proposing novel solutions to the important issues of the present. Further, the present state of society renders the way we have designed education more suspect than ever. No single profession has a monopoly on defining or solving the great issues of the day. At every twist and turn, we are constantly reminded of the overwhelming complexity and interdependency of all issues. We live in a world wherein the so-called technical aspects of issues cannot be clearly separated from the social, legal, political, and moral aspects, if the language of "aspects" is even an acceptable way to think anymore. I defy anyone to try to separate the so-called technical aspects of Three Mile Island or the abortion controversy from the legal, political, and moral aspects. Such a separation is, depending upon one's morality and politics, either immoral or politically irresponsible, if not just plain artificial and naive.

Alvin Toffler, in his book *The Third Wave*, may have put it best of all. Most of our institutions, including the modern university, were designed during the Second Wave, the age of the machine and the Industrial Revolution. One of the nice characteristics of a machine is that by definition it can be taken apart. It can be broken down into its separate parts, and the parts can be examined independently of one another. We cannot do this for social problems at all. Why? Because everything about them is subject to controversy. What's a "part" to one group is not to another, for example.

What then can we do? To start, we can recognize that at least four very different attitudes toward sociotechnical and social problems crop up repeatedly no matter what the issue. Second, our very survival, more than at any other time in our history, depends on our learning how to blend these four attitudes into a coordinated whole.

In their most extreme form, I have labeled these four attitudes or approaches: (1) the technological, quick-fix mentality; (2) the technological daydreaming mentality; (3) social daydreaming; and (4) social traditionalism.

Of these four approaches, the technological, quick-fix mentality is most prone to view problems in Rubik's Cube-like terms. This attitude also tends to dominate corporate and government life in America. When it comes to treating problems, despite insistence about problems' differences, for all practical purposes they are essentially the same. If problems cannot be defined and solved quickly (that is, in the very short run) and if complex problems do not have immediate, simple solutions, then this attitude leads to rejection; the problem is not worthy of even being considered a "problem."

A strong accompaniment of this attitude is a near exclusive focus on technical issues. Problems are discussed—even stronger, viewed—in highly complex technical terms, which are open only to "qualified experts." Some obvious examples are the economy, space research, almost all scientific research, and nuclear energy.

The near exclusive emphasis on technology means that those aspects of a problem that cannot be measured or are difficult to quantify are usually ignored. At its best, this position focuses on the doable, the feasible, and the sensible. Its insistence on measurement sets tough-minded standards of accountability; for something to be counted as worthy it must prove itself in the marketplace of goods, products, or ideas.

At its worst, this is short-term, myopic thinking. It sacrifices future businesses and ideas that, by definition, cannot be proven in the present for today's "bottom-line." Because problems are viewed as separate entities, each tends to be considered totally independent of the others. As a result, this attitude leads to a jump from issue to issue, problem to problem, without any overall scheme or plan.

Where the first attitude focuses on the here and now, the short term, what is known in terms of present, conventional, well-understood technology, the second attitude focuses on the technology of tomorrow. The best example of this approach is *Omni* magazine. The accent is on "the wonderful marvels of tomorrow's technology and how it is transforming our lives for the better." If we can only get through today's crises, then we are on "the verge of a revolution in thinking and technology that promises to transform us as 'never before'" or some such Sci-Fi public relations talk.

At its best, this attitude is marvelous for opening up new possibilities of what we might be, of suggesting sorely needed new ideas, and of reformulating old problems in such a way that entirely new solutions suggest themselves. At its worst, it is impractical daydreaming, of extending today's technologically fixated society indefinitely into the future and suggesting some marvelous technology wonder world without suggesting any sensible way of how to get it from horrible here to terrific there.

The third attitude is similar to the second in that the emphasis in both is on tomorrow. The main difference is that where the second attitude is focused exclusively on technology, the third is focused on people—on interpersonal relations at the community and societal levels. This attitude is concerned with the society of the future from a human standpoint. What new forms of human communities, living arrangements, and institutions will there be? What will it mean to be human in the future? Will our institutions be more effective from a human perspective? The best and the worst of this attitude parallels that of the second.

Finally, the last attitude parallels the first in that both are concerned with the here and now, the immediate short term, or the recent past. The difference is that the fourth attitude is concerned exclusively with people. The emphasis of this approach is on traditionally acceptable human behavior or time-tested standards of conduct. Religious fundamentalists are a good example. Anything that goes against the grain of traditional, sanctioned behavior is suspect, if not immoral.

Is it possible to get the best of each approach without the worst? Notice that we did not ask, "What is *the* answer?" for that would be to take us back into the exclusive clutches of the first approach.

Three considerations are critical. Unfortunately none of them are easy to realize, nor do we know how to do any of them truly well. The first, as I have pointed out, is to recognize that on all issues of any significance all four attitudes will either be present from the beginning or will surface in opposition to the others. By itself, this is healthy since it tends to counteract the one-sidedness of any approach. The second point is to appreciate that all four attitudes have a legitimate role to play in complex issues. This may be the hardest of all to do, for it demands distinguishing between legitimate and extreme forms of each attitude. By definition, an extreme position is one that recognizes only itself as legitimate. The difficulty with this is that nearly every position in our society thereby becomes extreme. Although difficult, this unfortunately may be the case. A pertinent example is, again, religious fundamentalism. More Americans than we may suspect may indeed identify with the issues raised by, say, the Christian Coalition. As Yankelovich pointed out in an article in *Psychology Today*, all of us, no matter what our social standing, have felt victimized by something in our society: crime, job insecurity, family instability, stress, anxiety, a general feeling of loss of control, or a growing inability to feel in charge of anything whatsoever. This does not mean, however, that Americans are ready to identify with the Christian Coalition's solution, their particular brand of social or moral traditionalism. The difficulty is to recognize *some* of the legitimacy of the concerns of religious fundamentalists even if—particularly all the more that—we do not like the form in which they are expressed or their proposed solutions.

The third point is no less difficult. This is the recognition that in reality all of the four approaches depend on one another, all the more that they oppose one another. No attitude can in actuality really go-it-alone. Consider former President Reagan's economic program. It was a mixture of all four attitudes. Despite all protests to the contrary, it certainly had its technological quick-fix aspects. Given the intolerance of doubt and uncertainty, characteristic of life at the national level, one had no option but to overstate its magic cure-alls, particularly their potency. At the same time, we were instructed to "give the program a chance to work, give it enough time to prove itself in the future." Whoever said that religious belief is not a strong factor in *every* economic program?

All of which finally leads me to the present book. This volume is one of the very few of which I know that is a serious and sustained effort at finding a methodology for accomplishing the difficult task of blending the different attitudes toward problem solving that I have been discussing. This would be reason enough to applaud it. That it is also an excellent example of what it preaches is added cause for celebration. If my joy is tempered at all, it is only because the world is probably still unprepared to hear this book's message, let alone really take it seriously. As a culture we are still too hooked on puzzles to appreciate the vital differences between serious problem solving and toying with games.

If ever there was a time when we needed to understand the dynamics of complex problems—how to change, renew our institutions, propose new solutions to old problems, and create new problems that are capable of revitalizing our will and spirit—then surely that time is now. The problems we face at present are so complex that they defy simple statements, let alone simple solutions. The age of simple solutions, like that of cheap energy, is over. The problems we face make Rubik's Cube seem literally like child's play.

Ian I. Mitroff
Harold Quinton Distinguished Professor of Business Policy
Department of Management and Policy Sciences
Graduate School of Business
University of Southern California

Preface

The concept of multiple perspectives is presented in this work as a practical means to bridge the wide gap that exists between analysis and decision making in the realm of sociotechnical systems. It is a revised and updated version of my book *Multiple Perspectives for Decision Making: Bridging the Gap Between Analysis and Action*, which was published in 1984 by North-Holland.

Following a brief introduction (Chapter 1), we discuss the traditional "technological" approach exemplified by systems analysis, management science, and similar methods and focus on its limitations (Chapter 2). Our proposed approach is presented in Chapter 3. In consonance with the law that "an ounce of application is worth a ton of abstraction," Chapters 4 to 6 focus on a wide spectrum of illustrations and applications, drawn from both public and private sectors, ranging from transportation system development (aircraft and airport) to severe industrial accidents (oil transportation and chemical manufacturing). The use of multiple perspectives in risk assessment is followed by its application to technological forecasting and corporate planning (Chapter 7). Next we look ahead with particular attention to the new developments in complexity science, its relation to our approach, and its potential benefits for sociotechnical system management (Chapter 8). The book concludes with guidelines for the practitioner (Chapter 9).

On the basis of the applications to date, we envision the user to be an executive or engineer in the private or public sector. Corporate managers and business strategists, policy and systems analysts, operations researchers and management scientists, government agency heads, and institutional administrators may also find the concept of practical value. Finally, it can add new dimensions to the education of students in fields such as engineering, computer science, business, and economics—who will be challenged in the twenty-first century by the increasingly complex, interconnected environment of the global village created by information technology.

Acknowledgments

The concept owes its development to Graham Allison's book, *Essence of Decision: Explaining the Cuban Missile Crisis*, and to West Churchman's writings on inquiring systems. It has also benefitted from two grants by the National Science Foundation. These debts are gratefully acknowledged.

I express my deep appreciation to the following contributors who helped to make this work possible. I would also like to thank my former colleagues at Hughes Aircraft and Lockheed who provided me with invaluable opportunities to observe and participate in real-life planning and decision making. Finally, I thank my doctoral students in the Systems Science Ph.D. Program at Portland State University for their faith, perceptions, and unstinting efforts to apply the concept.

HAROLD A. LINSTONE
Lake Oswego, Oregon
June 15, 1998

Contributors

Arnold J. Meltsner (Section 9.1 and Appendix A.5)
Professor Emeritus at the Graduate School of Public Policy, University of California, Berkeley, CA; author of *Policy Analysts in the Bureaucracy* and *Rules for Rulers*; and editor of *Politics and the Oval Office*.

B. Bowonder (Section 6.3)
Chairman, Centre for Energy, Environment, and Technology, Administrative Staff College of India, Hyderabad, India.

Bruce B. Clary (Section 4.2)
Professor and Chair of the Public Policy and Management Program in the Edmund F. Muskie School of Public Service, University of Southern Maine, Portland, ME; formerly Assistant Professor of Public Administration, Portland State University, Portland, OR.

Peter G. Cook (Section 5.2)

Formerly Manager of Software Development, Four-Phase Systems, Inc., Cupertino, CA, and student in Systems Science Ph.D. Program, Portland State University.

Andrew R. Goetz (Section 4.3)

Professor, Department of Geography and Center for Transportation Studies, University of Denver, Denver, CO.

Steve Hawke (Section 5.1)

Vice President, Delivery System Planning and Engineering, Portland General Electric Co., Portland, OR.

John S. Pearson, Jr. (Section 4.1)

Former Senior Vice President, Corporate Development, Surety Life Insurance Co., and student in Systems Science Ph.D. Program, Portland State University.

Joseph S. Szyliowicz (Section 4.3)

Professor, Graduate School of International Studies and Center for Transportation Studies, University of Denver, Denver, CO.

1

Introduction

Two things fill my heart with never-ending awe: the complexity of the total
social system . . . and the self within.

> Paraphrase of Immanuel Kant by C. West Churchman

The greatest danger in times of turbulence is not turbulence; it is to act
with yesterday's logic.

> Peter Drucker

We begin with three brief illustrations to indicate the path on which we are
embarking to recognize and bridge the gap between the technologist/engineer
and the executive/manager or between analysis and action. The approach we
shall use is that of viewing complex systems and decisions about them from
different perspectives, each providing insights not attainable with the others.

- Professor Jay Forrester of the Massachusetts Institute of Technology
  (MIT) has applied techniques from electrical engineering, specifically
  system dynamics, to model a corporation. His approach is known as
  Industrial Dynamics. Using key variables and their past relationships,
  he derives a set of equations that form the basis of computer runs that
  project the system behavior incrementally into the future. The model
  provides important insights about corporations, especially the flows of
  materials and personnel within various subunits over a period of time.
  In contrast, the brilliant Florentine civil servant Niccolò Machiavelli in

Discourses (1531) and *The Prince* (1532) offered very different insights concerning organizations, for example, practical guidelines on maintaining power and exercising effective control. Machiavelli's insights have been recognized to be quite relevant for the modern corporation, as evidenced in Antony Jay's 1948 book *Management and Machiavelli*. Both Forrester and Machiavelli are looking at organizations, but from very different angles: one through the eyes of an analyst, the other through the eyes of a political thinker.

- Harvard's Graham Allison examined the Cuban missile crisis and found some actions difficult to explain on rational grounds. For example, the shipping of the missiles from Russia to Cuba was camouflaged very carefully using freighters normally carrying cargo, such as lumber, and emptying the Cuban port of arrival of all Cubans. However, the building of the missile silos in Cuba by the Russians was easily visible from the air. The Russians knew we had U-2 spy planes (they had shot one down over Russia) and Cuba was less than one hundred miles from U.S. soil. This pattern makes no sense from a rational actor point of view—either use high security consistently or operate in the open. Only when Allison realized that the control of the shipping and the silo construction was split between two different organizations, the KGB and the military Corps of Engineers, respectively, each with distinct modus operandi, did the operation make sense.

- A corporate aerospace executive must make a decision about a new line of business. There is a detailed cost-benefit analysis conducted by his planning staff recommending this diversification as the "optimum" alternative. The executive does not make the final decision based on this report, which he considers a good one. He talks to various department heads to determine whether there is strong support or opposition to the proposal. Department B may oppose it on parochial grounds: the project would go to Department A and B would lose research and devlopment funding. Over the weekend he sees an old friend, the executive of a corporation in a different field, whose judgment he values and he discusses the idea with him. Of course, he also draws on his own intuition. On Monday he returns to the office and makes the decision to move forward. No formal weighting formula has been used in integrating his various inputs.

These three vignettes have one common characteristic: In every case we have more than one way of looking at a system and we find that each way yields insights about it that are not obtainable with the others.

"Scientific management" began with Frederick Taylor in 1911 and gathered steam with World War II's "operations research," a scientific method of providing managers with a quantitative basis for decisions regarding operations under their control [1]. The Battle of the Atlantic called for submarine search and the Battle of Britain for vectoring of interceptor aircraft. Mathematical analysis could and did offer significant help.[1] The War also was a turning point in the design of new systems, marking a level of complexity that required "systems analysis." Radar, fire control systems, and guided missiles, as well as nuclear weapon strategy created a strong need for scientific approaches in developing new mission requirements, system designs, and trade-offs. Researchers developed a game theory and decision analysis as well as technological forecasting tools. The flowering of Camelot-on-the-Potomac brought systems analysis to Washington. Cost-effectiveness analysis and the Planning-Programming-Budgeting System became de rigueur among the cognoscenti in the bureaucracy. And the industrial part of the defense complex had to learn to play the game.

By 1967, the Dean of the School of Electrical Engineering of MIT proclaimed:

> I doubt if there is any such thing as an urban crisis, but if there were, MIT
> could lick it in the same way we handled the Second World War [2].

The same year Congressman Emilio Q. Daddario introduced to Congress H.R. 6698, a bill designed to stimulate discussions to formalize the concept of technology assessment and strengthen the legislative process in the area of technology policy. The pinnacle of the expectations placed on systems analysis at the time is found in Max Ways' survey "The Road to 1977" in *Fortune*:

> The further advance of this new style [systems analysis] is the most significant prediction that can be made about the next ten years. By 1977 this new way of dealing with the future will be recognized at home and abroad as a salient American characteristic [3].

The optimism exuded by Ways and many others was based on solid evidence of the success of systems analysis[2] in dealing with purely technological

---

1. Subsequently, "management science" extended the approach to a wide spectrum of business operations.
2. For convenience we shall use this as an umbrella label to include at times various related subjects and spin-offs, such as operations research, management science, cost-benefit analysis, risk analysis, decision analysis, technological forecasting, technology assessment, and impact analysis.

systems and the anticipation of its wider application to the design of, and to decisions involving, systems that are not purely technological.

A decade later, bleak reality had displaced euphoria; this skepticism is reflected in the words of Ida Hoos:

> In our technological era, the dominant paradigm is so technically oriented that most of our problems are defined as technical in nature and assigned the same treatment—doctoring by systems analysts. The "experts" are methodological Merlins . . . Technology assessments are conducted by latter-day intellectual condottieri, the brains-for-hire . . . Most of the technology assessments I have reviewed . . . must be taken with a large measure of skepticism lest they lead us to regrettable, if not disastrous, conclusions [4].

Nuclear war, as exemplified by a U.S.–Soviet nuclear weapons exchange, had earlier been cited as ideally suitable to systems analysis. It was seen as a "well-structured" system, and endless computer modeling and gaming were conducted. But Fallows observed:

> The best minds of the defense conmmunity have been drawn toward nuclear analysis, but so were the best minds to be found in the monastery, arguing the Albigensian heresy in the fourteenth century [5].

The approach works as long as other nuclear powers do the same. But because no one has experience fighting a nuclear war, the theoretical scenarios had "no more foundation in fact than other theologians' fiery visions of hell" [5]. And in an era of nuclear proliferation, a heretic will arise sooner or later.[3]

Systems analysis may be well-intentioned in its approach to sociotechnical systems, but history is replete with examples of well-intentioned efforts culminating in evil. As the Declaration of the Rights of Man in 1789 ended in the Reign of Terror, the drive for quantifiable measures of effectiveness in Vietnam led "the best and the brightest" to the concept of the body count, which was then travestied in incidents such as the massacre of unarmed civilians at My Lai.

---

3. The whole deterrence concept depends on "rational" decision making. Yet history is hardly reassuring on this point when we look at other mass destruction decisions. One-quarter of Europe's population died in the Thirty Years' War over a religious question; one-third of Great Britain's population was killed in the War of the Roses over an argument between two families. In our time, six million Jews were killed by a culturally advanced nation to preserve its Aryan purity and millions were killed in Cambodia because they were not deemed reeducatable.

The routines of science and technology, development of information theory, and transformation of management and policy into "sciences" all made complex, living organisms into mechanistic feedback loops. Systems theorists' efforts at *Redesigning the Future* (Ackoff), creating a *Liberty Machine* (Beer), developing a *World Dynamics* model (Forrester), and *A Strategy for the Future* (Laszlo) are seen as the ultimate hubris.[4] To Thompson "the tongue cannot taste itself, the mind cannot know itself, and the system cannot model itself" [8]. To Adams, these models "can never be anything but cargo cult models, superficial caricatures of one minority's view of the world" [9].

Some mavericks had, in fact, questioned the paradigm of rationality for decades. Chester I. Barnard's work on executive decision making in 1938 recognized the inadequacy of the economists' concept of rationality as well as the distinction between organizational and personal decisions [10]. This work was a precursor to Nobel Laureate Herbert Simon's important principle of "bounded rationality" as an organizational phenomenon. In his own words:

> Rationality then does not determine behavior . . . [B]ehavior is determined by the irrational and nonrational elements that bound the area of rationality [11].

= we don't know what's going on.

Hugh Miser in his state-of-the-art review of systems analysis and operations research for the centennial issue of *Science* recalls Simon's description of systems analysis as a "celebration of human rationality" but, with the blinkered mindset of the analyst, interprets that statement to fit his own world view:

> The challenge is to enlarge this celebration to include the rational management of all of society's systems and their problems [12].

Ida Hoos [13] refers to this as the "man on the moon" magic: that is, the oft-repeated rhetorical question, "If we can put a man on the moon, why can't we _____?" where the blank can be filled in by (1) "reduce crime in our cities," (2) "develop an adequate public transportation system," (3) "rid America of poverty," (4) "improve our education system," and (5) "provide work for all," and so on.

In the area of corporate management, Hayes and Abernathy observed that principles of management fashionable in the 1960s and 1970s encour-

---

4. In fairness, we must also recognize that general systems theorists, such as Gerald Weinberg [6] and cyberneticists such as Heinz Von Foerster [7] have well understood the limitations of the conventional systems approach and the need for complementary world views.

aged in American managers a preference for "analytic detachment rather than insight that comes from 'hands-on' experience"[14]. Disillusionment and reaction became evident here also: by 1982 corporate strategists were "under fire" [15].

When Richard M. Cyert, coauthor of the classic *A Behavioral Theory of the Firm* later became president of Carnegie-Mellon University, he mused:

> As a professor of organization theory and management, I used to wonder about the practical value of these academic fields. For the last eight years, I've had some first-hand experience finding out . . . And I've concluded that the study of management makes a useful, but only a limited, contribution to the practicing manager.
>
> Organization theory hasn't provided me any framework to judge possible appointees. The theory hasn't even been very useful in developing new organizational structures . . . Finally, theory doesn't shed much light on how a manager should get information about how his organization operates [16].

My 20 years of systems analysis activity—in industry (corporate planning), a nonprofit institute (RAND), and academe (developing a systems science doctoral program)—mirrored this shift from confidence to concern. I experienced a deepening frustration with the chasm between systems analysis and decision making [17]. And my conviction grew that "better" systems analysis would not bridge this chasm. My 1976–1978 project on *The Use of Structural Modeling for Technology Assessment* for the National Science Foundation made the dilemma very vivid. In the "Conclusion" section of the final report, I wrote:

> There is still only lip service paid to any but "rational" or traditional "systems analysis" approaches and models in addressing the technology assessment process [18].

Decision making inherently involves organizations and individuals whose perspectives are very different from those of "rational" systems analysts or technology assessors. The signposts that showed me a way out of the dilemma were two books published in 1971: West Churchman's *The Design of Inquiring Systems* [19] and Graham Allison's *Essence Decision: Explaining the Cuban Missile Crisis* [20]. Churchman examined a variety of modes of systemic inquiry, such as data-based and model-based modes, and focused my attention on a "Singerian" mode that sweeps in all other inquiring systems. It is pragmatic, takes holistic thinking seriously, and recognizes that the system designer or analyst is inexorably a part of the system.

Allison used three "models" by which to "see" a single decision process: the rational actor model (I), the organizational process model (II), and the bureaucratic politics model (III). Not surprisingly, Allison himself found model III to be a more difficult challenge than models I and II: "Model III tells a fascinating story but is enormously complex. The information requirements are often overwhelming" [20]. It has taken the collapse of the Soviet Union and the opening up of secret files more than thirty years after the Cuban missile crisis to unearth significant details on Soviet operations and perspectives highly relevant for Allison's models II and III. Following Allison, Steinbruner's *The Cybernetic Theory of Decision* [21] also considered three paradigms: analytic, cybernetic, and cognitive. This work is the direct result of my encounters with Churchman and Allison.

Perspectives that differ in their underlying paradigms unavoidably create a kind of "Catch 22" situation. In consonance with the modes of inquiry preferred by scientists and technologists, we could regard analyses such as *technology assessment* (TA) as scientific endeavors and deal with the formulation of theorems, design of models, and validation of hypotheses. But virtually all writers on TA now agree that it is not a science—some call it an art. And our proposed concept, the use of multiple perspectives, inevitably moves us beyond the paradigms associated with science and technology. Experimental design and validation of hypotheses are intraparadigmatic: they operate only within the framework of a perspective. They cannot prove that any one model gives the most useful or "correct" representation of reality; they cannot give assurance that the variables chosen are sufficiently inclusive or appropriate. They tell us nothing about other models or perspectives.

Were we able to confine ourselves to the paradigms of science and technology, our work would be viewed with empathy by those who embrace that world view, including most practitioners of these analyses. Yet it is precisely the focus on a single perspective or world view—that of the "rational actor"—that is, in our opinion, the primary source of their inadequacy. Thus we may invoke the wrath of the purists; the use of multiple perspectives makes us *ipso facto* heretical to the fervent adherents of any one perspective. Orthodox systems analysts and management scientists are likely to view us as iconoclasts. Our purpose, however, is not to debunk or to urge abandonment of their conventional modes of analysis but to create or nourish an awareness of the need to step beyond the confines of their paradigms. The proposed route is that of pluralism or multiplicity of perspectives.

It is not an easy path for most. Westerners find it difficult to grasp the Japanese acceptance of two religions simultaneously: Buddhism and Shintoism.

Technologists may find it even more difficult to live with at least three perspectives simultaneously. Openness to other paradigms alien to one's own requires a level of empathy that is not common. But it may prove crucial.

Since its development, the concept of multiple perspectives has been demonstrated in a variety of contexts, for example, industrial accident examination, electronic funds transfer feasibility, and hydropower development. The illustrations in this book also cover a wide spectrum. They have in common the following factors:

- Ill-structured nature of the problem (typically sociotechnical systems);
- Significant organizational policy and/or decision aspects;
- Significant human aspects.

The innovation process from planning to implementation, public and private sector systems management, risk management, venture analysis, social/environmental impact assessment, and technology transfer all offer significant opportunities for the productive use of multiple perspectives.

References

[1]   Morse, P. M., and G.E. Kimball, *Methods of Operations Research*, New York, NY: MIT Press and John Wiley & Sons, Inc., 1952, p. 1.

[2]   Thompson, W. I., *At the Edge of History*, New York, NY: Harper and Row, 1971.

[3]   Ways, M., "The Road to 1977," *Fortune*, Vol. 75, No. 1, 1967, pp. 93–95 and 194–195.

[4]   Hoos, I. R., "Societal Aspects of Technology Assessment," *Technological Forecasting and Social Change*, Vol. 13, 1979, pp. 191–202.

[5]   Fallows, J., *National Defense*, New York, NY: Random House, 1981, pp. 140, 170.

[6]   Weinberg, G. M., *An Introduction to General Systems Thinking*, New York, NY: Wiley-Interscience, 1975.

[7]   Von Foerster, H., "The Curious Behavior of Complex Systems," *Futures Research: New Directions*, H. A. Linstone and W. H. C. Simmonds (eds.), Reading, MA: Addison-Wesley Publishing Co., 1977.

[8]   Thompson, W. I., *Evil and World Order*, New York, NY: Harper & Row, 1976.

[9]   Adams, J. G. U., "You're Never Alone with Schizophrenia," *Industrial Marketing Management.*, Vol. 4, 1972, pp. 441–447.

[10] Barnard, C. I., *The Functions of the Executive*, Cambridge, MA: Harvard University Press, 1938, pp. 187–189.

[11] Simon, H. A., *Administrative Behavior*, New York, NY: Macmillan, 1947, p. 241.

[12] Miser, H. J., "Operations Research and Systems Analysis," *Science,* Vol. 209, No. 4452, 1980, pp. 139–146.

[13] Hoos, I. R., *Systems Analysis in Public Policy: A Critique,* Berkeley, CA: University of California Press, 1972.

[14] Hayes, R. H., and W. J. Abernathy, "Managing Our Way to Economic Decline," *Harvard Business Review,* Vol. 58, No. 4, July–Aug. 1980, pp. 67–77.

[15] Kiechel, W., III, "Corporate Strategists Under Fire," *Fortune,* Vol. 106, 1982, pp. 34–39.

[16] Cyert, Richard M., *Wall Street Journal,* April 7, 1980.

[17] Linstone, H. A., "When Is a Need a Need?" *Technological Forecasting,* Vol. 1, 1969, pp. 55–71.

[18] Linstone, H. A., et al., "The Use of Structural Modeling for Technology Assessment," Futures Research Institute Report 78-1, Portland State University, Portland, OR, 1978, p. 132.

[19] Churchman, C. W., *The Design of Inquiring Systems,* New York, NY: Basic Books, 1971.

[20] Allison, G., *Essence of Decision: Explaining the Cuban Missile Crisis,* Boston, MA: Little, Brown and Co., 1971.

[21] Steinbruner, J. D., *The Cybernetic Theory of Decision,* Princeton, NJ: Princeton University Press, 1974.

2

The Usual Perspective and Its Limitations

Give a small boy a hammer, and he will find that everything he encounters
needs pounding.

Kaplan's Law of the Instrument

The greatest challenge today . . . in all of science is the accurate and complete description of complex systems. Scientists have broken down many
kinds of systems. The next step is to reassemble them, at least in mathematical models that capture the key properties of the entire ensembles . . .
That in simplest terms is the great challenge of scientific holism.

Edward O. Wilson, Consilience

Science and technology represent the most successful "religion" of modern
times. From Galileo to the Apollo lunar landing, from Darwin to recombinant
DNA, from Marconi to the internet, the operating principles or paradigms of
science and technology have yielded dazzling triumphs. In this world view,
which we shall label *the technical perspective* (or T), rationality and scientific
logic constitute the dominant paradigms (see Chapter 1, pp. 3–5). More specifically, it exhibits the following characteristics:

(1) The definition of "problems" abstracted from the world around us,
and the implicit assumption that problems can be "solved";

(2) Optimization, or the search for a best solution;

(3) Reductionism, that is, the study of a system in terms of a very limited
number of elements (or variables) and the interactions among them;

(4) Reliance on data and models, and combinations thereof, as modes of

inquiry;

(5) Quantification of information;

(6) Objectivity: the assumption that the scientist is an unbiased observer outside of the system he or she is studying; that is, truth is observer-invariant;

(7) Ignoring or avoiding the individual: a consequence of reductionism, perceived objectivity, and quantification (for example, the use of averages);

(8) A view of time movement as linear, that is, at a universally accepted pace reckoned by precise physical measurement with no consideration of differential time perceptions, planning horizons, and discount rates.

Applied mathematics and modeling have been used as tools by scientists and engineers for a very long time, and their evolution continues in accordance with these characteristics. They serve system designers remarkably well in the analysis of today's complex hardware and software.

Frequently, cause-and-effect modeling is carried out to study the static and dynamic behavior of the variables that describe the system and its environment. Structural models and system dynamics are illustrative of such tools [1]. Theoretical models are "validated" by empirical data. Rationality is assumed to determine decisions; for example, the alternative with the most efficient performance will be selected. Figure 2.1(a) schematically summarizes the general approach. A typical well-structured systems problem treated very successfully by such analysis is the optimization of the Long Island (NY) blood distribution system (from regional blood centers to hospitals). Because blood can be administered only within 21 days of collection, waste is a serious concern. The analysts were able to model the system and revise the distribution pattern to cut waste from 20% to 4% [2].

The success of this mode of thought and its paradigms led very naturally to increasing pressure to extend its use beyond science and technology, that is, to society and all its systems (Figure 2.1(b)). This attitude is typified by the planning, programming, and budgeting drive in the 1960s; the popularity of econometric and cost-benefit models in the 1970s; and corporate re-engineering in the 1990s. Organizations became cybernetic systems, utility theory determined preferences, social indicators were synthesized, decision analysis provided the key to decision making, and policy analysis selected strategies. There was a mathematical theory of war and, of course, "management science." Systems analysis was now described more broadly as the application of

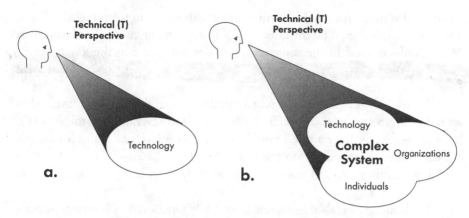

Figure 2.1 The technical perspective: (a) applied to purely technological systems and (b) extended to complex sociotechnical systems, which invariably involve social entities and individuals.

"the logical, quantitative, and structural tools of modern science and technology" to complex sociotechnical problems [3].

James Miller broke down all living systems, from cells to nations and supranational organizations, into subsystems that could be categorized in terms of 20 types. There are 8 subsystems that process matter and energy (for example, ingestion), 10 that process information (for example, memory and encoder), and 2 that process all three (for example, reproduction). Thus, the encoder in a cell is a component-producing hormone and in a national government a press secretary. All 20 subsystems are seen as critical to the continuation of life at any given level of living-system complexity and hence for the evolutionary process. This elaborate tour de force tried to do for systems what Mendeleyev's periodic table achieved for chemical elements [4].

Without question, the technical perspective is ideal for well-structured or "tame" systems problems. Why, then, does deep trouble result when relying on it in ill-structured or "wicked" problem areas? To answer this question, we will examine the eight characteristics listed previously in more detail.

2.1　The Problem-Solution View

When we talk about a "problem" we assume a solution exists. We have been brainwashed in school: a textbook presents a problem only if there is a solution (often in the back of the book). Such books do not point out that in the living world every new solution provided by a technology creates new problems.

Public health measures cut the death rate; but this result, in turn, fueled a global population explosion. The introduction of European agricultural techniques in Africa produces food in the short term and desertification in the long term. It would be more nearly correct to state that we shift problems rather than solve them.

Let us look at this situation schematically. A complex problem usually has several solution concepts (S), each of which leads to several new problems (P). In other words, we have a tree/branch structure with levels of P and S succeeding each other indefinitely into the future (Figure 2.2). Some Ps are of the diminishing ripple type, and some have an amplifying effect ("the cure is worse than the illness").

With complex real-life problems, we rarely have a clear statement or definition of the problem at the outset. If there are several stakeholders involved, each is likely to define the problem differently. One reason is that stakeholder A makes assumptions about stakeholder B that differ from those actually made by B (see Appendix A.3). Even if there is agreement as to the problem statement, we must recognize that it changes over time. Usually, a decision regarding a complex problem is made in steps and with each step the stakeholders and their assumptions are subject to change (see Appendix A.2).

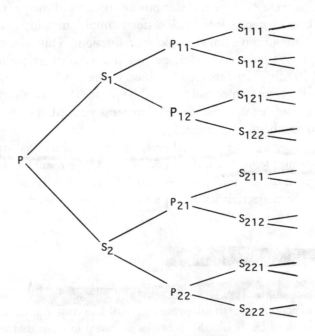

Figure 2.2 The problem-solution tree.

2.2 Optimization or the "Best" Solution Search

Cost-benefit analysis and linear programming are typical of the search for the optimal solution. It usually comes as a shock to those nurtured on this paradigm that complex living systems have not organized themselves in accordance with such an optimization principle. As Holling notes, ecological systems sacrifice efficiency for resilience or trade avoidance of failure (the *fail-safe* strategy familiar to engineers) for survival of failure (*safe-fail* strategy) [5]. They seek to minimize the cost of failure rather than the likelihood of failure. They strive to maximize their options rather than confine them by selecting the "best" one. They do not "manage" themselves by manacling themselves.[1] Evolution shows that their safe-fail strategy is eminently suited to a world that is inherently unpredictable at times.

2.3 Reductionism

Von Foerster's First Law [7] expresses the reductionist process rather well:

> The more complex the problem that is being ignored, the greater are the chances for fame and success.

If a system is complex, we simplify it by dividing it into subsystems. If we still cannot handle the subsystems, we reduce the system further. Finally we arrive at problems we can solve; fame and success come with publishing. The process leads inexorably to a plethora of papers that deal profoundly with unimportant, even trivial, problems.

A crucial assumption in reductionism is that the whole system is the sum of its parts and that, in splitting the system into its component parts, we can study each part in isolation. The implied assumption of linearity in the system unfortunately is quite uncharacteristic of complex systems. Indeed, the whole is more than the sum of its parts. There are few straight lines in our world. But the jump in difficulty of finding a solution when we move from linear to nonlinear

---

1. The dictionary tells us that "to manage" means "to control or direct the use of." As Von Foerster [6] notes, this implies that management reduces the degrees of freedom of the technological system being managed. In probing more deeply, it is ominous to find that "manage" is related to the word "manacle," which is "a device for confining the hands, usually consisting of two metal rings that are fastened about the wrist and joined by a metal chain." Much of American industry looks at technology assessment and environmental impact statements in precisely these terms, that is, as efforts to shackle technology.

systems is enormous.[2] Hence the predilection for linearization is as understandable in the case of scientists and technologists today as it was for physicists a century earlier.[3] As Berlinski so aptly put it:

> Complexity begets nonlinearity. But linear theory is where the theorems are. Buridan's ass perished between two such choices [8].

Another example of the reductionism common in analysis is the representation of a system as a set of elements with pairwise relationships denoting the interactions. If there are 3 elements (A, B, and C), there exist 6 possible relations (for example, A-B, C-B). If the pairwise qualification is removed, there are at least 49 interactions (for example, AB-ABC, B-B, BC-A). Anyone with a family or corporation knows that there are numerous nonpair relationships (for example, father-children). For a system of 10 elements, this number rises to over one million. (The formula is $(2^n - 1)^2$.) Such a calculation bares the vast simplification underlying conventional systems analysis: most potential interactions are ignored.

Modeling is undoubtedly the most pervasive means of simplifying complex systems for the purposes of analysis. We shall postpone a discussion of this subject to Section 2.4.

The use of averages (for example, statistical mechanics in physics and per capita gross national product in economics) and probabilities (for example, structural failure and health risk) has permitted the treatment of systems with very large numbers of elements, each behaving in a unique way. None will dispute the resulting success in effecting reduction of complexity. Not surprisingly, probabilities have been extended to areas such as planning. We hear talk of a "most probable" scenario. Unfortunately, it either comprises so few elements (events and trends) that it is meaningless or so many that, even if each had a 90% chance of occurrence, the product would have a very low likelihood. Let us say that a scenario encompasses for 20 events, each with an independent 90% likelihood. Then this scenario has only 12% probability of occurrence. If all

---

2. An example of a linear function is $F = a + bx + cy$; an example of a nonlinear function is $F = ax(y + bx)$, where a, b, and c are constants. For other examples of nonlinear equations, see Sections 7.2 and 8.2.

3. A personal note: I am reminded that, as a budding mathematician, I was duly impressed by the powerful theorems that can be derived for "regular" or "analytic" functions, that is, those that are differentiable in a region. Only much later was I made aware that, among all functions, those that are regular constitute "a set of measure zero." This translates into the statement that almost no functions are regular. Similarly, in the real world, linear systems are the exception rather than the rule.

alternative scenarios have a lower probability, does this make the 12% scenario a "most probable" one? History is strewn with events that had a powerful impact but were calculated to have a very low probability (see for example, the industrial accidents discussed in Chapter 6). The clients of the forecast are usually less interested in probabilities than in circumventing catastrophe and moderating the effects of failure. The analyst's familiar "expected value" calculation may miss the mark completely in providing a meaningful measure of risk for the decision maker.

A recent fashion in reductionism is the transfer of entire theories from one field to another (often falsely presented as an example of interdisciplinarity). One such case is the adoption of thermodynamics by some economists, for example, the "entropy state" of Georgescu-Roegen [9]. In the context of the science-technology world view it is tempting to reduce complexity by taking an existing law, albeit derived for closed physical systems, and applying it to open social systems. But the Second Law of Thermodynamics really does not address the evolution of living systems from single cells to Homo sapiens. Such systems are becoming increasingly organized, oblivious to the running-down postulated by the Law. In human beings, each fertilized egg recreates potential (that is, negentropy), and the transfer of information about technology among different cultures may have a similar effect. Berlinski [8] quotes Paul Samuelson in his Nobel lecture:

> There is really nothing more pathetic than to have an economist or a retired engineer trying to force analogies between the concepts of physics and the concepts of economics [10].

This should serve as a cautionary note to current researchers in evolutionary or emergent economics (see Section 8.1).

2.4 Reliance on Data and Models

A reflection of the reductionism just noted is the self-imposed constraint of the science-technology perspective to certain modes of inquiry [11, 12]:

- *Lockean:* Empirical, agreement on observations or data; truth is experiential and does not rest on any theoretical considerations;
- *Leibnizian:* Formal model and theoretical explanation; truth is analytic and does not rest on raw data of an external world;

[handwritten margin note: after saying how bad we are at understanding, he assumes he's good enough to put down a whole line of research!]

- *Kantian:* Theoretical model and empirical data complement each other and are inseparable; truth is a synthesis, multiple models provide synergism (for example, particle and wave theories in physics).

Not only the hard sciences, but the soft ones as well, see their legitimation almost exclusively in terms of these modes of inquiry. For example, one survey of "new" management strategies advised corporate planners to adopt the McKinsey S curves, Porter U curve, growth and market share matrix, Lewis strategy grid, and Mitchell price/equity return slope [13]. Such are the magic tonics peddled by the modern patent medicine salesmen to the corporate world [14]. They are essential elements in a process sometimes termed "the seagull model of consulting": "You fly out from Boston, make a couple of circles around the client's head, drop a strategy on him, and fly back" [15].

The widespread use of simple curves in economics reflects the dominance of models as a source of insight into economic processes. From supply and demand curves we moved to isoquants. The learning curve explained the benefits of increased production, namely, reduced cost; the Phillips curve suggested that unemployment and inflation were inversely related. The Laffer curve demonstrated that there is an optimal tax rate (that is, one that maximizes government revenue).[4]

Each curve represents an engagingly simple model and provides valuable, albeit limited, insights. The trouble begins when we overreach ourselves by claiming that the model approximates the real-world system. As we realize that, contrary to the Phillips curve, unemployment and inflation actually can rise simultaneously, as in the 1970s, we search for a more complex model, and we expect it to represent the system. In this way, an avalanche of increasingly detailed models is easily triggered. Their popularity is evident. As Daniel Bell put it, the Phillips curve "provided more employment for economists . . . than any public works program since the construction of the Erie Canal" [17].

Financial risk models have been the basis of the development of derivatives (dealing with currency devaluations and interest rate increases) and hedge

---

4. Economist John Kenneth Galbraith explains the aptly named Laffer curve as follows: "This economic formulation . . . held that when no taxes are levied, no revenue accrues to the government. An undoubted truth. And if taxes are so high that they absorb all income, nothing can be collected from the distraught, starving, and otherwise nonfunctional citizenry. Also almost certainly true. Between these two points a freehand curve, engagingly unsupported by evidence, showed the point where higher taxes would mean less revenue. According to accepted legend, the original curve had been drawn on a paper napkin, possibly toilet paper, and some critics of deficient imagination held that the paper could have been better put to its intended use" [16].

funds have relied on them—with disastrous results in 1998. As a Wall Street banking analyst has observed:

> [Computer models] only model whatever humans put into them. Are people putting in data that reflect the possibility of the financial equivalent of a nuclear meltdown? Usually not. And then they rely on computer models as if they're the word of God [18].

Science = our religion

Such models were caught by surprise, that is, their assumptions proven wrong, by currency meltdowns in Mexico (1994); Indonesia, Malaysia, and South Korea (1997); and Russia (1998). (See the discussion of "assumption drag" in Section 7.2.)

Emphasis on certain types of models easily leads to a kind of "group think." As system dynamics or input-output modeling proliferated and the number of modelers multiplied, conferences, papers, and books created a community. Shared interest and mutual reinforcement increasingly turned attention to baroque model improvements and compulsive extensions. In the process, the core assumptions were left behind untended.

Another facet of the problem is the jump from simulation to duplication, that is, the assumption that a computer can duplicate human behavior because it can simulate it. We understand the computer's operation; we do not yet understand that of the brain very well. The latter produces mental states; the former does not. A computer program can simulate a learning process but cannot create a thinking machine, regardless of its sophistication. The computer's formal operations, using symbols, do not imply that the symbols have meaning to the computer [19]. Thus, the reality created by the computer model in the mind of the programmer or user is not a duplication of a human or societal reality, a point often overlooked by those whose computer modeling experience was built on the simulation of purely technological systems. However, complexity science is currently making very significant advances in the computer simulation of living systems, and we sample them in Chapter 8.

more bad statements

In its most extreme form, modeling becomes an end rather than a means. The dedicated modeler reminds one of Pygmalion, the sculptor king of Greek mythology. He fashioned a statue of a beautiful girl and fell in love with it. Responding to his plea, the goddess Aphrodite brought the statue to life, and Pygmalion married his model. Today's modelers, mesmerized by the vast computer capacity, may also become wedded to their creations: the models become the reality. The computer's ability to handle large-scale models is confused with an ability to represent sociotechnical system complexity. Clearly, modeling seems to be fun for modelers, but it also can be a nightmare for the real-world problem solver.

? why

This discussion of the role of models suggests a subtle distinction between two approaches:

(1) Striving to represent a complex sociotechnical system realistically by replicating it in a mathematical format (for example, using a large-scale, computerized model to duplicate the real-world system);

(2) Seeking abstract models to serve as thinking aids, revealing possible clues or illuminating some aspect of the real system behavior in a different way; usually such models are simple enough to abandon without regret, occasionally elegant enough to cherish.

In the latter case, we harbor no illusion that the model represents the system realistically; we use the model merely as a key to unlock a new insight or point to a hidden link. Role 2 makes modeling an exceedingly valuable learning tool, but it is role 1 that has so frequently led us astray. Hence, the maxim suggested by Berlinski [8] for the mathematical modeler: "start simply and use to the fullest the resources of [mathematical] theory." As he observes, it is this prescription taken neatly in reverse that characterizes the world dynamics modeling of Forrester [20] and Meadows et al. [21], that is, an imposingly complex system of equations subjected to "an analysis of ineffable innocence." Role 1 is clearly reflected in Forrester's own stunning words in his explanation of system dynamics:

> All systems that change through time can be represented by using only levels and rates. The two kinds of variables are necessary but at the same time sufficient for representing any system [20].

Role 1 was also implied in the urban planners' growing conviction during the 1960s that they could rely on large-scale computer models to analyze urban structure and policy. But in 1973 Lee concluded in his *Requiem for Large-Scale Models*:

> None of the goals held out for large-scale models have been achieved, and there is little reason to expect anything different in the future. For each objective offered as a reason for building a model, there is either a better way of achieving the objective (more information at less cost) or a better objective (a more socially useful question to ask) [22].

Outstanding examples of role 2 are found in the work of Lotka [23] and Volterra on predator-prey relations, of Glansdorff and Prigogine [24], as well of Thom [25] on complex system stability and divergence effects, as well as in the writings of Marchetti [26]. The exciting recent work in computer simulation (Chapter 8) suggests that role 2 is currently being significantly advanced by the use of computer simulation. Using a bottom-up approach involving many system elements with behavior based on very simple rules, observation of the evolution of the system presents illuminating insights and provides new explanatory power significant for complex systems. As in role 1, computer simulation is used, but the purpose is quite different: the computer becomes a laboratory to substitute for undeveloped complexity theory rather than a means to represent an actual real-world system.

On the other hand, much of what has been termed General Systems Theory to date fails in role 2. It abstracts system models in general to such stratospheric levels that any potentially useful substance evaporates in the process, that is, it becomes an end in itself [8].

For analysts, it is difficult to appreciate that, as we move beyond the pure science-technology domain, other systems of inquiry may prove more fruitful. Here are several candidates:

- *Hegelian:* Dialectic confrontation between opposing models or plans leading to resolution; truth is conflictual as typified in a courtroom trial;
- *Merleau-Ponty:* Reality as currently shared assumptions about a specific situation; acceptance of a new reality is negotiated out of our experience; truth is agreement that permits action;
- *Singerian:* A pragmatic meta-inquiring system that includes the application of other inquiring systems as needed; the designer's psychology and sociology are considered inseparable from the physical system representation; ethics is swept into the design.

If we concentrate on the individual we should also mention Kant's *noumena,* which is reality beyond the perception of our senses, a world that we can only intuit, to which we are linked through our unconscious mind; in such a world there is no temporal distinction of past, present, and future.

Thus we see that there is much out there beyond data-based, model-based, and complementary multimodel systems of inquiry. Kellen urges us to:

> . . . realize the limitations of the knowledge you can obtain under the best of circumstances and with the most thorough use and study of the "data" . . . Some people are now fanatics in the realm of methodology . . . But any extensive use of, or trust in, any methodology can only lead you astray, and you can get the help that new methods and machines offer only

if your consumption remains sparing, your methodological diet balanced, and your attitude skeptical [27].

Plamenatz writes in his work on Machiavelli:

The ideas about the great man and his role in history of a sometimes careless historian may be more perceptive and realistic than those of the most scrupulous recorder of facts [28].

The science-technology world view also places great stress on cause-and-effect relationships. But pause to consider a comment of Toynbee:

In my search up to the present point, I have been experimenting with the play of soulless forces . . . and I have been thinking in deterministic terms of cause and effect . . . Have I not erred in applying to historical thought, which is a study of living creatures, a scientific method of thought that has been devised for thinking about inanimate nature? And have I not also erred further in treating the outcomes of encounters between persons as cases of the operation of cause and effect? The effect of a cause is inevitable, invariable, and predictable. But the initiative that is taken by one or the other of the live parties to an encounter is not a cause; it is a challenge. Its consequence is not an effect; it is a response. Challenge and response resembles cause and effect only in standing for a sequence of events. The character of the sequence is not the same. Unlike the effect of a cause, the response to a challenge is not predetermined . . . and is therefore intrinsically unpredictable [29].

2.5 Quantification

In ancient Greece the Pythagoreans attempted to preserve the purity of their mathematical expressions by putting to death the man who discovered incommensurables (that is, having no common measure or standard of comparison). Today the computer has become the ideal instrument to fuel the drive for quantification. A new version of Gresham's Law states that "quantitative analyses tend to drive out qualitative analyses." Zadeh's fuzzy set theory [30] has even been developed to quantify qualitative terms and, in the manner of a shoehorn, squeeze them into the computer input format. Churchman [31] points up the paradox: "fuzzy set theory runs the danger of becoming precise about fuzziness."

The developed nations are, culturally speaking, measuring societies. During the Cold War we measured national military strength by comparing the number of our strategic weapons systems with those of the Soviet Union, ignoring the fact that accuracy is far more significant than quantity and that the ability to destroy the enemy's industrial capacity four times may not be better than destroying it twice. We measure individuals by their "worth" in dollars and societies by their gross national products in dollars. No wonder, therefore, that the candid admission by David Stockman, one-time Director of the U.S. Office of Management and Budget that "none of us really understands what's going on with all these numbers" caused consternation in Washington [32]. Yankelovich's comment on the subject, his "McNamara fallacy," reminds one of the circles of Hell in Dante's *Inferno:*

> The first step is to measure whatever can be easily measured. This is OK as far as it goes. The second step is to disregard that which can't be measured or give it an arbitrary quantitative value. This is artificial and misleading. The third step is to presume that what can't be measured easily really isn't very important. This is blindness. The fourth step is to say that what can't be easily measured really doesn't exist. This is suicide [33].

Quantification engenders self-delusion. Tversky and Kahneman have found that

> People tend to overestimate the probability of conjunctive events and to underestimate the probability of disjunctive events . . . [Such biases] are particularly significant in the context of planning. The successful completion of an undertaking, such as the development of a new product, typically has a conjunctive character: for the undertaking to succeed, each of a series of events must occur. [This leads] to unwarranted optimism in the evaluation of the likelihood that a plan will succeed or that a project will be completed on time. Conversely, disjunctive structures are typically encountered in the evaluation of risks. A complex system, such as a nuclear reactor or a human body, will malfunction if any of its essential components fail. Even when the likelihood of failure is slight, the probability of an overall failure can be high if many components are involved . . . people will tend to underestimate the probabilities of failure in complex systems [34].

Economist John Maynard Keynes wrote his dissertation on the foundations of probability theory but became highly suspicious of mathematical models that claimed "false precision beyond what either the method or the statistics actually available can support." He viewed them as "charlatanism". In 1998 forecasts based on such models brought grief to the investors in the Long Term Capital Management Fund.

Finally, consider the observation of William Pfaff at one of our most prestigious think tanks:

> The fundamental claim of the think tank is that it deals with its materials objectively. But, of course, it cannot do so when the materials do not lend themselves to objective analysis . . . This is its great weakness when it ventures into policy matters . . . The nonscientific part has to be done in non-scientific ways, which is to say, non-think-tank ways. The characteristic error is to deal with the unquantifiable as if it were quantifiable.
>
> I once spent the better part of a week in argument with a remorselessly humorless colleague who wanted to assign numerical values to the phrases "desirable," "probably desirable," [etc.]. I said that language was used because language conveys certain things to the intelligence that numbers cannot. He regarded this as primitive prejudice or as "theology" [35].

2.6 Objectivity

Editors of scientific and technological publications have traditionally frowned on the use of the first-person singular or plural. Authors have resorted to arduous circumlocutions to banish "I" or "we" from their texts, lest they be tainted with subjectivity. Yet the assumption of objectivity on the part of scientists and technologists is revealed more and more frequently as a myth. Churchman writes of the social sciences:

> One of the most absurd myths of the social sciences is the "objectivity" that is alleged to occur in the relation between the scientist-as-observer and the people he observes. He really thinks he can stand apart and objectively observe how people behave, what their attitudes are, how they think, how they decide . . . [it is a] silly and empty claim that an observation is objective if it resides in the brain of an unbiased observer [36].

Mitroff lays to rest objectivity in its traditional meaning in the physical sciences with his study of Apollo moon scientists:

> It is humanly impossible to eliminate all bias and commitment from science . . . [we cannot] pin our hopes for the existence of any objective science on the existence of passionless unbiased individuals [37].

Heinz Von Foerster, a cyberneticist, insists that objectivity cannot occur in the relation between the scientist as observer and the people he observes.

The claim that the properties of an observer must not enter into the description of his observation is nonsense, because without the observer there are no descriptions; the observer's faculty of describing enters, by necessity, into his descriptions.

If objectivity cannot be assumed for the scientist in his proverbial ivory tower, it would seem foolhardy indeed to carry this assumption over to technology management in a real-world setting. The "real world" is a complex system in which virtually "everything interacts with everything"—and this includes the manager. That being the case, the choice of model and data, of problem definition and boundaries, is always partly subjective.

2.7 Ignoring or Avoiding the Individual

From Adam Smith to West Churchman, concern has been expressed over the danger of ignoring the individual and losing him in the aggregate view. Smith said 200 years ago:

> The man of system . . . seems to imagine that he can arrange the different members of a great society with as much ease as the hand arranges the different pieces upon a chessboard; he does not consider that the pieces upon the chessboard have no other principle of motion besides that which the hand impresses upon them; but that, in the great chessboard of human society, every single piece has a principle of motion of its own altogether different from that which the legislature might choose to impress upon it [38].

Churchman makes the following observations:

> Economic models have to aggregate a number of things, and one of the things they aggregate is you! In great globs you are aggregated into statistical classes . . . Jung says that, until you have gone through the process of individuation . . . you will not be able to face the social problems. You will not be able to build your models and tell the world what to do . . .
>
> From the perspective of the unique individual, it is not counting up how many people on this side and how many on that side. All the global systems things go out: there are no trade-offs in this world, in this immense world of the inner self . . . All our concepts that work so well in the global world do not work in the inner world . . . We have great trouble describing it very well in scientific language, but it is there, and is important . . .

To be able to see the world globally, which you are going to have to be able to do, and to see it as a world of unique individuals . . . that is really complexity [39].

In retrospect we encounter instance after instance where individuals were crucial in the interaction of a technology with society: Wernher Von Braun's leadership in rocket and space vehicle development, Bill Gates and Andy Grove in information technology development, and Rachel Carson's book *The Silent Spring* in environmental concerns. In these cases we have an impact of individuals on technology. Conversely, technology may have a tremendous impact on the individual. Television ended the career of Senator Joseph McCarthy, radio broadcasts of fireside chats worked powerfully for President Franklin Roosevelt, and television coverage of the space program made folk heroes of the astronauts.

2.8 Perceptions of Time

The science-technology world view is concerned with physical space-time, with time as a dimension or variable essential in grasping the dynamics of a complex system. Distortions intrude through the relativity theory as, for example, perceptions of time vary with observer velocity in an Einsteinian universe. Similarly, economists apply a discount rate to future dollars to determine their present value; the basis traditionally is the cost of capital. Aside from such rather mechanistic alterations, this perspective sees time as moving linearly, to a universally accepted pace determined by precise physical measurement. Thus Forrester, Meadows, Mesarovic, and Pestel exercised their system dynamics models over 50- to 130-year periods, but their computational time increment is independent of society and individuals, geographical locale, and era. We shall use the term *technological time* for this case.

By contrast, every individual has a *personal time* conception. A person's time horizon is dictated by the expected life span, position in Maslow's hierarchy of human needs, and/or other individual considerations. The individual applies a psychological discount rate to his perception of future problems and opportunities, which is totally distinct from the economist's dollar discount rate based on the cost of capital. The psychological discount rate means, in effect, that the individual looks at the future as if through the wrong end of a telescope [40]. Distant objects appear smaller than they really are. Similarly, problems far in the future are of less concern to us than equally serious problems in the near term. The highest discounting occurs where immediate personal survival is the prime concern; the lowest rate occurs in an affluent, well-educated family in a stable Western or Japanese setting. Time discounting varies with age and with psychological type. Leaders in a society are often distinguished by their atypical time orientations, that is, their far-sightedness.

Table 2.1 suggests the Jung typology and related time orientations. Even our daily newspaper raises the subject:

> The dimension of time has become a great paradox of the modern world. Words and images are transmitted instantly, people almost as fast. But the context and the meaning do not come through the blur of impression, which seems to make adjustment slower and more difficult [41].

Historian Fernand Braudel divides his distinguished work on *The Mediterranean* into three parts:

1. The almost timeless history of man and his interaction with the physical, inanimate environment;
2. The social history of groups and groupings that generate forces leading, for example, to wars;
3. History on the scale of individual men.

> . . . a history of brief, rapid, nervous fluctuations, by definition ultra-sensitive; the least tremor sets all its antennae quivering . . . as such it is the most exciting of all, the richest in human interest, and also the most dangerous [42].

don't like it.

Table 2.1
Jung's Typology and Time Orientations [40]

Jung type	Time focus	Discounting
Sensation	Present	Highest
Feeling	Past	Selective bias
Intuition	Future	High/moderate
Thinking	Past-present-future	Moderate

He sees historical time as "geographical time, social time, and individual time."

Let us now turn from the individual to organizations or social entities. Neither technological time nor personal time prevails. Organizations have a longer time horizon than individuals; they do not expect to die like human beings. This does not mean they use a zero discount rate, merely a lower one than individuals. *Social time* is multigenerational. Organizations have, in fact, a curious blend of long- and short-time horizons. There is the motivation of self-perpetuation and the pressure of meeting next month's payroll and protecting next year's budget. As in the case of individuals, organizations have a spectrum of time horizons. Small companies contrast with large ones, medieval Christian with modern Western societies, rich European with poor African states. Thus, the discount rate depends both on the conception of time and, to a lesser degree, organizational and individual differences (Figure 2.3).

The importance of such discounting in the decision-making context can hardly be overestimated: the decision maker's preference is strongly dependent on the assumed discount rate. We will say more on the subject of discounting in Section 7.1.

These, then, are eight important paradigms that govern our usual perspective of complex systems. They also suggest why so much of systems analysis is an "inside job," performed for other analysts who share the same paradigms and not necessarily for the audience that needs it.

Having reviewed the principal characteristics of the technical perspective and its limitations, we now introduce other perspectives to augment it.

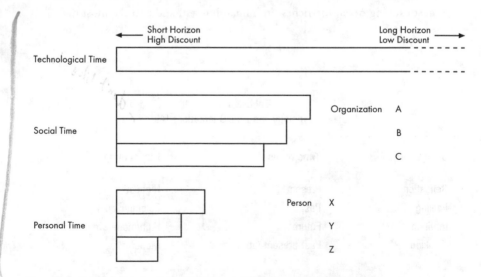

Figure 2.3 Relative time horizons: a schematic. Note: For qualifications see text.

References

[1]   Linstone, H. A., et al., "The Use of Structural Modeling for Technology Assessment," *Futures Research Institute Report 78-1*, Portland, OR: Portland State University, 1978.

[2]   Brodheim, E., and G. P. Prastacos, "The Long Island Blood Distribution System as a Prototype for Regional Blood Management," *Interfaces,* Vol. 9, 1979, pp. 3–20.

[3]   Miser, H. J., and E. S. Quade (eds.), *Handbook of Systems Analysis: Overview.* New York: North-Holland, 1985, p. 2.

[4]   Miller, J. G., *Living Systems.* New York: McGraw Hill, 1978.

[5]   Holling, C. S., "The Curious Behavior of Complex Systems: Lessons from Ecology," in *Futures Research: New Directions,* H. A. Linstone and W. H. C. Simmonds (eds.), Reading, MA: Addison-Wesley Publishing Co., 1977, p. 129.

[6]   Von Foerster, H., "The Curious Behavior of Complex Systems: Lessons from Biology," in *Futures Research: New Directions,* H. A. Linstone and W. H. C. Simmonds (eds.), Reading, MA: Addison-Wesley Publishing Co., 1977, pp. 107–108.

[7]   Von Foerster, H., "Responsibilities of Competence," *J. Cybernetics,* Vol. 2, No. 2, 1972, p. 1.

[8]   Berlinski, D., *On Systems Analysis: An Essay Concerning the Limitations of Some Mathematical Methods in the Social, Political, and Biological Sciences,* Cambridge, MA: MIT Press, 1976, pp. 131–132.

[9]   Georgescu-Roegen, N., *The Entropy Law and the Economic Process,* Cambridge, MA: Harvard University Press, 1972.

[10] Samuelson, P., "Maximum Principles in Analytical Economics," *Science,* Vol. 172, Sept. 10, 1971, p. 994.

[11] Churchman, C. W., *The Design of Inquiring Systems,* New York: Basic Books, 1971.

[12] Mitroff, I. I., and M. Turoff, "Technological Forecasting and Assessment: Science and/or Mythology?" *Technological Forecasting and Social Change,* Vol. 5, 1973, pp. 113–134.

[13] Kiechel, W., III, "New Management Strategies," *Fortune,* Vol. 104, 1981, No. 7, pp. 111–126; No. 8, pp. 139–146; No. 9, pp. 181–188; No. 10, pp. 148–154.

[14] Cicco, J. A., Jr., "Wanna Fix Your Firm?" *New York Times,* Jan. 5, 1982, p. 25.

[15] Kiechel, W., III, "Corporate Strategists Under Fire," *Fortune,* Vol. 106, 1982, p. 36.

[16] Galbraith, J. K., *A Tenured Professor,* Boston, MA: Houghton Mifflin Co., 1990, pp. 75–76.

[17] Gardner, M., "Mathematical Games," *Scientific American,* Dec. 1981, p. 23.

[18] *New York Times,* Oct. 4, 1998, Sec. 3, p. 4.

[19] Searle, J. R., "Minds, Brains, and Programs," in *The Mind's I: Fantasies and Reflections on Self and Soul,* D. R. Hofstadter and D. C. Dennett (eds.), New York: Basic Books, 1982.

[20] Forrester, J., *World Dynamics,* Cambridge, MA: Wright-Allen Press, 1971, p. 18.

[21] Meadows, D., et al. *The Limits to Growth,* New York: Universe Books, 1972.

[22] Lee, D. B., Jr., "Requiem for Large-Scale Models," *AIP Journal,* May 1973, p. 163.

[23] Lotka, A. J., *Elements of Mathematical Biology,* New York: Dover Books, 1956.

[24] Glansdorff, P., and I. Prigogine, *Structure, Stability, and Fluctuations,*, London: Wiley Interscience, 1971.

[25] Thom, R., *Structural Stability and Morphogenesis,* Reading, MA: W. A. Benjamin, Inc., 1975.

[26] Marchetti, C., various articles in *Technological Forecasting and Social Change,* beginning with Vol. 10, 1977, pp. 345–356.

[27] Kellen, K., "On Problems in Perceiving Other Nations and Systems," Security Studies Paper No. 15, Los Angeles, CA: University of California, pp. 24–25.

[28] Plamenatz, J. (ed.), *Machiavelli,* London: Fontana/Collins, 1972, p. 45.

[29] Toynbee, A., *A Study of History.* (revised and abridged by A. Toynbee and J. Caplan), Fairlawn, NJ: Oxford University Press, 1972, p. 97.

[30] Zadeh, L., "Fuzzy Sets," *Information Control,* Vol. 8, 1965.

[31] Churchman, C. W., *The Systems Approach and Its Enemies,* New York: Basic Books, 1979, p. 20.

[32] *New York Times,* Nov. 13, 1981, p. 17.

[33] Yankelovich, D., quoted in A. Smith, *Supermoney,* New York: Popular Library, 1972, pp. 271–272.

[34] Tversky, A., and D. Kahneman, "Judgement Under Uncertainty: Heuristics and Biases," *Science,* Vol. 185, Sept. 27, 1974, p. 1129.

[35] Pfaff, W., "Think Tanks: Think Again," *Quest/81,* May 1980, pp. 79–80.

[36] Churchman, C. W., *Challenge to Reason,* New York: McGraw Hill, 1968, p. 86.

[37] Mitroff, I. I., *The Subjective Side of Science,* New York: North-Holland, 1974, p. 248.

[38] Schneider, H. W. (ed.), *Adam Smith's Moral and Political Philosophy,* New York: Hafner Publishing Co., 1948, p. 247.

[39] Churchman, C. W., "A Philosophy for Planning," in *Futures Research: New Directions,* H. A. Linstone and W. H. C. Simmonds (eds.), Reading, MA: Addison-Wesley Publishing Co., 1977, pp. 82–90.

[40] Linstone, H. A., and W. H. C. Simmonds (eds.), *Futures Research: New Directions.* Reading, MA: Addison-Wesley Publishing Co., 1977, pp. 5–6, 10.

[41] *New York Times,* Dec. 28, 1979.

[42] Braudel, F., *The Mediterranean and the Mediterranean World in the Age of Philip II,* Vol. 1, New York: Harper & Row, 1972, pp. 20–21.

3

Our Proposed Perspectives

I have said it thrice: What I tell you three times is true.

Lewis Carroll, *The Hunting of the Snark*

Woodcutter: All those different stories—I began to doubt my senses. I couldn't understand—I still can't understand—why they all lied.

Wigmaker: Did they?

Woodcutter: They must have! I know what I saw with my own eyes.

Wigmaker: Why should I trust your eyes any more than those of the other three? Like I told you—people see what they want to see and say what they want to hear.

Fay and Michael Kanin, *Rashomon*

3.1 Introduction

In its most general form, a system involves nature, man, society, and technology, singly or in combination. Here are some examples:

- Man—a biological system;
- Nature—the solar system;
- Technology—a communications satellite;
- Nature/technology—a waterwheel;
- Man/society—a legal system;

31

- Nature/man/society—a primitive village;
- Man/society/technology—an information system.

Our primary concern will be the last in this list. In Chapter 2 we reviewed a series of paradigms integral to the way we normally look at such systems. Technological systems never exist in isolation but always involve technology *and* human beings, both organizationally and individually. Technology is, after all, a product of human minds and interfaces with them in numerous ways at all stages from creation to obsolescence. Corporations that produce and service the hardware and software, regulatory agencies, and advocacy groups, as well as political bodies, educational, religious, and ethnic groups may be linked to the technological aspect of the system.

The individual also affects the system and may be affected by it. Computers constitute a prosthesis of certain parts of the brain and the impact may vary from one individual to another. Computer output may overrule common sense because of its aura of scientific quantification. Television creates a reality of its own; in Paddy Chayefsky's film *Network* the desperate commentator, anchorman Howard Beale, rants:

> You people sit there, night after night. You're beginning to believe this illusion we're spinning here. You're beginning to think the tube is reality, and your own lives are unreal. This is mass madness.

The diverse "actors" that impinge on the typical decision process dealing with a complex system are sampled in Appendix A.2.

We focus here on distinct ways of looking at a system. In a narrow sense, the concept of multiple models is widely recognized. For example, there are the Ptolemaic and Copernican solar system models, one replacing the other as the "correct" view of the world. However, our interest is in the use of multiple models simultaneously or in parallel, not sequentially.

Accepting multiple models requires a considerable degree of intellectual sophistication or maturity. Religions strongly depend on conformism, on *one* belief system, as a base for authority. Even science has its accepted dogma. The fear of unsettling alternative perspectives was, and is, reflected in inquisitions, witch hunts, denunciations, ostracism by colleagues, and other techniques of persecution. But there were occasionally mavericks who were comfortable with conflicting *Weltanschauungen*. Thus, by the nineteenth century, mathematics challenged us with parallel multiple models—Euclidean, Riemannian, and Lobachevskian geometries—and physics soon posited the wave and particle theories of light.

In this chapter we will introduce three ways of viewing a sociotechnical system, that is, looking at it through three different kinds of filter. We prefer the word "perspective" over "model" (which Allison used) to emphasize that each way of viewing involves distinct paradigms, not merely different mathematical formulations or computer models.

We propose a technical perspective (T), an organizational perspective (O), and a personal perspective (P).[1] Consider, for example, an organization such as a corporation. Using the technical perspective, we may see the organization as a hierarchical structure, model it using system dynamics, and apply decision analysis or other tools of management science. The organizational perspective sees the same organization as a powerful or weak unit; a living system fighting competitors, cohesive or divided; a collection of baronies (divisions, departments) with a weak king (president, chief executive officer); or a strong chief with loyal lieutenants running the subunits, a powerful staff and weak line, or vice versa. The personal perspective may see the same organization as job security, an opportunity to exert power, or a step to gain prestige. Thus each perspective sees the world through a different filter.

We shall find that *each perspective yields insights about the system not obtainable with the others;* it is this realization that motivates our entire effort. Using only one perspective is analogous to seeing a one-dimensional representation of a three-dimensional object. Integration of the three perspectives reflects the fact that the whole is more than the sum of its parts. A balance of attention to all three perspectives is clearly desirable; *we seek to avoid gross imbalances so often evident when technologists grapple with issues that are not purely technological.*

Perspectives may conflict or support each other. An apt analogy is the American courtroom. Every witness presents a perspective, and the prosecutor and defense attorney each perform an integration or synthesis (using and weighting witness testimonies in unique ways). In striving for a decision, the jury may then accept one integration or the other or reject both and do its own integration. Observe that, unlike the case in the scientific world, there does not exist one "correct" weighting or integration.

Perspectives are also dynamic—they change over time. Even retrospectively we observe this characteristic: each generation reinterprets the past. Historians writing in different generations view a specific past event or culture in very different ways. The impacts of a 1990 technology as seen in a 1998 evaluation may appear significantly changed in a 2008 study.

---

1. Earlier and less detailed versions of this work were published in [1, 2].

3.2 The Technical Perspective

Historically, this perspective is much newer than the organizational and personal perspectives. It may be formally traced to Francis Bacon (1561–1621), who galvanized the Age of Reason. He was convinced that *ipsa scientia protestas est*—knowledge itself is power—and saw the need "to commence a total reconstruction of sciences, [practical arts], and all human knowledge, raised upon the proper foundation" [3].

This perspective has assumed ever-greater significance as exemplified by post-World War II think tanks such as the RAND Corporation, the Institute for Applied Systems Analysis, and the Santa Fe Institute, as well as the systems, risk, and impact analysis literature. The first book on the subject of technology assessment announced that

> Technology assessment is a systems analysis approach to providing a whole conceptual framework, complete both in scope and time, for decisions about the appropriate utilization of technology for social purposes [4].

The technology and its environment are viewed as a system in the now-familiar way sketched in Chapter 2. The world is seen in quantitative ways, so popular with management consultants, such as curves or computer models. Terms like alternatives, trade-offs, optimization, data, and models suggest the rational, analytic nature of the technical perspective. In fact, Allison [5] used the label "rational actor" for his first model, which is equivalent to our T perspective. We avoid his label because it suggests that the other perspectives are irrational, an implication that we reject. Rationality can only be judged from within, that is, in the context of a given perspective.

The "tools" include among others probability and game theory, decision and cost-benefit analysis, system dynamics, structural modeling, and econometrics. There is significant interest in the classification and categorization of information, in preparing lists and matrices, and in structuring organization charts and graphs. Axelrod's cognitive maps (the signed, directed graphs or "digraphs" in Appendix A.1) constitute a T perspective technique to depict an individual's belief system or, more accurately, his assertions of causal links. A valiant effort has been made to apply this tool to political decision analyses, such as the deliberations of the British Eastern Committee in 1918, Gouverneur Morris' arguments on the U.S. presidency at the 1787 Constitutional Convention, and proposed international control of the oceans [6].

The United States as a culture is the most strongly T-oriented culture in the world. We love statistics and polls. A true baseball fan is awash in statistics and a beautiful girl is a "10." We define *quality of life* (QOL) in terms of numerical indicators—so that it would be more precise to label it quantity of life. The bias toward the T perspective is seen in the Central Intelligence Agency:

> Technological cleverness is the pride of the U.S. intelligence . . . But American supremacy in technical intelligence is profoundly misleading. It is not representative of the U.S. intelligence capabilities as a whole but stands in stark contrast. For in every other intelligence field—human spies, analysis of data collected, and ability to conduct secret operations the U.S. intelligence community appears to be dangerously deficient [7].

It is probably not a coincidence that the means of obtaining input (personal contact) and the type of input obtained with the O and P perspectives are not those accessible to surveillance satellites and other high-technology sensors.

The theory of games was the brilliant brainchild of John von Neumann and Oskar Morgenstern [8]. In its simplest form there are two players and each has several options. The payoffs associated with every pair of choices are known to them, as are their objectives, that is, maximizing or minimizing the payoff. The calculus then determines the best strategy for each player. Like probability theory, game theory originated in conjunction with social games. As Schelling observed, the idealization of a conflict required by the theory drastically alters the character of the game. "There is a danger in too much abstractness" [9]. It might be said that Schelling anticipated Allison's models. He recognized the unrealistic restrictiveness of the "rationality" assumption and saw the need for a theory of strategy that encompassed what appears to the analyst as "irrationality." Multiple perspectives certainly help to avoid the game theory trap. Consider Schelling's recommendation:

> We may wish to solicit advice from the underworld, or from ancient despotisms, on how to make agreements work when trust and good faith are lacking and there is no legal recourse for breach of contract. The ancients exchanged hostages, drank wine from the same glass to demonstrate the absence of poison, met in public places to inhibit the massacre of one by the other, and even deliberately exchanged spies to facilitate transmittal of authentic information [9].

In our framework, game theory is inexorably tied to the T perspective and Schelling's discussion recognizes its limitations.

Utility theory transforms a general measure, such as dollars, into a personal preference scale (also known as a utility scale or utiles). This step would seem to take into account other perspectives (for example, predilection of an individual for risk taking). However, the concept, dubious at best, is often doomed to failure by the attempt to calibrate the scale in a pseudoanalytic manner (that is, via the T perspective). Typically, the subject individual is asked a series of standard questions about his risk propensities using a highly idealized, hypothetical situation. Example: On a new project described in two sentences, which alternative do you prefer, (1) the certainty of making $100,000 profit or (2) an 80% chance of making a $200,000 profit and a 20% chance of losing $50,000? The resulting scale is then used to predict the respondent's preferred decision (highest expected utility) in a complex real-life problem. Further, individuals are compared on the basis of such utility profiles. The resulting "realism" offers as much illusion as instant antiquing applied to new furniture. The complexity of human decision making simply cannot be captured by such superficial number crunching.

The computer's inherent preference for T perspective tools makes it tempting to focus even more strongly on the T perspective than has been the habit of analysts to date. Its universal language is particularly appealing when contrasted with the Tower of Babel suggested by the pluralism of O and P perspectives.

Since the T perspective is such a well-mined lode, we will now focus our attention on the other perspectives. We will have more to say about the T perspective in later chapters.

3.3 The Organizational Perspective

The organizational perspective sees the world through a different filter, from the point of view of affected and affecting organizations. There is great concern whether a new policy will threaten the organization's rights, standing or stability, whether it fits the current *standard operating procedures* (SOPs) and parochial priorities. In this perspective, we deal with power: Where is the real leverage? How can conflicts among units be turned to constructive use? There is no intensive search for analytic tools; in fact, often there is a mistrust of "academic" techniques. They are viewed either as unrealistic or as unpredictable and uncontrollable. For example, if a banking commission of senior civil servants and bank representatives is created to analyze the impact of electronic funds transfer, finding each member using an organizational perspective rather than a technical perspective would not be unexpected. Although uniqueness of the technical perspective is the norm, each organization may have a different O perspective on the same sociotechnical system.

For our purposes, "organizations" may be formal or informal, hierarchical or egalitarian, permanent or ad hoc.[2] They may be traditional structures (for example, corporations or bureaucracies) or they may be bound by substantive activities or interests. The fact that a collective may not be formally organized does not invalidate its significance.

Sometimes a postulated "public attitude" can alter (or sustain) an impact as if it were a powerful advocacy group. Alexis de Tocqueville eloquently described this condition:

> Time, events, or the unaided individual action of the mind will sometimes undermine or destroy an opinion, without any outward sign of the change. It has not been openly assailed, no conspiracy has been formed to make war on it, but its followers, one by one, noiselessly secede; day by day a few of them abandon it, until at last it is only professed by a minority. In this state it will still continue to prevail. As its enemies remain mute or only interchange their thoughts by stealth, they are themselves unaware for a long period that a great revolution has actually been effected; and in this state of uncertainty they take no steps; they observe one another and are silent. The majority have ceased to believe what they believed before, but they still affect to believe, and this empty phantom of public opinion is strong enough to chill innovators and to keep them silent and at a respectful distance [10].

At other times a group opinion can modify or distort individual judgments. Solomon Asch's experiments clearly show this phenomenon [11]. His subjects were isolated and shown two lines A and B of substantially different lengths. They each recognized the difference. In the next phase, a group of six "confederates" were taken aside and asked to say that the lengths were the same. One of the unwitting subjects was then introduced to the confederates and, after listening to each of them claim the lengths were the same, asked to state his view. In 58% of the tests, the unwitting subject agreed with the group view that the lengths were the same. The experiment convincingly demonstrates that people are not necssarily objective observers who trust the reality of their senses.

The world seen from the pure O perspective in ideal form is an orderly progression from state to state, with an occasional minor crisis along the way,

---

2. Permanence often becomes a top priority internal organizational objective. This may lead to perpetuation of the organization far beyond its raison d'etre. For example, the U.S. Assay Commission, appointed each year since 1792 to ascertain that U.S. coins contain as much silver or gold as promised (a chore routinely duplicated by the Bureau of Standards), was abolished only in 1980 by President Carter.

for which experience and the procedural manual have the answers. Rules and procedures are there to be followed: policy is quasi-sacred once it is promulgated.

With all human beings socialized into some sociocultural organization, this perspective influences all actions and decisions ("Is this right?" "Do I have a right to?"). Perhaps the strongest argument for inclusion of this perspective is the realization that, in the political arena, highly technical information is usually, and properly, discounted in favor of social interests and considerations of values involved—and these can never be adequately encompassed by a T perspective. Pressures emanate from institutions, regulatory agencies, special interest groups, and mass social movements. Illumination of the interplay of these pressures necessitates the O perspective.

The O perspective also reflects the culture and myths that have helped to mold and bind the organization, group, or society as a distinct entity in the eyes of its members. Outstanding companies have strong cultures that reflect their values. Myths and legends accumulate over the years to reinforce these values [12]. Later we will see glimpses of such corporate cultures in the cases of a utility company, an electronics company, and an aircraft company (Chapter 5) and find them essential in understanding their decision making. In the U.S. Army, the Western marksmanship tradition has had a profound impact on modern rifle procurement (Chapter 4). Engineering laboratories, too, have distinct cultures. Churchman [13] recalls his experience during World War II at the Army's Frankfort Arsenal. Requests to 20 metallurgical laboratories to calibrate the hardness of a steel bar produced significant differences among them. The unique training pattern in each laboratory was probably responsible.

The social psychologist Kurt Lewin has posited that all actions have some specific "background" and are at least partly determined by it. He insists that this background is of crucial importance for the perception of reality and is intimately bound to the need for security, that is, for "belonging" [14]. Often, we can identify individuals who create, amplify, or manipulate myths: Bill Gates, Steve Jobs, and Andy Grove are recent examples.

In the political arena, Adolf Hitler almost singlehandedly presented the German people with the myth of racial superiority and national destiny to create a Thousand-Year Reich. His charisma transformed a personal (P) perspective into a collective O perspective so successfully that his party won 37% of the popular vote in the July 1932 Reichstag election. The power of O perspectives to create illusions was evident in the enthusiastic acceptance of ludicrous doctrines about Aryan physical characteristics and racial purity and superiority by millions of Germans (and Austrians). The points we want to emphasize here are these: (1) a group's O perspective is crucial as a basis for its members' decision making, whether or not it corresponds to outsiders' perceptions of reality; and

(2) the perspective may be subtle and require more than superficial probing to bring to light.

There is another aspect of interest: future problems are discounted in contrast to near-term problems; that is, short-range consequences for the organization and its actions are given priority. Here this perspective deals with organizational or social time (see Section 2.8). Each organizational actor is cognizant of parochial priorities and interests; they are distinctive to his or her organization. The same applies to standard operating procedures; they go far toward limiting potential decision alternatives. Seen from the organizational perspective, a technology appears to create problems or solve problems for the organization. There is concern that the technology may disturb the functioning of an organization, that is, become a disruptive force. Interest in a technology also is a function of the amount of "noise" made about it (inquiries from "above," mention in the media). There is a strong tendency to break down problems in accordance with organizational responsibilities. The Department of Defense may be interested in exotic new nuclear, chemical, and biological weapons, but not in their long-term storage and disposal problems.

Another characteristic common to many organization staffs is the fear of making errors. This is reflected in the utility curves of executives. These curves are typically asymmetric; that is, in absolute numbers the value (on a utility scale) of making x dollars for the company is not nearly as high as the value of losing x dollars. As a city manager pointed out to us,

> Innovation does not occur within a governmental agency unless someone internal is interested in it or unless some fairly steady external pressure is applied . . . There are two reasons for this: you have a certain amount of priorities and the inability to answer them all . . . The second one is . . . the tremendous price that anyone in government pays for failure.
>
> An example in the private sector: The Edsel was a tremendous failure of the Ford Motor Company. The guy who headed that program later went on to become president of Ford Motor Company. Because all Ford asked after the catastrophe was, "Did you know what the hell went wrong?" And the project manager said, "Sure we do, we know that our pre-World War II marketing methods are totally unreliable in today's marketing. We've analyzed what went wrong . . . and so we totally revamped our marketing techniques." The Ford Motor Company went on with the Falcon and Mustang and just one success after the other from a marketing standpoint. And that's all that they asked—do you know what you did wrong? The private sector accepts failure, and that's part of the price you pay for progress.
>
> Government can't accept failure. If somebody fails in the public sector, the political people are all over him because they've got to protect their

ass . . . and it's this inability to accept failure that has made government officials very rigid about trying something new. [If the innovation fails] you'd expect the resignation of whoever was connected with it, or the demotion, or certainly the end of their career [15].

In an era of transition, as experienced by today's advanced societies, this fear is deplored as a serious weakness in the organizational ability to adapt to changing needs. Complex sociotechnical systems cannot be adequately modeled, so experimentation is vital and, in Don Michael's terms, we must be "willing to embrace error" [16]. (The Germans use the term *fehlerfreundlich* or "error-friendly.")

Machiavelli was a champion of a vital organization, the state, and Antony Jay, himself an executive, has observed in his book, *Management and Machiavelli:*

> Machiavelli . . . is bursting with urgent advice and acute observations for top management of the great private and public corporations all over the world . . . It means looking at the corporation in a new way: looking not through the eyes of the accountant and systems analyst and economist and mathematician, but through those of the historian and political scientist [17].

Machiavelli recognizes the difference between an O and a P perspectives. He sees morality as necessary to guide individual conduct but not to guide state conduct. Thus, a diplomat as representative of the state is not bound by the moral code of its people: "No good man will ever reproach another who endeavors to defend his country, whatever be his mode of doing so." The modern executive faces the same dichotomy: he may recommend corporate actions that he would never condone in his personal life. (See, for example, Section 5.3.)

In sum, the organizational perspective helps us with sociotechnical systems in at least the following ways:

- Identification of the pressures in support of, and opposition to, the technology;
- Insight into the societal ability to absorb a technology—the incrementalism common in organizations is an important constraint;
- Increasing ability to facilitate or retard implementation of technology by understanding how to gain organizational support;

- Drawing forth impacts not apparent with other perspectives, for example, based on realities created within an organization;
- Development of practical policy (for example, new coalitions).

It might well be argued that reductionism, noted as a characteristic of the technical perspective, is in evidence also in the organizational perspective. The point to be made, however, is that it takes quite a different form. We are not concerned here with a reduced number of quantified variables but rather with such "reductions" as the application of a discount rate and use of standard operating procedures. All of these characteristics are simplifications, but fundamentally different from those associated with the T perspective.

A list of characteristics of the O perspective as well as a comparison with those of the other perspectives will follow in Section 3.5.

3.4 The Personal Perspective

The personal (P) perspective is the most subtle and elusive, the most difficult to define. Here the world is seen through the filter of the individual's eyes and brain. The P perspective should sweep in any aspects that relate individuals to the sociotechnical system and cannot be brought out by the other perspectives. Thus we exclude from this perspective the purely physical impacts of a technology on the individual, for example, medical technology on life expectancy. But intuition, charisma, leadership, and self-interest, which play vital roles in matters of policy and decision, may only be understood through the P perspective. The systems philosopher sees the "unique individual," the clinician talks about "specificity of behavior."

Freud, in his epochal *Interpretation of Dreams,* perceived three layers: professional, political, and persona. He found the first to be the most current and accessible; the third to be the deepest, least current, and least accessible [18]. The analogy to our three perspectives is self-evident. As would be anticipated with Freud's psychoarcheological conception, we will find most difficulty with the personal perspective.

A T-oriented analysis of selected individuals' decision-making processes has clearly shown that their cognitive maps of causal linkages are remarkably free of feedback, that is, cycles. Axelrod attributes this to people having more beliefs than they can handle [6]. They simplify by considering the one-directional policy-consequence linkages and avoiding the complication of doubling back. Military planners exhibit this tendency in studying future enemy strategies and tactics: they develop our responses to them and then fail to consider what the enemy might do to minimize the effectiveness of these responses. Technologists start with a problem and develop a solution, but neglect to go the next step, that is, probe the problems created by such a solution (see Section 2.1).

Thus we have at least a partial rational explanation of the "irrational" behavior of the individual as well as the group. Incidentally, as Hofstadter points out, the computer can be as irrational as the human mind [19]. The notion that "irrationality is incompatible with computers" rests on a serious misconception. A computer working perfectly can be instructed to print out illogical statements. Similarly, a brain with faultlessly working neurons may support "irrational" human behavior; that is, a belief held in the software of the mind may clash with the hardware of a perfectly functioning brain.

There are clearly many individuals who interact, directly or indirectly, with a sociotechnical system. There are beneficiaries and victims, entrepreneurs and users, regulators and lobbyists. There are the "hidden movers." These are individuals who, from a second- or third-level position, pull the strings that determine how things progress. (Attention is usually so keenly focused on the behavior of the puppets, which is overt, that the effect of the puppeteer, who is hidden from view, is ignored.) In the case of a very prominent power position, we need to look for the "power behind the throne," especially if we suspect that the ostensible power person is not operating under his own steam. This is difficult enough, but at least in such a case—because of the interest of historians and political analysts, for example—the persons surrounding the power position are in the public eye and therefore subject to scrutiny. Still, the "gatekeeper," or person who controls the information flow in an organization, is often difficult to identify.

For less publicly prominent positions, the powers behind the throne usually remain obscure. They may not even appear on the organizational chart. One way of possibly identifying them is to look for the individuals who do the writing in an organization (policy statements, position papers, and standard operating procedures or regulations, for example). Their writing frequently sets the tone for the organization or else becomes a point of departure for discussion within the organization. If such persons hold their position for any length of time, it may be assumed that they wield considerable influence.

Personal probing is essential in identifying key individuals. In cases of an emerging technology there may not yet be identifiable individuals. In such instances, types and their characteristics must be sketched. And here, too, the P perspective is of value that cannot be estimated. What makes a future Sammy run can often be predicted by analogy with past movers. In fact, an interview might elicit interesting insights on how to "beat the system" or outflank recalcitrant bureaucracies.

Intuition is a well-appreciated trait in the world of business, as the following quotes suggest:

- R. P. Jensen, Chairman of General Cable Corp.: "On each decision, the mathematical analysis only got me to the point where my intuition had to take over" [20].
- J. Fetzer, Chairman of Fetzer Broadcasting Co.: "Walk through an office, and intuition tells you if things are going well" [20].
- R. Siu, Management Consultant: "Effective CEOs . . . are aware that rationality and the scientific method provide critical inputs to only one of three crucial questions overarching key decisions. These are: (a) Does it add up? (b) Does it sound okay? and (c) Does it feel right? Logic and science contribute primarily to the first question, less to the second, and even less to the third" [21].

The typical T-trained mind usually balks at the mention of intuition. Some individuals' P perspective is virtually a T perspective, that is, T dominates in their own world view. A quintessential T-focused executive is Robert S. McNamara, the former Secretary of Defense. He perceived the Vietnamese conflict in strictly systems-analytic terms—with disastrous results. Even three decades later, he still cannot grasp that war deals with human beings and cannot be managed without giving full attention to the O and P perspectives.

It is significant that some T-oriented, highly respected scientists have not been afraid to pay homage to intuition and accept it as an important concept. Consider Jacques Hadamard's classic, *The Psychology of Invention in the Mathematical Field*. He writes:

> That those sudden enlightenments which can be called inspirations cannot be produced by chance alone is already evident . . . there can be no doubt of the necessary intervention of some previous mental process unknown to the inventor, in other terms, of an unconscious one [22].

He quotes the German physicist Helmholtz, who observed that "happy ideas" never came to him when his mind was fatigued or when he was seated at his work table. "After the fatigue . . . has passed away, there must come an hour of complete physical freshness before the good ideas arrive."

Poincaré, another well-known French mathematician, distinguishes (1) fully conscious work, (2) illumination ("happy ideas") preceded by incubation, and (3) the quite peculiar process of the first sleepless night. The unconscious appears to consist of several levels. Hadamard writes:

It is quite natural to speak of a more intuitive mind if the zone where ideas are combined is deeper and of a logical one if that zone is rather superficial. This manner of facing the distinction is the one I should believe to be the most important [22].

In the case of exceptionally intuitive minds, even important links of deduction may remain unknown to the thinker who has himself found them. Hadamard cites examples: mathematicians Fermat, Riemann, Galois, and Cardan. Cardan's invention of imaginary numbers ($i = \sqrt{-1}$) is a beautiful example of the use of the nontraditional to leap from one rational to another rational domain.

More recently, Nobel laureate Herbert Simon and associates explored the differences between experts and novices in solving physics problems. They found that the expert is mentally guided by large numbers of patterns serving as an index to relevant parts of the knowledge store. The patterns are:

. . . rich schemata that can guide a problem's interpretation and solution and add crucial pieces of information. This capacity to use pattern-indexed schemata is probably a large part of what we call physical intuition [23].

Each individual has a unique set of patterns that inform his intuition. In calling on the P perspective, we are thus augmenting the conscious, logical T process by opening ourselves to the deeper mental levels that store patterns of great potential value. Salk specifically stresses the need to cultivate both intuitive and reasoning realms—separately and together. Indeed the evolution of the human mind depends on this binary relationship [24].

Isaiah Berlin insists that a superior P perspective affords a sense of greater vision, a more profound feeling for the flow of life in which we are immersed [25]. It sees what can be and what cannot; it has an awareness of the interplay of the imponderables with the ponderables.

Leadership is a quality of recognized importance in science and business as well as in politics and the military. "He who knows how to summon the forces from the deep, him they will follow" [26]. This applies not only to political demagogues and statesmen but to influential academics and dynamic entrepreneurs. Courant in applied mathematics, Rabi in atomic structure, von Braun in rocketry, and Ford in automobile production were leaders. Disciples, students, and imitators built on these leaders' innovative ideas and magnified their impact.

Self-interest motivates most of us, although it is usually hidden. It may take the form of prestige, profit, power, or pleasure. Florman writes in *The Existential Pleasures of Engineering:*

As an engineer, I have an instinctive flush of pride in the machine . . . every man-made structure has a little bit of cathedral in it, since man cannot help but transcend himself as soon as he begins to design and construct [27].

The felt need to mask this energizing factor generates deceptions and illusions that may be difficult to penetrate. Successful technological innovation and policy change implementation require leadership; leadership is driven by self-interest.

Effective organizations are those that have found successful ways of making the self-interest of the members work constructively and in unison to support the goals of the organization. And one guideline to pursue self-interest in organizations successfully is to:

provide others a personal perspective on what you are trying to accomplish and the importance it holds in terms of what matters to you [28].

And "what matters to you" is found in each person's unique reality, his or her "alignment":

There is no way of comprehending the rationale behind someone's behavior . . . until you understand the alignment that underlies that person's orientation [28].

Mitroff's detailed study of more than forty scientists who participated in the Apollo lunar missions clearly determined that they often had very good reasons for behaving irrationally [29].

It is their intense, raw, and even brutal aggressiveness that stands out . . . As one of the respondents put it, "if you want to get anybody to believe your hypothesis, you've got to beat them down with numbers; you've got to hit them again and again over the head with hard data until they're stupified into believing it" [29].

Specifically, we see the P perspective in four roles, which we discuss in the following sections.

An Understanding of the Total Decision Process Is Enhanced Through the Participating Actors

Political activity involves the interactions of organizations and individuals. Usually we cannot grasp the political process without knowing the characteristics of the individual players; they are illuminated by the P perspective.

Voter attitudes may be better understood by selected in-depth interviews than by polls. Reporters often find in hindsight that they would have been much better served by relying on their own legwork, which in turn produces their own political instincts [30].

Insiders' books on the Kennedy and Nixon White Houses and works such as Truman Capote's *In Cold Blood* give us other examples of the insights dug up from the deep layer of the P perspective.

In many top-level corporate and governmental decision-making settings the staff is highly sensitive to the chief executive's P perspective. They therefore filter incoming information for him so that it conforms as much as possible to that perspective. This process has disastrous effects at times. The filtered intelligence provided to President Lyndon Johnson on Vietnam, Presidents Nixon and Carter on Iran, President Reagan on the Soviet Union, and President Bush on Iraq all reflect a kind of "sanitized groupthink" molded by loyal subordinates anxious to support and enhance their superior's P perspective.

The P Perspective Serves as a Precursor to a Better Understanding of the O Perspective

The affected persons may be considered as a group, but the impact may be comprehensible only by dealing directly with individuals and their perspectives on a one-to-one basis. By learning individual beliefs, we can separate those that are widely shared (that is, collective beliefs) from those that are not. For example, union reactions can be gauged better by knowing the attitudes of individual union members, the reaction of blacks to automatic teller machines could be fathomed by direct dialog, and the understanding of the impact of television on children or of mobility on the aged benefits from personal contacts.

Individuals May Matter, and This Perspective Identifies Their Characteristics and Behavior

It was the grand old man of forecasting, Bertrand de Jouvenel, who observed that:

who sits up there makes a major difference . . . and it seems foolish not to recognize that individual decisions are historical causes in their own right [31].

Individuals can bring about change more easily than can institutions. Salk sees this as a prime reason to focus on the individual [24].

Robert Goddard, Andrew Carnegie, and Admiral Rickover had recognizable impact on the course of technology. Yet, we have found that there is a strong temptation on the part of T-oriented individuals to downplay the P perspective. Among the arguments are four that will be considered in turn.

Only in Rare Cases Does the Individual Make a Difference

The criterion as to whether an individual makes a difference is often difficult to apply. Would the American Revolution have had the same outcome if the roles of Generals Washington and Gates had been reversed? There are obvious situations, but more frequently it is possible to provide a meaningful answer only in hindsight.

"Crazy Judah" (Theodore D. Judah) was the brilliant railroad engineer whose enthusiasm—or fanaticism—galvanized the largest and most important engineering enterprise of America's first century, a transcontinental railroad. It was a technological project comparable in its challenge to the Apollo manned lunar landing in this country's second century. Not one man in 50 in 1860 believed that rails would ever cross the rugged Sierra Nevada mountain range. Judah was the conceptualizer, money raiser, engineering supervisor, and lobbyist. He convinced several Sacramento merchants—among them Huntington, Stanford, Crocker, and Hopkins—to form the Central Pacific Railroad Company. He wrote impact assessments, determined the route, and arranged to be on the staffs of both the House and Senate Committees dealing with the Railroad Bill to support the project. On July 1, 1862, in the midst of the Civil War, President Lincoln signed the crucial bill. Judah then had the difficult task of keeping the effort steadfastly directed at his long-range objective rather than becoming sidetracked for attractive short-term profits. Undoubtedly, a railroad would have been constructed after the Civil War, but the changed timing and nature would have affected the course of California's development.

Suppose there had been no Wright brothers. Someone else would have initiated powered flight, possibly in Germany or France. Would it have made a difference? The American aerospace industry might have been a German or French one. It frequently does matter who is first.

Dr. Frances Kelsey of the U.S. Food and Drug Administration was a key figure in preventing the sale of thalidomide, a drug introduced in Europe to treat headaches. It proved to have a most serious side effect in pregnant women: deformed children. Did she make a difference? Had another, less stubborn, person handled this New Drug Application, the ultimate result would have been the same, although a great deal of human suffering would have been precipitated. In the Kelsey case, public attitudes toward government regulation, toward the ethics of drug manufacturers, and toward chemicals generally could have been significantly different. If we contend that anyone in Dr. Kelsey's position might have resisted the pressures equally well, we are saying that decisions do not matter, only roles do. And if decisions do not matter, what is the point of decision and policy analysis at all? Is not the purpose to aid the decision process? If decisions do matter, they must not be treated as though they do not; thus, the people who make them also matter. Moreover, such analysis is concerned with the short and intermediate, as well as the long-term future, and the transient effects of individual decisions are of the essence since they influence the trajectory and its practical concomitants.

Holsti lists seven circumstances in which the individual decision maker may be of significance:

1. Nonroutine situations where standard operating procedures (SOPs) do not apply;
2. Decisions made at the top of the organizational hierarchy by leaders free from constraints;
3. Long-range policy planning, where there is wide variation among policy makers on "what is desirable" and "what is important";
4. When the situation itself is highly ambiguous;
5. When there is information overload, and such strategies as filtering, queuing, and omission must be used;
6. Unanticipated events unleashing individual initial reactions that may be decisive;
7. Circumstances in which complex cognitive tasks associated with decision making may be impaired by stresses on decision makers [32].

There Are Too Many Individuals to Be Considered

This argument assumes that a P perspective is useful only if a very large number of individuals with different perspectives is included. This is analogous to the contention that a decision maker cannot make a decision unless he has obtained input from every affected individual. Recognizing that this is impractical, the decision maker does not jump to the other extreme and argue that he should not talk to any affected party.

The most widely articulated argument among political scientists against cognitive approaches to foreign policy decision making is based on "theoretical parsimony and research economy" [32]. Not surprisingly, the T-oriented researcher is readily convinced that he can get more mileage from T than from P; in other words, with his very limited resources, the benefit-cost ratio of T appears higher to him.

P Provides a Carte Blanche for Baseless Claims

It may be argued that our ability to analyze a sociotechnical system is very modest, even with the perspective that is most "scientific." After all, the T perspective involves conjectures about consequences, assumptions about models, and at best, partial evidence. The lack of rigor characterizing P provides the analyst leeway for all kinds of gratuitous interpretations and attributions. When it comes to assessing, by way of anticipation, the influence of an individual actor on the development or implementation of a technology (or, more generally, on historical processes), the criterion of "reasonableness of conjecture" should be applied. Certain "wild" speculations should be eschewed, even though it can be demonstrated that there are historical precedents for the projected scenario. Because the Roman emperor Caligula appointed a horse to the position of consul, we are not justified to spin out extraordinary possibilities of a similar nature. Unfortunately, history is a cautionary tale of the chameleon nature of the reasonableness criterion itself.

One cannot pose an a priori argument that multiple perspectives are invariably superior to a single (T) perspective. Obviously, three poorly done perspectives will be inferior to one excellent T perspective. As in aerial photography, three overexposed shots from different angles will tell us less than one sharp shot. The answer lies with the quality of the multiple perspectives, that is, the integrity, appropriateness, and experience of the analysts. As a general rule, well-drawn multiple perspectives are nearly always preferable to a single perspective.

The Analysis Would Become Too Sensitive, That Is, Politicized

The argument assumes that the analysis can be apolitical and operate effectively at a macrolevel, where individuals are seen far below as so many ants. Those most comfortable with the T perspective are also most likely to be made nervous by the political sensitivity of the perspectives that are most appropriate to what Allison calls bureaucratic politics [5]. They nearly always prefer to shun these aspects, although doing so may strip the work of much of its value and submerge some of the very things that should be brought to the surface. A noncontroversial impact assessment is also likely to be an assessment of very modest usefulness.

Some of the consequences of descending from the Olympian heights, where objectivity reigns and politics can be disdained, are as follows:

- The sponsor may be displeased and withhold further contracts or assignments from the analysts;
- Other clients may withhold contracts or assignments;
- The report may be buried by the client;
- If care is not exercised by the analysts, confidentiality of input may be breached through attribution, with resulting embarrassment to informants;
- Individuals and organizations may be helped or hurt.

Despite these concerns, we cannot escape the fact that a sociotechnical systems analysis, like any policy analysis, is inherently political.

Communication of Complex Problems and Issues May Be Made More Effective by Means of the Personal Perspective

Novelists and playwrights successfully express social issues through the words of individuals. Shaw uses the unique Liza Doolittle and her father to portray class problems in England. Arthur Miller uses Willie Loman to describe the American urge to be well liked. Barbara Tuchman uses a single person, Enguerrand de Coucy, as the local point of her sweeping survey of fourteenth-century Europe. Hauptmann's *Rose Bernd,* Ibsen's *The Wild Duck,* Solzhenitsyn's *Gulag Archipelago,* Burgess' *1985,* and television's *Upstairs, Downstairs* are other striking illustrations of the use of the P perspective to communicate social concepts. The enormity of the Nazi holocaust cannot be told at all by the T perspective (statistics of six million murders), but it is at least partly communicated by the P perspective *Diary of Anne Frank* and Spielberg's motion picture *Schindler's List.*

Focusing on the business world, Peters and Waterman also find that

we are more influenced by stories (vignettes that are whole and make sense in themselves) than by data (which are, by definition, utterly abstract) [12, p. 61].

Tolstoy's struggle with the P perspective is most revealing. In the epilogue to *War and Peace,* he addresses himself to the historian's eternal question: were Napoleon and Alexander the cause of the effects they produced, or was the movement of nations produced by the activity of all the people who participated in the events? His answer:

> Morally, the wielder of power appears to cause the event; physically it is those who submit to the power . . . The cause of the event is neither in the one nor in the other but in the union of the two [33].

Tolstoy had a marvelous feeling for piercing the heart of a P perspective; he recognized the importance of each individual. He felt it was essential to present the invasion of Russia through the eyes of individuals, not organizations and abstract forces. His unresolved dilemma was his inability to integrate a vast number of P perspectives. He could not do what, say, the physicist does in dealing with the immense number of particles in a gas, that is, integrate the individual effects into a very meaningful gas law. Focusing on Napoleon is clearly not the way to integrate the individuals involved with the invasion of Russia. But neither does this mean that Napoleon as an individual is immaterial. As Isaiah Berlin observes:

> Napoleon may not be a demigod, but neither is he a mere epiphenomenon of a process that would have occurred unaltered without him [25].

It is the rare individual who can incorporate in his own thinking the appropriate balance among the T, O, and P perspectives and thus can apply the multiple perspective concept effectively as a one-person effort.

3.5 T + O + P: Characteristics and Comparisons

Table 3.1 summarizes the distinctive characteristics of the three perspectives.

Together, T, O, and P constitute, in Churchman's terms, a Singerian inquiring system.

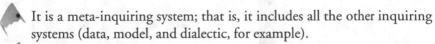

- It is a meta-inquiring system; that is, it includes all the other inquiring systems (data, model, and dialectic, for example).
- It is pragmatic; that is, the truth content is relative to the overall goals and objectives of the inquiry.
- It takes holistic thinking so seriously that it constantly attempts to "sweep in" new components; it is, in fact, nonterminating and explicitly concerned with the future.

Table 3.1
Characteristics of Multiple Perspectives

	Technical (T)	Organizational (O)	Personal (P)
Worldview	Science-technology	Unique group or institutional view	Individual, the self
Objective	Problem solving, product	Action, process, stability	Power, influence, prestige
System focus	Artificial construct	Social	Genetic, psychological
Mode of inquiry	Observation, analysis: data and models	Consensual, adversary, bargaining and compromise	Intuition, learning, experience
Ethical basis	Logic, rationality	Justice, fairness	Morality, personal ethics
Planning horizon	Far (low discounting)	Intermediate (moderate discounting)	Short for most (high discounting)
Other descriptors	Cause and effect	Agenda (problem of the moment)	Challenge and response, leaders and followers
	Optimization	Satisfying	Ability to cope with only a few alternatives
	Quantification, trade-offs, cost-benefit analysis	Incremental change	Fear of change
	Probabilities, averages, statistics, expected value	Reliance on experts, internal training of practitioners	Need for beliefs, illusions, misperception of probabilities
	Problem simplified and idealized, reductionism	Problem delegated, factored, issues and crisis management	Hierarchy of individual needs (survival, . . .)
	Need validation, replicability	Need standard operating procedures, routinization	Need to filter out inconsistent images
	Conceptualization, systems theories	Reasonableness	Creativity, vision by the few, improvisation
	Uncertainties noted	Uncertainty used for organizational self-preservation	Need for certainty
Criteria for "acceptable risk"	Logical soundness, openness to evaluation, decision analysis	Institutional compatibility, political acceptability, practicality	Conduciveness to learning, focus on "me-now"
Communications	Technical report, briefing	Insider language, outsiders' assumptions often misperceived	Personality and charisma desirable

• It postulates that the system designer is a fundamental part of the system; his psychology and sociology are inseparable from the system's physical representation [34].

A subtle, but important, advantage in the use of such a pragmatic Singerian approach is the automatic reduction in the reliance on shaky theoretical analysis in decision making. The strength of the quasi-theological faith in models developed via the T perspective is awe inspiring and frightening. Multiple perspectives should minimize this self-delusion because the T perspective no longer dominates the analysis.

The schematic in Figure 3.1 shows the typical case of a single T perspective (one vertex) and multiple O and P perspectives (multiple vertices) illuminating a system consisting of interacting technology, organizations, and individuals.

We do not consider the differences between disciplines (for example, aeronautical engineering, electronic engineering, and economics) as reflecting different inquiring systems. They all use the same data/model-based paradigms, the same mode of perceiving, but they do look at different parts of the problem

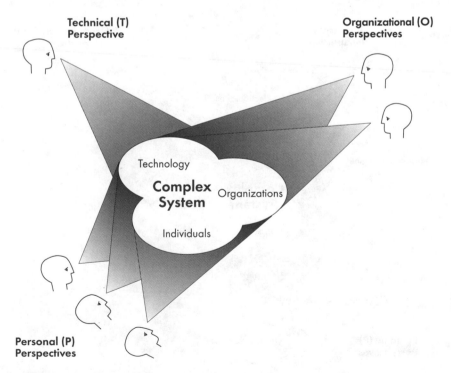

Figure 3.1 T, O, and P perspectives on a complex sociotechnical system.

(usually using different variables and mathematical models). The aeronautical engineer, electronic engineer, and economist may look at the same aircraft design and focus on different problems (for instance, lift, avionics, and cost per mile). But they all use the T perspective: they develop models (wind tunnel or computer) and seek to quantify and optimize. This is denoted in Figure 3.2 using a single vertex for T. Putting it simply, they all use the same kind of lens to "see" the system, whereas each organization O and individual P uses a unique lens. This is not to deny the change, over time, of the accepted scientific paradigm as well as the simultaneous existence of distinct paradigms, as with the Ptolemaic and Copernican cosmological theories and the wave and particle theories of light. It is, however, far less common with T while it is the norm in the O and P. Kuhn's *Structure of Scientific Revolutions* deals with this process in the hard sciences.

Another example of opposing T perspectives is the split among T-oriented forecasters between technological optimists (for example, physicist Herman Kahn and economist Julian Simon) and pessimists (for example, the *Limits to Growth* and *Global 2000* Reports). Dunlap [35] sees them in terms of two sets of paradigms: exemptionalist and ecological. In the former, culture and technol-

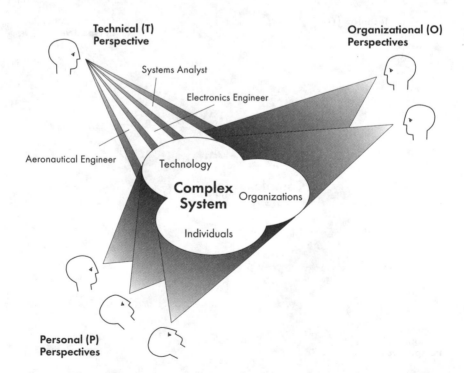

Figure 3.2 Multiple disciplines are not multiple perspectives.

ogy enable Homo sapiens to adapt nature to human ends, that is, man possesses characteristics such as intellect and organizational capability, which make him an exceptional species "exempt" from the ecological principles that govern all other forms of life. In the ecological paradigm, man cannot evade ecological laws and is dependent on the continued stability of the global ecosystem (for example, on finite resources).

The difference between technological optimists and pessimists may also be interpreted as follows. A problem may have several possible technological solutions, with each solution creating new problems. For example, advances in medical, sanitation, and food production technology raise global life expectancy and, in turn, exacerbate overpopulation and pollution. Such a "tree" was represented in Figure 2.2. The optimists focus on the solutions, the pessimists on the new problems.

Turning to O and P, we depict in Figure 3.3 the quasi-continuous range of perspectives for individuals and organizations. There are various individuals, informal groupings, formal small and large organizations, or social entities, Each has a unique *Weltanschauung,* a distinct perspective. We could subdivide

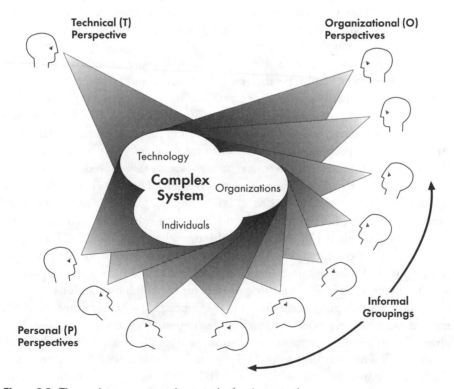

Figure 3.3 The continuum—personal to organizational perspectives.

O and P perspectives into various categories, such as institutional and cultural perspectives, individual-personal and situational-personal perspectives. We have chosen not to complicate the basic concept; to follow this path could easily lead us into a morass of semantic and sterile academic debates.

We have already noted in Section 3.2 that the T perspective is a distinctly modern phenomenon. For millenia of human existence, the O and P perspectives were dominant. Western medieval man, for example, used the O and P perspectives almost exclusively: his society and religion were his world, and these "organizations" prescribed his perspectives. His space and time were finite: the world was 4000 years old and would soon end. The realm of knowledge was also assumed to be bounded. But the past years of exploration and scientific discovery have resulted in the ascendancy of the T perspective to a level of importance unknown in any previous era. By no means, however, has it replaced the other perspectives. A look at Germany, the world's leading country in science and technology during the 1920s and 1930s, should make this very apparent.

The perspectives may also be considered in an ethical context. The T perspective avoids involvement with moral concerns; it affects neutrality and perceives any system through the eyes of an external observer assumed to be objective. It searches for cause and effect, for solvable problems.

The scientist/technologist, initiated into the multiple perspective concept, may assert that the T perspective ought to have more normative force and authority than the O and P perspectives. This view is not far removed from the notion that the T perspective is the correct one and that the others simply reflect irrational human beings interferring with it. We do not share this quasi-technocratic attitude. Science's very modest level of understanding of the human brain suggests that the proposed reliance of sociotechnical systems on the T perspective, even if only for normative considerations, seems rash indeed.

The O and P perspectives sweep in human beings, their emotions and ethics. The difference between O and P is exemplified ethically as that between organizational and individual dominance, between subservience to the society and personal freedom [36]. In a hierarchical, authoritarian society, P perspectives are unimportant; only the O perspective matters (except for the person at the top of the hierarchy). In a heterarchical, democratic society, P perspectives are important; each individual is responsible for his or her own actions.

The technologist's preference for the T perspective commonly mirrors a natural bent: he feels more comfortable dealing with objects than people. It is, after all, the people orientation that most profoundly distinguishes O and P from T. It has recently been suggested that in the business world, what truly sets the bootstrapping manager without an MBA apart from the stereotypical MBA and "what seems to account in large measure for his success is an almost passionate focus upon people" [37]. The MBA training emphasizes the technique-oriented, T perspective approach to management; it is much less effective in enhancing the ability to deal with people—and this is often where the degreeless executives excel. It is significant that Swiss banks and Israeli industrial enterprises draw many of their leaders from their respective military establishments. The demonstrated ability to lead and inspire people seems more important to them than a classroom-trained MBA. And this is precisely where the O and P perspectives come to the forefront. We suspect that an effective executive exhibits a good balance of T, O, and P. This would explain at once why T-focused professors of management can learn more from practicing managers than the practicing managers can learn from the academics. The academics have to observe the managers before they can write their "how to" books. In the words of CEO Tom Monaghan of Domino's Pizza,

> I didn't really learn much that was new to me . . . I found as I was reading it
> that I knew the sense of what it was going to say next even before I read the
> words [38].

Indeed, I would have never developed the multiple perspective concept if I had not spent half my career in industry.

Most individuals appear to constitute a dynamic mixture of perspective types. We rarely deal with either a pure T-, O-, or P-oriented person or with one exhibiting a perfect balance among the perspective types. The "norm" is apparently a presence of all three perspective types in an unbalanced way. The ivory-tower scientist should be expected to have a dominant T perspective in the contacts we are most likely to have with him. But we have also observed the presence of the P perspective in the scientist, in terms of intuition, drive, and prestige concerns. On the other hand, the successful "organization man" [39] should have a particularly well-developed O perspective but should not completely lack T or P perspectives. Genetic as well as environmental factors may underlie the unique mix or dominance of perspective types in each person. Since we need diverse perspectives, research to improve our ability to identify the individual's characteristic imbalance would be most helpful.

The preceding discussion raises an intriguing philosophical question: If the P perspective is defined as the individual's view of the world, does it not encompass whatever mix of T, O, and P types resides in the mind of that person? In other words, is it proper in our context to discuss an individual's world view in terms of T, O, and P balance and imbalance or is that world view indivisible? We postulate that a qualitative discussion of the individual's personal balance or bias in perspective types can be meaningful and useful. The characteristics of the types are usually distinguishable (see Table 3.1). Freud's analogy of the three psychoarcheological layers in the individual (Section 3.3) assumes a similar separability of types. We do, in fact, often distinguish in our own decision making what is best objectively, what is best for our organization, and what is best for us personally.

We conclude this section with a review of the key characteristics.

1. *We have considered three perspective types: T, O, and P. Each yields insights not obtainable with the others, and this is the justification for using multiple perspectives.* None by itself suffices to deal with a complex system, but together they provide a richer base for decision and action. Using a single perspective is analogous to employing a single dimension to depict a three-dimensional object. Each added dimension facilitates comprehension. At the same time we must remember that the ability to live comfortably with, and tolerate, multiple perspectives is exceedingly difficult for many people. No matter how much additional insight they provide, some people simply cannot tolerate three very different perspectives of a single system (just as they cannot handle multiple religions).

2. *Any system may be viewed from any perspective.* For example, an organization may be viewed from a T perspective as well as an O perspective; an engineering project may be viewed from a P perspective as well as a T perspective. A given system decision usually involves a number of organizational and individual actors, each with a distinct O or P perspective. Two perspectives may reinforce one another or cancel each other.

3. *The paradigms associated with T are not appropriate for O and P.* Thus, terms such as "proof," "replicability," and "validation," standard in science and technology, are not suitable for O and P. For example, decisions (like jury trials and sports events) are one-time occurrences and can never be replicated.

4. *The choice of which particular perspectives to bring to bear or emphasize in a specific problem is a matter of one's ethical values and judgments.* We cannot "prove" that any set is the "right" one any more than an executive can prove that he or she consulted the "right" sources before making an important decision.

5. *The systems designer, analyst, or manager is a fundamental part of the system or problem being analyzed.* The individual's psychology as well as social context are inseparable from how he or she represents a system or problem.

6. *Perspectives are dynamic and can change over time, suggesting the value of periodic iteration.* New technological factors come into play and the organizational and key individual actors change.

7. *It is not always easy to distinguish between an O and a P perspectives.* Is the person giving his or her own or the organization's perspective? Effective organizations are usually characterized by a strong congruence between the O perspective and their members' P perspectives.

8. *In a decision process, T tends to dominate in the early planning phases, giving way to O/P dominance in the later action phases.*

We now turn to the important task of integrating perspectives.

3.6 Integration of Perspectives

President John F. Kennedy wrote in 1963:

The essence of an ultimate decision remains impenetrable to the observer—often, indeed, to the decider himself . . . There will always be the dark and tangled stretches in the decision-making process—mysterious even to those who may be most intimately involved [40].

"Ultimate decision" involves the final integration of input, usually of various perspectives. How should we deal with it?

In Section 3.1 we introduced the American courtroom trial to illustrate multiple perspectives (witness testimonies). We pointed out that the jury can accept the integration of the prosecutor or that of the defense attorney or reject both and do its own integration of the testimony. Neither a jury nor an executive can reconstruct precisely how the integration occurred and the decision was reached.

Most decision makers find it quite difficult to describe this process explicitly, although they execute it every day. Consider the case of General Motors' decision to downsize in consequence of the oil crisis.

As reported by William Halal [39]:

An awareness of the energy crisis . . . during the early 1970s increased the emphasis on strategic planning at GM. The "down-sizing" decision . . . was formulated in a process of "logical incrementalism" that includes successive steps searching for marginal improvements that comprise the formulation of a new strategic posture. Some major advances in this direction included: the formation of an ad hoc task force on energy in 1972, the approval of the Seville [K] and Chevette [T] car programs which proposed 800–1000 pound weight reductions across the entire product line . . . [These steps were followed by] formation of a strategic planning department in 1977 at the corporate level.

As reported by Joseph Kraft [40]:

I asked Murphy [Chairman of the Board] when that decision had been made . . . Pointing to the sheets he held in his hand, he said, "This is an official schedule of major actions by GM. It says here that the executive committee approved the K-Car decision on Jan. 23, 1974, and the T-Car on the same day. But I know it's wrong. We didn't make the decision in the executive committee. We made it in the engineering-policy group. It was on December 23."

There had, in fact, been no high-level meetings at GM on the date described by the Chairman of the Board as D-Day. [The interviewer then talked to Gerstenberg, Chairman of the Board 1972–74.] Gerstenberg's account . . . was just as flawed as that given by Murphy. For one thing Gerstenberg was wrong about the committee that made things happen. [It was not all forgetfulness. Tactics were also involved.]

An official of the Department of Transportation said, "Nobody at GM could tell you exactly how the downsizing decision was made because nobody knows. Without the [government's] miles-per-gallon standards, GM would never have downsized the way it did." That view was endorsed by a Washington lawyer who works for the auto industry . . . He wrote me: "Only when the fuel economy standards were enacted in 1975 did a comprehensive approach to downsizing begin."

The process of integration is not merely one of assembling a composite picture from jigsaw puzzle pieces, nor ironing out contradictions by some rules of thumb, nor arranging the information hierarchically. Integration resembles the task of conceptualizing a three-dimensional object from a series of one-dimensional descriptions and two-dimensional drawings.

In the integration process the perspectives *cross-cue* each other: they may reinforce each other or cancel each other out. In the jury case, the prosecutor and defense attorney each cross-cue witness statements in preparing their respective summations to strengthen their case and weaken the opponent's. In the case of the executive, the staff may provide a series of perspectives and a proto-type integration, but here, as with the jury, the final integration must be left to the decision maker. It is hazardous and counterproductive for the staff analyst to do the integration and provide only that as input to the decision maker. This would correspond to the jury only hearing the summations and not the witness testimonies. It would mean that the decision maker cannot introduce his or her own weighting of the perspectives. The prototype integrations may be of considerable value to the decision maker, but they may also fail to include considerations only known at the highest level (including intuitive ones).

There are arguments for providing a *prototype* integration. One is the possibility that an inexperienced client may misuse the perspectives. For example, he or she might choose a "best" perspective and ignore the others. Or, the analysis might be thrown out because there appears to be disagreement among perspectives. The technologist is not accustomed to dialectic inquiring systems.

There are special circumstances where the integration without presentation of contributing perspectives might be justified. It may be desirable to "launder" or neutralize politically sensitive insights obtained from the O and P perspectives. But it is our view that, in general, the decision maker is poorly served by receiving only the integrated product.

Two words that should be tabu in any discussion of the study of sociotechnical systems are *comprehensive* and *definitive,* as in "a risk analysis should be comprehensive" or "the described perspectives are definitive." Only a T perspective mind is likely to use these words. Anyone who has tried to determine the number of interactions possible with a small number of elements in a system (see Section 2.3) will understand the unreality of comprehensiveness. So will anyone who has studied the impacts of technologies in history.

3.7 Linkages and the Interactions of Perspectives

We will now probe cross-cuing of perspectives in another way. Figure 3.4 schematically suggests the basic relationships among the perspective types, and Figure 3.5 is a simplified schematic version that we will find useful. We will briefly illustrate the connections.

T and O: Information Technology and Societal Organization

A particularly fascinating and timely issue of technology in its complex systemic setting is that of the impact of information technology on societal organization.

A useful metaphor for the evolutionary growth of complex societal systems and its cyclic nature is the spiral shown in Figure 3.6 [41, 42]. There is an alternation between two stable states, centralized and decentralized or integrated and separated. A simple, hierarchical system, say, a tribe or small

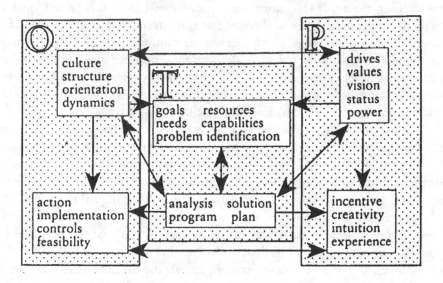

Figure 3.4 Perspective interactions. (*Source:* [41] © 1994, Reprinted with permission. All rights reserved.)

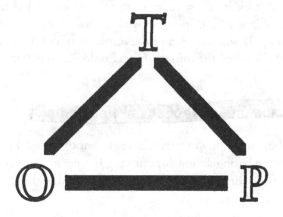

Figure 3.5 Another schematic for T-O-P (*Source:* [41] © 1994, Reprinted with permission. All rights reserved.)

company, grows until it can no longer be effectively managed centrally. It then separates into smaller units with considerable local autonomy. After some time a growing ineffectiveness is observed that leads to reunification. Each shift may invoke a chaotic phase. In other words, successful evolution proceeds to increasing complexity by periodic restructuring involving swings between integration

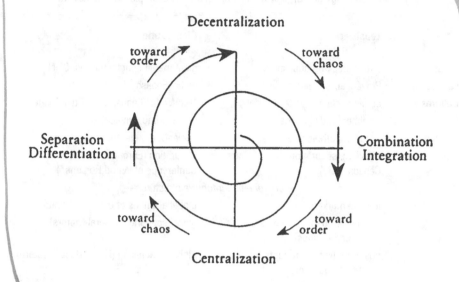

Figure 3.6 The evolution of complex systems. (*Source:* © 1994, Reprinted with permission. All rights reserved.)

and differentiation. We find this behavior at scales ranging from business to cosmology. In particular, history is replete with a cyclical pattern of this kind, from primitive clans to the city-states to empires.[3] Even American history exhibits the swing between decentralized states (eighteenth century) and a strong national government (twentieth century). Today we are in the midst of such a shift: a distinct devolution of power from the federal government.

Now information technology is opening up powerful possibilities of facilitating shifts between centralization and decentralization. We see centralized organizations becoming more decentralized and vice versa. Indeed, we observe *simultaneous* localization and globalization as suggested in Table 3.2.

The crucial questions are: what is the desirable balance between these two organizational states and how can information technology assist in attaining it?

In Nobel laureate Herbert Simon's words,

The question is not whether to decentralize, but to what extent . . . Once more we are trying to define a golden rule: we want to find the exact level

---

3. One can construct a similar spiral for chemical elements, with hydrogen at the center and the heaviest elements at the rim.

Table 3.2
Information Technology and Organizational Change: Some Examples of "Glocalization"

	Localization	Globalization
Media	e-mail, desktop publishing	giant media conglomerates, CNN
Languages	Provençal, Catalan	global English
Cultures	ethnic enclaves	"McWorld" (jeans, Coca-Cola, Disney)
Crime	neighborhood violence	global crime syndicates
Conflicts	terrorism, ethnic war	nuclear war, electronic war
Governance	tribalism, separation (Soviet Union, Canada, Italy)	integration (European Union, NAFTA, Conference of World Regions*)
Corporations	*—coordination-intensive structures—*	
	internal markets	global alliances of enterprise units
	decentralized information services (American Airlines)	global sourcing (General Motors)
	customization of products (clothes manufactured to order)	global franchising (Hertz, Best Western)
	—the internet: consumers and e-corporations—	
	individual consumer-directed rather than seller-directed purchasing on the internet	individual consumer access to worldwide market on the internet
	—multilocal or glocal (global-local) companies—	
	McDonald's	
	local ownership	
	local food variations (different chicken sandwiches in UK, Germany)	
	regional supplies/sourcing (Poland: meat, potatoes, bread)	
		global management concepts
		global quality standards
		global sourcing (Mexico: sesame seeds)
	—virtual corporations—	
	Nokia Display Products	
	Marketing and sales done by International Technology Associates Inc.	
	Customer services and tech. support done by Trillium Industries Inc.	

* A relatively new nonprofit organization that seeks to represent the global interests of subnational economic regions and their leading industries from around the world with the objective of strengthening transnational linkages in areas such as free trade, law enforcement, environmental protection, scientific research and development.

within the organizational hierarchy—neither too high nor too low—best suited to each category of decisions [43].

Voge has used the analogy of telephone switching and finds that "switches in the ideal structure are equally distributed among all [hierarchical] levels" [44].

Drawing on his studies of the coevolution of biological systems and their self-organizing behavior, Kauffman has arrived at the idea that complex organizations develop best when "well-chosen" or optimally sized local subunits, nonoverlapping and semiautonomous, act in their own perceived best interest. For example, a stable effective organizational size in both emergent biological systems and human working groups appears to be about 150. This is the group size predicted for modern man based on the relationship between group size and neocortex size for primates. Petrich cites modern examples where similar size stable social groups evolved, ranging from Microsoft to Booz, Allen & Hamilton [45].

Despite conflicting constraints such complex systems appear to achieve coordination and coevolve even without a central administrator [46]. The optimal degree of decentralization or subunit size appears to be close to the transition between ordered and chaotic states, that is, "at the edge of chaos." At the same time Kauffman is acutely aware of the emergence of globalization. The real significance of these ideas for business organizations in a twenty-first century setting dominated by information technology is becoming apparent. As Table 3.2 shows, we are already observing coordination-intensive, global-local, and virtual structures, de facto efforts to address the crucial balance question. They portend striking new networking arrangements to assure unprecedented flexibility and dynamism [47].

Inevitably, they also raise new concerns. Microsoft has recognized the power of its dominance of the personal computer operating system market (currently about 90%) in controlling the development of other technological innovations in the on-line information field. Among the possible means: bundling its Internet Explorer with Windows 95 and premature announcements of nonexistent future software ("vaporware") to discourage competition. The monopoly potential is raising concerns in the Antitrust Division of the U.S. Justice Department.

Another concern is the ability of the individual in the organization to coevolve with the fluid organization. The need for compatibility between individual and organization will inform the self-organizing process and affect the balance between localization and globalization in unanticipated ways. Fluid organizations require highly adaptive individuals.

O and P: The Extra-Constitutional Corporation

The most basic O-P relationship is that between the society and the individual, usually framed in terms of the individual's rights and responsibilities to the society. John F. Kennedy articulated the challenge in his inaugural presidential speech: "ask not what your country can do for you, but what you can do for your country." The imbalance has been increasingly distorted since World War II, aided and abetted by an explosive growth of the litigious society. But even the corporation must address this problem.

Corporations are "persons" under the U.S. Constitution. They have rights but are not recognized as parts of the society that wield considerable power. This power is exercised through lobbies to assure a favorable operating environment. The power is also seen in their position in communities and their transnational modus operandi. As Constitutional law expert Arthur S. Miller observes:

> America's political economy is dominated by business enterprises not even remotely in the contemplation of the Founding Fathers. Some super-corporations overshadow in economic importance most of the 50 states and many nations of the world. Both domestic and transnational corporations . . . have in significant respects taken over some of the substance of sovereignty and also are warping original constitutional structures. Decisions made in corporate boardrooms, on such matters as investment, prices, and plant location, directly affect (and thereby govern) Americans as well as people elsewhere . . . Corporations are private governments [48].

Yet many corporations show concern neither for the local community in which their business evolved nor for the nation whose soil nurtured them.

> The governing power of corporations should be legitimated. That is two-pronged: first, corporate decisions in some way should further the interests of both the entity and the larger corporation called society; secondly, members of the corporate community who are directly affected by corporate decisions should be protected against arbitrariness . . . In a democratic society, power, to be legitimate, must be responsible, that is, "accountable" [48].

As with natural persons, the corporate persons must assume responsibilities to the society as well as accept rights. One effective step in this direction would be mandatory jail sentences for the top executives for major corporate crimes. It is hard to rationalize jail sentences for the petty theft of $100 and only wrist-slapping fines for billion dollar corporate frauds. The "Catch 22" is that their enormous financial resources give corporations vast political power that translates into the ability to resist imposition of meaningful corporate responsibility to the society.

Another O-P relation, the Asch effect, was discussed in Section 3.3.

T and P: Measurement

As the U.S. Bureau of the Census has found, simple counting of populations raises significant problems that call for perspectives other than T. Consider the census taker knocking on a door in an urban ghetto area. The woman opens the door and he shows his identification card. The door is promptly slammed in his face. The reason: fear that the government might discover a hidden male whereas the woman has been collecting government checks as an abandoned mother with children and no wage-earning father. Another factor is the vast number of illegal aliens. It thus becomes clear why an accurate count of the population is impossible in the United States. It has been proposed that the country adopt a system of mandatory registration of all its inhabitants, as is the norm in Japan and Germany. This idea is strongly opposed by many Americans as an invasion of privacy, an attitude recalling the America of the nineteenth century and its wide open West.

The same situation viewed from an O perspective raises the problems of undercounting and the resulting shortage in federal funds distributed to certain states and cities (such funds being a function of the population count). Congressional apportionment is similarly dependent on the census. Consequently, the "simple" counting problem becomes a highly politicized, rather than a strictly statistical, issue.

T and O and P: The Technological Frontier and the Creative Individual

Figure 3.7 suggests the relationships among the perspectives in facilitating the creative process [49, 50]. Important organizational needs are an open environment with freedom to pursue untried ideas, minimum external constraints, encouragement, recognition, challenge, and stimulation. We can readily point out interactions among all these perspectives:

- P + O → T: The creative individual provides input to the organization on the needed technical resources.

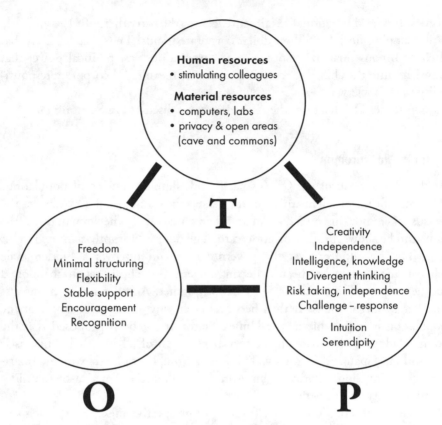

Figure 3.7 Perspectives on creativity (*Source:* [41], © 1994, Reprinted with permission. All rights reserved.)

- • P + T → O: The creative individuals and the technical resources determine the target areas for investigation and the scope of innovations to be pursued by the organization.
- • T + O → P: The technical supporting staff often performs detailed, behind-the-scenes tasks and provide input to the organization that determines how best to proceed toward successful innovations.

The relationship of age to creativity is a significant aspect that affects the interactions among T, O, and P. Young individuals and organizations are more creative than old ones and more open to novelty. As Max Planck once observed, established generations of scientists never accept new theories; they die first. Some studies suggest that the key is not chronological age but "disciplinary" age, that is, how much time has been spent in one working environment. Thus shifting careers can lead to creative rejuvenation.

3.8 Other Perspectives

The R Perspective

Two thousand years ago Cicero was convinced that religion is indispensable to private morals and public order. Over the past two millenia we have had frequent, dreadful breakdowns of institutional and cultural order, many incited by religious differences. Today, despite the rise of science as a quasi-religion, the pattern continues. Still, the late Willis Harman believed that our society is undergoing a fundamental transformation. He saw forces at work that suggest an emerging "transmodern society" characterized neither by a scientific/material nor by a religious/spiritual worldview. Rather, it is a fusion of "scientific inquiry with the perennial wisdom at the core of the world's spiritual traditions" [51]. While it maintains confidence in scientific inquiry, it recognizes the limitations of science, including reductionism and objectivism, in other words, the limitations of the technical perspective.

It is useful to recall that O and P deal with human beings whereas T is an artificial creation of the human mind. As already noted, in evolutionary terms, O and P are much older than T. As the human mind developed, it created spiritual/mythological/religious perspectives, which we label R, in other words the triad O-P-R (Figure 3.8). T and R both constitute human creations, but they exhibit fundamental differences: T is reductionist and seeks to be objective,

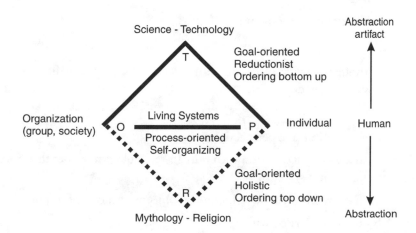

Figure 3.8 The R perspective: a counterpoint to T.

whereas R is holistic and unabashedly subjective. Science struggles with the laws of self-organization (autopoiesis) bubbling up from lower to higher levels, while religion accepts a top-down systemic view (the myth of God the purposeful creator). T and R also have striking similarities: both are goal-driven and employ abstract idealizations. Harman's conviction is that they will jointly form the basis of the transmodern society. Alternatively, there is the prospect of increasingly grave confrontations between T and R as we embark on the age of biotechnology. Technologists are already plunging deeply into areas such as human embryonic cell isolation and the development of cells to produce "improved" animals and repair human organs.

A plea for the integration of natural and social sciences with the humanities by the eminent sociobiologist Edward O. Wilson is also relevant in this connection. He uses the label *consilience* to articulate a scientific vision that encompasses ethics and religion [52].

Chinese Perspectives

Zhichang Zhu has introduced a Chinese set of three multiple perspective types, based on neo-Confucianism, to deal with complex sociotechnical systems. They are labeled WSR:

- *wuli:* denoting knowledge about physical world phenomena, material conditions as well as man-made constructions;
- *shili:* ways of seeing, modeling, doing, relating humans to the physical world;
- *renli:* relations among human beings.

Even though they use different cultural languages, commonalities between TOP and WSR are evident [53]:

- Both involve three perspective types.
- Both are designed to deal with human-technological rather than merely technological systems.
- Both move beyond the reductionist, objectivist mode of inquiry.
- Both are concerned with action.
- Both eschew cookbook or *n*-step procedures.

In our interpretation, *wuli* corresponds to T, *shili* to the relationships T-O and T-P, while *renli* deals with the relation O-P. Figure 3.9 schematically suggests the relationships.

Zhu sees WSR as a practical Oriental systems methodology to bridge the gulf between Western systems practice and Eastern culture. The concept of *li* is rooted in Confucianism and does not have a precise English translation. It may be rendered as "patterns or ways man's thinking and acting should take." Key neo-Confucian principles underlying WSR are the harmonious view of oneness, belief in the unity of knowledge and action, and the pursuit of multiple means of investigation.

The Pervasiveness of Multiple Perspectives

Finally, it is fascinating to observe how frequently human beings have resorted to three ways of looking, the spectrum ranging from the great religions to historical and psychoanalytic studies to recent systems analysis (Table 3.3). Our multiple perspectives do indeed rest on a long tradition.

Acknowledgments

Portions of Sections 3.1 to 3.5 and 3.7 reprinted with permission from *The Challenge of the 21st Century* by Harold Linstone with Ian I. Mitroff by the State University of New York Press, 1994, State University of New York. Quotation from *Rashomon* by Fay and Michael Kanin reprinted with permission of Random House, Inc.

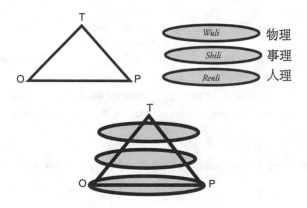

Figure 3.9 Comparison of T-O-P with a Chinese set of perspectives.

Table 3.3
Multiple Perspectives: The Curious Persistence of Trinities

RELIGION			
Judaism	God as nature (malhuyot)	God as history (zihronot)	God as revelation (shoferot)
Christianity	God the Father	God the son: Jesus	God the Holy Ghost
Hinduism	Brahma the creator	Vishnu the preserver	Siva the destroyer
SOCIOLOGY			
Weber's kinds of legitimacy			
	other-directed rational	tradition-directed traditional	inner-directed charismatic
Mingers (1996)	the material world	the social world	the personal world
PSYCHOANALYSIS			
Freud's psycho-archeological layers			
	professional	political	personal
HISTORY			
Braudel's historical time			
	geographical time—man's interaction with physical, inanimate environment	social time—social history of groups	individual time—history on scale of individual men
SYSTEMS ANALYSIS			
Allison (1971 Harvard)	rational actor	organizational process	bureaucratic politics
Steinbruner (1974 MIT)	analytic paradigm	cybernetic paradigm	cognitive paradigm
Andersen (1977 MIT)	rational perspective	organizational perspective	cognitive perspective
Linstone (1981 PSU)	technical perspective	organizational perspective	personal perspective
DeRaadt (1989, Lulea, Sweden)	physical modality	social modality	lingual modality
Warfield (1991)	situational complexity	pluralistic complexity	cognitive complexity
Zhu (1996, Lincoln, UK)	*wuli*	*shili*	*renli*

Note. Appearance of two items in the same column does not imply their equivalence.

References

[1]   Linstone, H. A., "On the Management of Technology: Old and New Perspectives," in *Decision Models for Industrial Systems Engineers and Managers,* P. Adulbhan and M. T. Tabucanon (eds.), Bangkok: Asian Institute of Technology, 1980.

[2]   Linstone, H. A., et al., "The Multiple Perspective Concept," *Technological Forecasting and Social Change,* Vol. 20, 1981, pp. 275–325.

[3]   Bacon, F., *Philosophical Works,* J. M. Robertson (ed.), London, 1905, p. 241.

[4]   Hetman, F., *Society and the Assessment of Technology,* Paris: Organization for Economic Co-operation and Development, 1973.

[5]   Allison, G., *Essence of Decision: Explaining the Cuban Missile Crisis,* Boston, MA: Little, Brown and Co., 1971.

[6]   Axelrod, R. (ed.), *Structure of Decision,* Princeton, NJ: Princeton University Press, 1976.

[7]   Toth, R., *New York Times,* Dec. 30, 1980, p. 1.

[8]   Von Neumann, J., and O. Morgenstern, *Theory of Games and Economic Behavior,* Princeton, NJ: Princeton University Press, 1944.

[9]   Schelling, T. C., *The Strategy of Conflict,* Cambridge, MA: Harvard University Press, 1960, p. 162.

[10] DeToqueville, A., *Democracy in America,* Vol. II, New York: Knopf, 1966.

[11] Asch, S. E., "Effects of Group Pressure Upon the Modification and Distortion of Judgments," in H. Guetzkow (ed.), *Groups, Leadership, and Men,* New York: Russell & Russell, 1963, pp. 177–190.

[12] Peters, T. J., and R. H. Waterman, Jr., *In Search of Excellence,* New York: Harper & Row, 1982.

[13] Churchman, C. W., *Thought and Wisdom,* Seaside, CA: Intersystems Publications, 1982.

[14] Lewin, K., *Resolving Social Conflicts: Selected Papers on Group Dynamics,* New York: Harper & Row, 1948.

[15] Linstone, H. A., et al., "The Multiple Perspective Concept with Applications to Technology Assessment and Other Decision Areas," Futures Research Institute Report 81-1. Portland, OR: Portland State University, 1981, pp. 234–235.

[16] Michael, D. N., *On Planning to Learn—And Learning to Plan,* San Francisco, CA: Jossey-Bass Publications, 1973.

[17] Jay, A., *Management and Machiavelli,* New York: Holt, Rinehart, and Winston, 1968.

[18] Schorske, C. E., *Fin-de-Siecle Vienna: Politics and Culture,* New York: Vintage Books, 1981.

[19] Hofstadter, P., *Gödel, Escher, Bach: The Eternal Golden Braid,* New York: Vintage Books, 1980.

[20] Rowan, R., "Those Business Hunches Are More Than Blind Faith," *Fortune,* Vol. 99, April 23, 1979, pp. 110–114.

[21] Siu, R. G. H., "Management and the Art of Chinese Baseball," *Sloan Management Review,* Vol. 19, Spring 1978, pp. 83–89.

[22] Hadamard, J., *The Psychology of Invention in the Mathematical Field*, Princeton, NJ: Princeton University Press, 1945, pp. 21, 113.

[23] Larkin, J. et al., "Expert and Novice Performance in Solving Physics Problems," *Science*, Vol. 208 (4450), June 20, 1980, pp. 1335–1342.

[24] Salk, J., *Anatomy of Reality: Merging of Intuition and Reason*, New York: Columbia University Press, 1983, pp. 79, 120.

[25] Berlin, I., *The Hedgehog and the Fox*, London: Weidenfeld and Nicholson, 1967, p. 34.

[26] Hoffmansthal, Hugo, quoted in Schorske, *Fin-de-Siecle Vienna: Politics and Culture*, New York: Vintage Books, 1981, p. 172.

[27] Florman, S. C., *The Existential Pleasures of Engineering*, New York: St. Martins Press, 1976.

[28] Culbert, S. A., and J. J. McDonough, *The Invisible War: Pursuing Self-Interests at Work*, New York: Wiley and Sons, 1980, p. 204.

[29] Mitroff, I. I., *The Subjective Side of Science*, Amsterdam: Elsevier Scientific Publishing Co., 1974, pp. xiii, 144–145.

[30] *Time*, Dec. 8, 1980, p. 101.

[31] de Jouvenel, B., *The Art of Conjecture*, New York: Basic Books, 1967, p. 108.

[32] Holsti, O., "Foreign Policy Formation Viewed Cognitively," in *Structure of Decision*, R. Axelrod (ed.), Princeton, NJ: Princeton University Press, 1976, pp. 26, 30.

[33] Tolstoy, L., *War and Peace*, Epilogue II (1869), L. and A. Maude, transl., New York: Simon and Schuster, 1958.

[34] Churchman, C. W., *The Design of Inquiring Systems*, New York: Basic Books, 1971.

[35] Dunlap, R. E., "Paradigmatic Change in Social Science," *American Behavioral Science*, vol. 24, 1980, pp. 5–14.

[36] Von Foerster, H., "The Curious Behavior of Complex Systems: Lessons from Biology," in H. A. Linstone and W. H. C. Simmonds (eds.), *Futures Research: New Directions*, Reading, MA: Addison-Wesley Publishing Co., 1977.

[37] Kiechel, W., III, "Executives Without Degrees," *Fortune*, Vol. 105, No. 13, June 1982, pp. 119–120.

[38] Krass, P., *The Book of Business Wisdom*, New York: John Wiley and Sons, 1998.

[39] Halal, W. E., *Strategic Planning in Major U.S. Corporations*. Study prepared for General Motors Corp. at George Washington University, Washington, D.C. See also *Technological Forecasting and Social Change*, Vol. 25, 1984, pp. 239–261.

[40] Kraft, J., "Annals of History: The Downsizing Decision," *New Yorker*, May 5, 1980, pp. 134–162.

[41] Linstone, H. A., *The Challenge of the 21st Century*, Albany, NY: State University of New York Press, p. 117.

[42] Linstone, H. A., and W. H. C. Simmonds (eds.), *Futures Research: New Directions*, Reading, MA: Addison-Wesley Publishing Co., 1977, p. 258. See also [41, p. 324].

[43] Simon, H., *The New Science of Management Decision*, Englewood Cliffs, NJ: Prentice-Hall, 1977, Chap. 4.

[44] Voge, J., "Management of Complexity," in *The Science and Praxis of Complexity*, Contributions to the Symposium at Montpellier, France, May 9–11, 1984, Tokyo: The United Nations University, 1985.

[45] Petrich, C. H., "Organization Science: Oxymoron or Opportunity?" *Complexity*, Vol. 3, No. 4, 1998, pp. 23–26.

[46] Kauffman, S., *At Home in the Universe*, New York: Oxford University Press, 1995, p. 262.

[47] Hawryszkiewycz, I., *Designing the Networked Enterprise*, Norwood, MA: Artech House, Inc., 1997.

[48] Miller, A., "Constitutionalizing the Corporation," *Technological Forecasting and Social Change*, Vol. 22, 1982, pp. 96, 101.

[49] Udwadia, F. E., "Creativity and Innovation in Organizations: Two Models and Managerial Implications," *Technological Forecasting and Social Change*, Vol. 38, 1990, pp. 65–80.

[50] Evans, J. R., "Creativity in MS/OR: The Multiple Dimensions of Creativity," *Interfaces*, Vol. 23, No. 2, 1993, pp. 80–83.

[51] Harman, W. W., "Bringing About the Transition to Sustainable Peace," Speech prepared for the International Society for the Systems Sciences, Budapest, Hungary, Sept. 1996.

[52] Wilson, E. O., *Consilience: The Unity of Knowledge*, New York: A. A. Knopf, 1998.

[53] Zhu, Z., "Systems Approaches: Where the East Meets the West," Hull, United Kingdom: Centre for Systems Studies, University of Hull, 1996.

4

Illustrations from the Public Sector

By intervening in the Vietnamese struggle, the United States was attempting to fit its global strategies into a world of hillocks and hamlets, to reduce its majestic concerns for the containment of Communism and the security of the Free World to a dimension where governments rose and fell as a result of arguments between two colonels' wives . . . For the Americans in Vietnam, it would be difficult to make this leap of perspective.

F. Fitzgerald, *Fire in the Lake*

I believe that ideas such as absolute certainty, absolute exactness, final truth, and so on are figments of the imagination that should not be admitted in any field of science . . . the belief in a single truth, and in being the possessor thereof, is the deepest root of all evil in the world.

Max Born, *Symbol und Wirklichkeit*

In this chapter, we begin our look at the application of multiple perspectives. We first consider the public sector. The illustrations range from the Civil War to the 1980s, from local to national governments, and from simple technology (rifles) to sophisticated systems (atomic bomb). In Chapter 5, we will examine illustrations from the private sector.

4.1 Military Technology

The T perspective has been extensively used in forecasting and assessing military technology since World War II. During the Cold War the study of the impact

ᴸnot before?

of a potential new U.S. weapon system on Soviet strategy may not have been labeled a technology assessment, but it essentially was one. We recall that the pioneering work of Allison (Chapter 1) involved an application of multiple perspectives to a military-political problem [1].

We consider three innovations in military technology and examine the significance of the O and P perspectives:

1. Introduction of a new ship concept into the U.S. Navy;
2. Introduction of new rifles into the U.S. Army;
3. Introduction of nuclear weapons into a war by the U.S. government.

The USS *Wampanoag*

The *Wampanoag* was a 4,200-ton "advanced technology" destroyer built for the U.S. Navy and commissioned in 1868. She had sails and a steam engine and was fast (over 17 knots). Sea trials proved her to be a magnificent technical achievement, ahead of ships in any navy at that time [2].

In 1869 all naval steamships were scrutinized by a board of naval officers. The mood of the Board is documented. The steam vessel, said the Board, was not a school of seamanship for officers or men:

> Lounging through the watches of a steamer, or acting as firemen and coal heavers, will not produce in a seaman that combination of boldness, strength, and skill that characterized the American sailor of an elder day; and the habitual exercise by an officer of a command, the execution of which is not under his own eye, is a poor substitute for the school of observation, promptness, and command found only on the deck of a sailing vessel [2, p. 114].

The Board examined the *Wampanoag* and developed a bill of particulars leading to the conclusion that the ship was "a sad and signal failure" and could not be made acceptable. The country was in a state of peace, and the Board opposed building ironclads, needed in war, to avoid unnecessary alarm. There was a large supply of timber in the Navy Yards "which the interests of economy demand should be utilized." They noted the familiarity of the workmen with wooden ship building and their dependence on it for a livelihood.

The ship was laid up for a year and soon sold by the Navy. Morison ponders this strange turn of events:

Now it must be obvious that the members of this Naval Board were stupid. They had, on its technical merits, a bad case, and they made it worse by the way they tried to argue it . . . [But after a time] I began to be aware of a growing sense of dis-ease . . . Could it be that these stupid officers were right? I recalled the sagacious judgment of Sherlock Holmes. The great detective, you will remember, withheld the facts in the incident of the light-house and the trained cormorant because, as he said, it was a case for which the world was not yet fully prepared. Was this also the case with the *Wampanoag?* What these officers were saying was that the *Wampanoag* was a destructive energy in their society. Setting the extraordinary force of her engines against the weight of their way of life, they had a sudden insight into the nature of machinery. They perceived that a machine, any machine, if left to itself, tends to establish its own conditions, to create its own environment and draw men into it. Since a machine, any machine, is designed to do only a part of what a whole man can do, it tends to wear down those parts of a man that are not included in the design. I don't happen to admire their solution, but I respect their awareness that they had a problem . . . [It] is not primarily engineering or scientific in character. It's simply human [2, pp. 116–122].

In these passages Morison shifts perspectives, from T to O. A decision that appeared "stupid" when viewed from the former suddenly became reasonable when seen from the latter. Thus, a new technological system was held back for reasons that would be exceedingly difficult to uncover with a T perspective. As a postscript, the introduction of the revolving turret rendered all navies obsolete. The Naval Board could have rejected the *Wampanoag* on technical grounds.

The M-16 Rifle

Only joint consideration of T, O, and P perspectives can explain the complex decision process culminating in the selection of the technically superior M-16 rifle as the standard weapon in the 1960s. The attitude of a U.S. Army organization is shown to be consistent in the face of externally generated technological innovations over a 100-year period. Its actions in the defense of its position may have been extreme.

The rifle is the most basic weapon system in any army. Therefore, decisions to replace a rifle are a very serious matter. Since the Civil War, the history of the U.S. Army rifle has been an interesting one, presenting us with technical, organizational, and personal aspects.

Figure 4.1 schematically describes the decision process that finally led to the selection of the M-16 rifle. It is based on the analyses of McNaugher [3] and

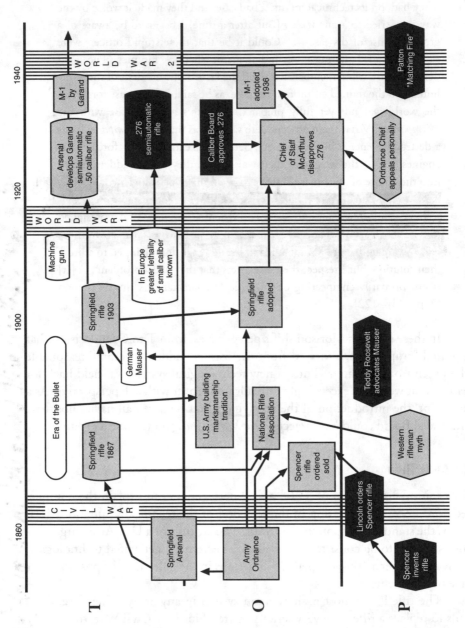

Figure 4.1 The M-16 rifle: a historical chart.

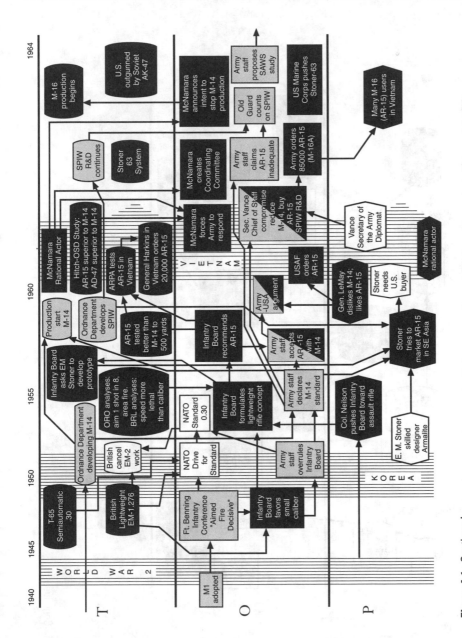

Figure 4.1 Continued.

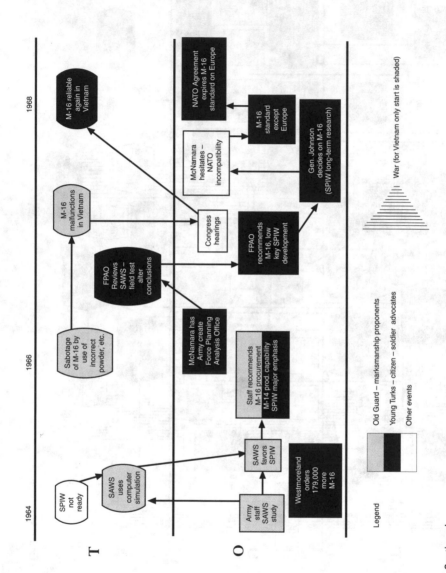

Figure 4.1 Continued.

Fallows [4] as well as discussions with former key individuals in the Department of Defense.

The past 100 years can be seen as a struggle between marksman and citizen-soldier weapon proponents or between the old Army Ordnance/Springfield Arsenal establishment and the newer Infantry Board/Secretary of Defense organizations.

The Civil War inaugurated the era of the bullet. A precursor to the M-16 story is told about the first reliable repeating rifle for military use [4, p. 80]. When the Civil War began, Union troops carried a cumbersome muzzle-loading rifle. A young inventor named Spencer, who came from outside the Army's Ordnance establishment, had developed the repeating rifle. When he could not get the Army's attention, he wangled an appointment with President Lincoln. They went behind the White House and the President, who was a good shot, test fired the rifle. The Secretary of War had been invited but declined to attend. Lincoln liked the rifle and sent the Secretary a note ordering the Army to procure it. They bought the minimum amount, assigned the weapons mostly to the cavalry, and indicated that they were not suitable for infantry use. Several Union regiments, however, bought the Spencer rifles with their own money rather than use the approved rifle. After Lincoln's assassination, the head of the Ordnance Corps quickly declared the Spencer rifles obsolete and ordered them sold. (Ironically many of these superior rifles were bought by the Indians and used in the attack on Custer at Little Bighorn.)

After the Civil War, the myth of the Western sharpshooter and the formation of the National Rifle Association reflected the development of a uniquely American marksmanship tradition. A marksman firing in a long-range rifle competition needed a large, heavy round to maximize steadiness in flight and minimize sensitivity to wind. The Army Ordnance Corps, responsible for small arms, adopted the marksmanship concept as its own creed. Its Springfield Arsenal produced the first breech-loading rifle to fill this indicated need in 1867.

Again, in the Spanish-American War, Theodore Roosevelt's Rough Riders, with their ordnance-approved rifle, found themselves facing troops equipped with a superior rifle, the Mauser. When he became President, Roosevelt ordered the unenthusiastic War Department to buy Mausers.

Every modern conflict has raised doubts about the Ordnance Corps' criteria, that is, the appropriateness of the marksman's rifle for the citizen-soldier. World War I introduced the machine gun, and the semiautomatic rifle followed; suppression fire became an important consideration. In Europe, the smaller .276 semi-automatic rifle was introduced, and a specially appointed Army Caliber Board approved a similar version in 1932. But Chief of Staff

General MacArthur sided with the traditionalists and disapproved. Instead, the .30 caliber M-1 became the standard Army weapon in 1936.

In World War II, assault tactics relying on volume of fire, rather than accuracy, became important. General Patton wanted "marching fire": several steps, then a short burst, more steps, another burst. It was recognized that lethality is enhanced by bullet speed more than by caliber size, making a smaller caliber rifle clearly preferable as a weapon. It was also found that few soldiers in combat fired their rifles at targets over 300 yards in the distance. In fact, nearly 80% of the combat soldiers never fired their weapons at all during battles. The exceptions to this rule were those who carried the Browning automatic rifle, a portable machine gun that could spray continuous fire and "hose down" an area.

After the war, the British developed a small, lightweight .276 caliber assault rifle. The U.S. Infantry Board tested and accepted the British weapon. There was the additional argument of standardization within NATO. Once again tradition overruled the recommendation, and in 1957 the Army Staff and Ordnance Corps (more precisely, the Army Materiel Command) responded with the M-14. It was an automatic-firing direct descendant of their .30 caliber M-1.

At this time Eugene Stoner of the Armalite Corporation completed the design of the AR-15, which used the smaller, faster, and more lethal .22 caliber bullet as well as a plastic stock, thus weighing less. A soldier could carry nearly three times as many rounds as with the M-14.

Extensive Army field tests and analyses led to the embarrassing conclusion that the AR-15 was superior to the M-14. The organization men predictably applied the NIH factor ("not invented here"), ignored these results, and ordered full production of the M-14 and its round. One individual who did not go along with the "party line" was General Curtis LeMay of the U.S. Air Force. In 1962, USAF declared the AR-15 its standard and ordered the rifle.

Another individual now came onstage, Secretary of Defense McNamara, a "rational actor" par excellence. Tests in Vietnam conducted by the Advanced Research Projects Agency (not a part of the Army) concluded:

> In overall squad kill potential the AR-15 is up to 5 times as effective as the M-14 rifle. [The AR-15] can be produced with less difficulty, to a higher quality, and at a lower cost than the M-14 rifle. In reliability, durability, ruggedness, performance under adverse circumstances, and ease of maintenance, the AR-15 is a significant improvement over any of the standard weapons including the M-14 rifle [4].

The Ordnance establishment countered with its own tests and found the M-14 a "radically" better model. Later these tests were found to have been rigged [4].

Secretary McNamara overrode the Army and sent more AR-15s to Vietnam; the reports coming back on their performance were enthusiastic. The AR-15 was renamed the M-16. Meanwhile the Army Ordnance hit on a diversionary tactic, development of a *Special Purpose Infantry Weapon* (SPIW). The Marine Corps, on the other hand, requested Stoner's type of weapon. To head off another confrontation, the Army Staff proposed a new study: the *Small Arms Weapons System Study* (SAWS). Since SPIW was not yet ready, computer simulation had to be used, and it "proved" SPIW to be superior to any other rifle. McNamara responded by creating a new *Force Planning and Analysis Office* (FPAO). It reviewed SAWS and concluded that the computer simulations were logically inconsistent. Its field tests again showed the M-16 to be superior.

Perhaps the most stunning phase in the organizational struggle was the sudden epidemic of malfunctions of the M-16 in Vietnam. The weapon that had been glowingly praised now jammed and misfired. The reason was found in the Ordnance Corps' "modifications" imposed on the M-16. A useless manual bolt closure was added, personally ordered by the Army Chief of Staff; the "twist" of the rifle barrel was increased, reducing lethality; most important of all, Stoner's ammunition was replaced by unsuitable ball powder that effectively increased the failure rate by 600%.

> The Army's modifications had very little to do with . . . warfare, but quite a lot to do with settling organizational scores [4, p. 77].

When more and more soldiers wrote letters home about the unreliable M-16, Congress went into action and conducted an exhaustive inquiry. Their report charged that the M-16 had been sabotaged by the Ordnance Corps.

> The most striking aspect of the testimony was its humdrum routine tone. When representatives of the Ordnance Corps were pressed to explain their decisions, they fell back on citations from the rule books, like characters in a parody of the bureaucratic temperament. They seemed to have a hard time remembering who was responsible for crucial decisions; they tended to explain things by saying, "the feeling was," or "the practice has been" . . . They could list with careful bureaucratic logic the reasonableness of each step they had taken [4, pp. 93–94].

The modifications that were so damaging were never properly corrected. The O perspective is blindingly evident. Fallows adds a postscript to this tale. In 1980 when Army troops went on exercises in Egypt, unattributed comments began to appear: visibility is so good in the desert that a sharpshooter rifle is really needed, not a popgun like the M-16. The struggle of one organization to control the course of a technology was not yet over.

We draw a number of implications from this illustration.

- The rational actor's selection of the "best" system hardly reflects the real-life decision process, that is, the T perspective does not suffice to understand the management of technological change. In this case the O perspective is central.

- The Army does not operate as a unitary decision maker. For example, the Infantry Board and Army Staff were on opposite sides of the argument.

- Individuals play a vital role in the process. For example, civilians in the Office of the Secretary of Defense—McNamara, Hitch, and Vance— as well as certain generals—LeMay and Wyman—were instrumental in shifting decisions.

- The overt and hidden motivations for actions must be clearly distinguished if the decision process is to be understood. Examples: the ordering of the SAWS project by the Army Staff and McNamara's creation of FPAO were indirect means to achieve certain objectives.

- The organizational actors may go to remarkable lengths to attain parochial objectives.

The Decision to Use the Atomic Bomb (Pearson)

This illustration deals with the most influential innovation in military technology of modern times, the atomic bomb–specifically, the world-shaking decision whether or not to use it. The T perspective dominates but is reinforced by the O and P perspectives.[1]

---

1. Subsequent to Pearson's work on this case, it has come to our attention that Davidson and Lytle have published a book on "the art of historical detection" that also tackles the decision to drop the atomic bomb on Japan via multiple perspectives, specifically, using Allison's original models. They conclude that:

  If historians based their interpretations on a single model, they would never satisfy their desire to understand the sequence of events leading to Hiroshima . . . The use of several models allows the historian the same advantage enjoyed by writers of fiction who employ more than one narrator. Each narrator, like every model, affords the writer a new vantage point from which to tell the story . . . Thus, as organizations grow more complex, models afford historians multiple perspectives from which to interpret the same reality [5].

On June 1, 1945, the situation was as follows: Truman had been President only seven weeks following Roosevelt's death. He had not only inherited a war but the organization, plans, and capabilities of winning it. Germany had tendered its unconditional surrender on May 8 and Japan had no prospects of winning. Unconditional surrender was being demanded of Japan; U.S. public opinion, ignited by Pearl Harbor and fanned by years of propaganda, would accept no less. Although its navy and air force had been destroyed, Japan was not yet ready to accept the humiliation of unconditional surrender.

The atomic bomb was being developed in an atmosphere of secrecy and uncertainty. Security had been a target throughout the weapon's development. On June 1, an atomic bomb had not yet been exploded; no one knew for sure that it would work.

T Perspective

Henry L. Stimson's article "The Decision to Use the Atomic Bomb" is a model case of the technical approach to decision making. He portrays a unitary decision maker, President Truman, with Stimson as senior advisor. *ideal T*

The problem was bounded, and the goal was clear: "The principal political, social, and military objective of the United States in the summer of 1945 was the prompt and complete surrender of Japan" [6, p. 101]. This objective was to be achieved as quickly as possible with minimal cost, physical destruction, and loss of American and Japanese lives. The alternatives were set out and their consequences assessed, as summarized in Table 4.1.

Stimson, as Secretary of War, found in his analysis total justification for the decision to drop the bomb.

> [These reasons] have always seemed compelling and clear, and I cannot see how any person vested with such responsibilities as mine could have taken any other course or given any other advice to his chiefs . . . I believe that no man . . . could have failed to use it [6].

Whether these reasons provide full justification remains controversial. However, what they do not provide is a full explanation; so we turn to other perspectives. *ha. is that so?*

O Perspective

If Stimson saw the use of the atomic bomb as the only logical means to end the War, P. M. S. Blackett, a British Nobel Laureate, saw it quite differently: "The dropping of the atomic bomb was not so much the last military act of the Second World War, as the first major operation of the cold diplomatic war with

didn't limestone also say that people's choices are more a product of their environment rather than their self? i.e. been exam ple

Table 4.1

The Technical Perspectives in the Atomic Bomb Decision

	Conventional Bombing and Blockade	Invasion	A-Bomb Japan without Warning	A-Bomb Japan after Warning	A-Bomb Uninhabited Island
Unified decision maker	Collective will unified in President Truman				
Bounded problem	Japan's unconditional surrender				
Goal	Obtain unconditional surrender as quickly as possible with minimum loss of Allied lives and (secondarily) with a minimum of cost, physical destruction, and loss of Japanese lives.				
Options	Conventional Bombing and Blockade	Invasion	A-Bomb Japan without Warning	A-Bomb Japan after Warning	A-Bomb Uninhabited Island
Consequences Unconditional surrender	Uncertain	Highly likely	Highly likely	Uncertain	Uncertain
Time to surrender	Lengthy	November 1946	Short	Uncertain	Uncertain
Allied lives lost	Moderate	1,000,000+	None	None or few	None
Japanese lives lost	Many	2,000,000+	20,000–200,000	Few	None
Cost	High	Very high	Low	Low	Low
Destruction	Very high	Very high	High	High	Low
Other consequences	Thousands of U.S. prisoners of war sure to die			Would use one of only two bombs, perhaps without the desired effect. If demonstration failed, then lower U.S. morale, higher Japanese morale, loss of international prestige. Japan might attempt to defend target. Japan might move POWs to target site.	Would use one of only two bombs, perhaps without the desired effect. Shock effect reduced. If demonstration failed, then lower U.S. morale, higher Japanese morale, loss of international prestige.
Trade-offs	Between lives, time, money, extent of destruction				
Choice	As an optimum				

Russia" [7]. The organizational perspective helps us to understand his statement and provides the second view of the decision.

The major Allied powers were the United States, Britain, and Russia, with leaders Truman, Churchill, and Stalin, respectively. As long as their mutual survival demanded the defeat of the Axis, these nations were able to work together. But with Germany's surrender in Europe and Japan's retreat in the Pacific, their common goal was largely achieved. Attention shifted to new goals, reflecting each country's parochial priorities, perceptions, and interests.

Russia sought to ensure its defense and national well-being by imperialistic expansion in Europe (Romania, Bulgaria, Yugoslavia, Czechoslovakia, Poland, and Hungary). It had similar goals in Korea, China, and the North Pacific. As old problems were solved and old goals achieved, new problems and new goals directed the search for new solutions.

Due to its closeness to the continent, Great Britain was most concerned about Soviet expansion in Europe. Churchill enthusiastically supported the use of the bomb. He saw it bringing ". . . a speedy end to the Second World War, and perhaps much else besides" [8, p. 259]. Far more than Truman, Churchill distrusted and feared the Russians.

American perceptions were changing, too. Russian entry into the Pacific conflict was still being sought by the allied military, but not by the diplomatic corps. The change in policy was incremental: the United States continued its official stance of welcoming Russian participation but unofficially worked to avoid it. The United States wanted to contain Russian expansion in the Far East. And Russia's challenge in Europe was not forgotten. According to Leo Szilard, one of the top Manhattan Project scientists, Secretary of State James Byrnes argued that the bomb need not be used to defeat Japan but rather to "make Russia more manageable in Europe" [9]. The O perspective might therefore "see" a Soviet challenge, expansion in the Pacific, and the U.S. response, detonation of an atomic bomb, to demonstrate power and to accelerate the Japanese surrender before Soviet entry into the Pacific War.

An organizational perspective can also be applied on a different level. From this perspective, we view the nation as the organization and focus on several units within it: (1) the Executive Branch of government, including specifically the President, his advisors, the War Department, and the military; (2) the Congress; (3) the public, perhaps as represented by the press; and (4) the Manhattan Project scientists. Examining the relationships among these units—each with its own priorities, perceptions, and prerogatives—provides yet another view of the decision.

We begin with the relationship between the Congress and the Executive Branch. The checks-and-balances system gives Congress authority over appropriations. Yet secrecy required that the vast sums of money needed for the

Manhattan Project be obtained without the informed approval of the legislators. The procedures employed can be characterized most charitably as highly irregular. That the Executive Branch was worried about possible postwar repercussions is clear from the following statements.

General Leslie Groves, Head of the Manhattan Project:

If we succeed, they won't investigate us at all; if we fail, Congress for a long time won't investigate anything else [7, p. 28].

Admiral William Leahy, Chief of Staff for Presidents Roosevelt and Truman:

I know F.D.R. would have used it in a minute to prove that he had not wasted two billion dollars [8, p. 5].

A student of the decision, Walter Schoenberger has written:

The halls of Congress might very well have echoed and re-echoed with angry denunciations of the war's greatest boondoggle . . . This was probably a consideration in quickly testing and using [the bombs]. Their successful use turned what might have been a political liability into what was a great political asset. What administrative foresight . . . [that] the atomic bombs had been produced just in time to effect the surrender of Japan.

Truman was a man who would have reasonably been sympathetic to arguments that the two billion dollars spent on the project should not prove to be a waste and, more important, that it should not appear as a waste to Congress and to the people of the United States [8, pp. 105, 299].

A less forceful argument can be made that the agreement negotiated by Roosevelt with Churchill to jointly develop the bomb was a treaty that should have been approved by the Senate. Whether those still living were influenced to drop the bomb by this potential postwar problem seems unlikely but cannot be ruled out completely. The separation of powers required by the Constitution ran headlong into the secrecy required by the War. Secrecy won. The successful development and use of the bomb absolved the Executive Branch. An important characteristic of organizations is their propensity to change only incrementally over time. This limited flexibility of organizations goes a long way in explaining the decision to use the bomb.

Statements by some of the major actors give a general sense of the strong momentum that the project assumed.

Henry L. Stimson, Secretary of War:

At no time, from 1941 to 1945, did I ever hear it suggested by the President, or any other responsible member of government, that atomic energy should not be used in the war [6, p. 98].

J. Robert Oppenheimer, Manhattan Project:

We always assumed if they were needed, they would be used [9, p. 335].

Winston Churchill:

The decision whether or not to use the atomic bomb to compel the surrender of Japan was never even an issue. There was unanimous, automatic, unquestioned agreement . . . nor did I ever hear the slightest suggestion that we should do otherwise [8, p. 259].

Harry S Truman:

The final decision of where and when to use the bomb was up to me. Let there be no mistake about it. I regarded the bomb as a military weapon and never had any doubt that it should be used [8, p. 25].

As a new President, Truman might have abruptly reversed policy; but his role in the organizational structure made that highly unlikely. He inherited a war and with it a winning strategy. Why increase uncertainty by changing the policies that were working? During the early days of his administration Truman told his Cabinet, the Joint Chiefs of Staff, Prime Minister Churchill, and the U.S. Congress that he planned to carry on the policies of Roosevelt. Although never a man to duck a decision, Truman freely delegated authority and responsibility to his advisors (the same men who had worked with Roosevelt). Roosevelt's and Truman's advisors included military men. In popular opinion, at least, the military mentality is equated with tradition, maintenance of the status quo, and standard operating procedures. To the military mind, the objective of war is victory. That was U.S. policy, and the continuity of policy was not going to be upset by the new President.

Of the particular policies that Truman retained, none was more important than the demand for unconditional surrender. He probably had no choice:

- The attack on Pearl Harbor provoked a response of righteous indignation in the American people. Their hurt pride demanded revenge and retribution.

- Roosevelt capitalized on the emotional response to boost morale and rally the public to the battle cry.
- "Complete victory," "no compromise," "total elimination," "unconditional surrender,"—these phrases laced the speeches of U.S. leaders throughout the war.
- Suggestions for deviation from this policy were met by charges of appeasement in the press and from Congress.

Given the Japanese peace overtures during the summer of 1945, a more flexible stance on the terms of surrender might well have led to a negotiated settlement without the use of the atomic bomb. But a legacy of past policies and pronouncements permitted Truman only limited flexibility.

A type of Newtonian Law of Inertia applies to organizations: "An organizational policy that is in effect stays in effect unless acted on by new information." In organizations, information flows only in certain channels. Secrecy requirements surrounding the atomic project inhibited information flow even more than normal. No information flowed outward to the public, press, or Congress. Outside opposition to the use of the bomb simply could not develop.

On the inside, among all groups involved with the weapon, only the scientists were not unanimous in supporting its use. The Frank Committee consisted of a group of scientists in the Chicago Laboratory that opposed an unannounced nuclear attack on Japan. The Committee prepared a report outlining its objections. This report did not reach Truman and probably was not seen by Stimson. Instead it was channeled to the bottom rung of the organizational hierarchy.

The scientific panel, which received the Frank Committee Report, found it unconvincing and concluded, "We see no acceptable alternative to direct military intervention" [6, p. 101]. Thus, the only potentially effective counteropinion to the use of the bomb was drowned in the communication stream.

The communication system also failed to deliver much of the available information regarding Japan's peace feelers. There was some awareness at the highest levels of government that the Japanese had initiated peace-oriented contacts with the Russians; but the intelligence of the OSS, Navy, and Foreign Morale Analysis Division, which emphasized the urgency and importance of the contacts, probably never reached Truman.

A new world political order, Constitutional violations, continuity of policy, mass psychology, restricted information flows—these are the factors the organizational perspective brings to the analysis.

P Perspective

This perspective is most helpful in explaining how some of the results already discussed may have come about.

One of the reasons the information contained in the Frank Committee Report did not reach the President was the tendency of the human mind to filter out inconsistent images. The President was new and an outsider to the 12-year, F.D.R.-oriented executive establishment. He could not afford to challenge policies and fiefdoms so early in his presidency. Intelligence information regarding Japan's peace moves did not reach responsible U.S. government officials, in part because of their own and the system's limited information processing capacities. Stimson's article shows a willingness to focus on only one possible goal, unconditional surrender, rather than scan for alternatives like negotiated settlement.

There is evidence that on several occasions members of the Joint Chiefs and members of the Interim Committee silenced their own personal disagreements in order to present a unanimous opinion to the President, probable instances of peer group reinforcement of the generally accepted view (see the Asch effect in Section 3.3).

The earlier quotations from Oppenheimer, Churchill, Truman, and Stimson clearly indicate their strongly held belief that using the bomb was the correct decision. Their statements convey a sense that dropping the bomb was really right: "There was unanimous, automatic, unquestioned agreement" [8, p. 259].

The P perspective may also explain Truman's continuation of Roosevelt's policies. Fear of change and of the unknown are present in his rather unguarded remark to a group of reporters the day after Roosevelt's death:

> Boys, if you pray, pray for me now. I don't know whether you fellows ever had a load of hay fall on you, but when they told me yesterday what had happened, I felt like the moon, the stars, and all the planets had fallen on me. I've got the most terribly responsible job a man ever had [8, p. 107].

There is also the need of a new President to appear decisive and bold. Truman had a strong sense of history. We may speculate that a decision not to drop the bomb would later be viewed by historians as a sign of weakness.

Stimson picked the members of the Interim Committee that were to advise the President on matters of nuclear policy. It has been suggested that he picked them specifically because they would tend to agree with his views. Perhaps personal interests were at work.

One might also look to possible personal interests as the cause of the change of opinion by certain scientists to oppose the use of the bomb. Many were Europeans who had helped develop the bomb in a race against Nazi Germany. With Germany's surrender, the nightmare of Hitler vanished, and their motivation was gone. Yet we have seen that they had little real effect on the decision.

Lessons

This illustration shows how the three perspectives join to give a more fully rounded picture and higher degree of realism than the T perspective can provide by itself.

- The T perspective presents the decision as the only rational choice among alternatives because the strategy to use the bomb without warning virtually dominated all other alternatives; that is, this strategy was at least as good as any other on all important choice criteria then enunciated.

- The O perspective provides much of the motivation for allowing the unconditional surrender goal to stand unchallenged. It suited the international political needs of the United States and Great Britain: inhibiting the imperialistic expansion of the Soviet Union. The goal also suited the needs of the Executive Branch, justifying the constitutional breach and the "unauthorized" expenditure of $2 billion. It was consistent with past government policy; dropping the bomb at this time was compatible with the propaganda of earlier times.

- The P perspective suggests that the key individuals believed deeply in the rightness of unconditional surrender. The new President was in a difficult position, succeeding a tremendously popular President who had in 12 years molded the Executive Branch completely in his own image. Truman had to make his mark quickly by decisiveness and boldness. The one effort in opposition to the use of the bomb was that of a group of scientists (the Frank Committee). It was probably influenced by the refugees among them, whose overriding motivation, fighting Nazi Germany, vanished with Hitler's death and Germany's surrender.

- Given the needs of so many people and so many organizational units, the organizational perspective suggests that they would create a socially constructed reality that made the decision appear rational, even inevitable.

[handwritten margin note: the three served as both explanation of what did happen and deeper insight into what could have happened.]

- The personal perspective was used in several instances to show that the other perspectives were not exhaustive in their treatment of the decision; more was still to be learned. However, diminishing returns and the absence of first-hand commentary are reasons the personal perspective was not developed more fully.

- Each perspective was used, by itself, to explain aspects of the decision. Each proved useful and revealed features not captured by the others. This alone shows the value of adopting multiple perspectives. It is, however, only by weaving the strands of the perspectives together that the pattern of the whole cloth is revealed.

Further Comments

In moving from the first illustration, the *Wampanoag*, to the third, the atomic bomb, we have increasingly swept in higher levels of the federal government. In this section we augment the illustrations with a few vignettes that vividly bring into view the O and P perspectives in national and global contexts.

O Perspectives as Seen by Observers of the Washington Scene

In our exposition of the O perspective (Section 3.2) we drew on Machiavelli. In the following comments on the operation of the federal government we see that such a perspective is as applicable to Washington in 1999 as it was to Florence in 1530.

Peters

The Editor-in-Chief of the *Washington Monthly,* Charles Peters, gives us insights on "how Washington really works" that are far removed from the civics textbooks but would appear familiar to readers of *The Prince.*

On shadow organizations:

> Clubs are just part of a larger social bond that exists everywhere but is especially prevalent in Washington, where private life is so much an extension of professional life. This bond is the "survival network" and it is the key to understanding how Washington really works . . . Almost everyone in the government, whether he works on Capitol Hill or in the bureaucracy, is primarily concerned with his own survival. He wants to remain in Washington or in what the city symbolizes—some form of public power. Therefore, from the day these people arrive in Washington they are busy building networks of people who will assure their survival in power [10, p. 5].

Peters quotes Nicholas Lemann of the *Washington Post:*

[Washington is] a place where every person you deal with is someone who is either helping you survive now or might conceivably later on [10, p. 7].

On the use of delay:

Often delay will serve the client [company] just as well as outright victory [in fighting regulatory agencies] . . . The client could go on making money doing whatever he was doing wrong for those ten years . . . But what about the $5 million to $10 million it would have cost the client? . . . Legal fees are tax deductible [10, pp. 94–95].

On protection of turf:

The Firemen First Principle: . . . when faced with a budget cut, the bureaucrat chops where it will hurt constituents the most, not the least. The howls of protest will then force the cuts to be restored [10, p. 40].

On power:

In a recent survey [lobbyists] rated the congressional staffs as their number one lobbying target (by contrast, the White House ranked sixth) [10, p. 115].

On isolation:

Except for . . . rare occasions . . . the congressman's isolation is complete. He shakes hands with hundreds of people every day, but he really talks to no one. It is easy for those enveloped in this cocoon [the Capitol and its five satellite office buildings] to imagine that it is the real world . . . This is the ultimate make believe [10, p. 117].

On the irrational actions fostered by SOPs:

No military officer who wants to advance himself can afford a bad report. From the moment the top officials at the Pentagon instituted the body count as the measure of success in Vietnam, commanders began to pressure their subordinates to produce bodies [My Lai was one result] [10, p. 77].

On relations with the press:

The press, instead of exposing the make believe, is part of the show . . . [the reporters] are too bound up . . . in the ease of being stenographers for government press agents [10, pp. 17, 32].

On this subject, Dieter Schwebs, in his review of Peters' work, adds an interesting organizational insider's view [11]. This dedicated former systems analyst in the *Department of Defense* (DOD) and *General Accounting Office* (GAO) notes that the taxpayer pays the salaries of many thousands of employees whose job is manipulating the press to make their bosses look good and to sell their programs. One effective tool of the bureaucracy is the judicious use of "sensitive," "confidential," and "secret" stamps. According to Schwebs, classification is readily used to cover up waste and declassification to fuel self-serving hype and help in the fierce competition for public funds. Declassification is even carried out illegally with impunity. For example, a controlled leak may be orchestrated by affixing a "top secret" stamp to a document and then providing it to an eager journalist who is delighted to print such "hot" information.

Kissinger

On the State Department:

> The system lends itself to manipulation. A bureau chief who disagrees with the Secretary can exploit it for procrastination. In 1975, the Assistant Secretary in charge of Africa managed to delay my dealing with Angola simply by using the splendid machinery so methodically to "clear" a memorandum I had requested that it took months to reach me. When it arrived, it was diluted of all sharpness, and my own staff bounced it back again and again for greater precision—thereby serving the bureau chief's purposes better than my own. Alternatively, the machinery may permit a strategically placed official's hobbyhorse to gallop through, eliciting an innocent nod from a Secretary unfamiliar with all the code words and implications [12].

On the DOD, Henry Kissinger provides a fine example of astute political behavior on the part of the Secretary of Defense Melvin Laird:

> Laird acted on the assumption that he had a constitutional right to seek to outsmart and outmaneuver anyone with whom his office brought him into contact. I eventually learned that it was safest to begin a battle with Laird by closing off all his bureaucratic or congressional escape routes, provided I could figure them out. Only then would I broach substance. But even with such tactics, I lost as often as I won. John Ehrlichman considered mine a cowardly procedure and decided he would teach me how to deal with

Laird. Following the best administrative theory of White House predomi-
nance, Ehrlichman, without troubling to touch any bureaucratic or congressional bases, transmitted a direct order to Laird to relinquish some
Army-owned land in Hawaii for a national park. Laird treated this clumsy
procedure the way a matador handles the lunges of a bull. He accelerated
his plan to use the land for two Army recreation hotels. Using his old congressional connections, he put a bill through the Congress that neatly overrode the directive, all the time protesting that he would carry out any
White House orders permitted by the Congress. The hotels are still there
under Army control; the national park is still a planner's dream. Ehrlichman learned the hard way that there are dimensions of political science not
taught at universities and that being right on substance does not always
guarantee success in Washington [13].

Ehrlichman's own perspective on Laird shows that such lessons were not
lost on him.

Camp David's telephones went through an Army Signal Corps switch-
board . . . The Camp David operators were all Army enlisted men, and
their supervisors were Army officers. The only question was: how closely
did Mel Laird monitor the President and the rest of us at Camp David
when we called someone on his Army telephone system? Did he just keep
track of whom we called, or did he also know what was said [14]?

Rickover

Admiral Rickover was once asked by a Congressional Committee why so many
"unqualified" officials rose to the top of the military structure. His answer:

The only rationale I can come to is that everything in life has been easy for
these officials. They have been carried along by family, by wealth, by
friends, possibly by political considerations. In a position requiring technical expertise for the first time in their lives, they believe themselves capable
of solving these problems by their "personality" methods that have previously gotten them by [15].

In other words, the military academy ideal of the presentable, well-
rounded, loyal defender of the service tradition is an important contributor to
the O perspective and usually outweighs technical excellence as a criterion for
promotion.

Borsting

A thoughtful discussion of "Decision-Making at the Top" by a former Assistant Secretary of Defense (Comptroller), Jack R. Borsting, also reveals the significance of perspectives other than the technical one [16]. He notes that top-level DOD decision making is

- Nonalgorithmic, creative, and free-form (O, P);
- Very data oriented (T);
- Basically open loop, tending to give rudder directions but not looking at the wake (O);
- Very short-term oriented (O, P);
- Teamwork oriented (O);
- Very personal—the judgment of one's close advisors is extremely important (P);
- Creating a need to budget time for important decisions (O);
- Demonstrating that external forces—Congress, the White House—are often more important than a rational systems analysis (O);
- Subject to conflicting goals, for example, between public and private sectors (O);
- Dealing with "messes" rather than well-structured problems; they must be treated holistically (T, O, P).

What makes this picture especially interesting is that it is drawn by a past-president of the Operations Research Society of America!

4.2 Local Crisis: The Mount St. Helens Eruption (Clary)

Mt. St. Helens, one of the dormant Cascades Range volcanoes in the state of Washington, showed signs of life in March 1980 and became fully active with a dramatic explosion on May 18 of that year. The top of the mountain was blown off, reducing its height from 9700 feet to 8300 feet. The amount of energy released has been calculated as equivalent to 500 times that of the atomic bomb dropped on Hiroshima. More than 44,000 acres of fir trees were leveled; stream flooding as well as mud flows caused extensive damage; and more than 60 persons were reported dead or missing. Sporadic activity continues at intervals.

Long-term watershed management has become a major concern. Communities in Southwest Washington, downstream from the volcano, face a constant flood hazard because of the unstable sediment produced by earlier activity as well as the possibility of new eruptions.

T Perspective

Historically, the U.S. Army Corps of Engineers has responded to flood control problems with structural solutions, that is, building dams and levees or dredging river channels. In view of the suddenness and magnitude of the May 18 eruption, structural measures by a military agency were the only feasible short-term response. Emergency funds were authorized by the President, and the Corps began a construction and dredging program southwest of the mountain. Some nonstructural solutions, such as property acquisition, were examined and rejected on cost-benefit grounds.

The following year (1981), the situation changed. The crisis mentality faded, federal cutbacks reduced the Corps' allocation of funds for this operation, and a new *Federal Emergency Management Agency* (FEMA) report on hazard mitigation focused on nonstructural measures outside of large urban areas.

At this stage, the T perspective no longer suffices because there are more organizations and actors. Problems of politics, communication, and coordination come to the fore. It should be noted that White [17] had recognized the emergence of these problems in the case of multiple mitigation approaches to flood control over a decade earlier.

O Perspective

The first issue is historic: which federal agency is the lead agency—the Corps, the U.S. Forest Service, the *U.S. Geological Survey* (USGS), or FEMA? Interestingly, the O perspective affected technical as well as organizational questions. For example, the Corps and USGS continually disagreed on sediment estimates. Acceptance by the Corps of the USGS data would create a dilemma in justifying its decision to build debris dams on the Toutle River, the stream most affected by the eruption.

The *National Flood Insurance Program* (NFIP) has been in effect since 1968. A community that wishes to participate in NFIP is required to have a floodplain ordinance. Thus, the communities west of Mt. St. Helens were spurred to develop at least minimal regulations. From their O perspective, the possible eruption of a long-dormant volcano was certainly no stimulus for contingency action that would tie up potential industrial land. The societal discount rate (see Section 7.1) eliminated any consideration of tectonic history and geologists' forecasts in 1975 of a major eruption before the end of the century [18].

Even after the May 18 eruption, organizational resistance to change was widespread. The "crisis of the moment," which altered the five-century-old topography drastically, forced little change in local floodplain ordinances. Cowlitz County was the one county that shifted its attitude significantly on land use control. Subjected to the most severe damage in the eruption, it alone placed a moratorium on building. Its officials exerted pressure to change existing federal policy. They noted that (1) 16 federal agencies had been given funds to assist the recovery and (2) only one or two had fully spent their appropriations. The conclusion was obvious:

> If the money has been appropriated and we have legitimate needs to be addressed, then we should be able to pool our resources and direct them to these problems [19].

The County specifically wanted permission to acquire property in the floodplains of the Toutle and Cowlitz Rivers rather than rebuild damaged structures. It would thus be able to exercise better control over development. Not surprisingly, this request was turned down; it ran counter to federal SOPs.

The societal discount rate also affected posteruption planning. A new flood warning and emergency preparedness program was considered—and forgotten—when the winter of 1980–1981 produced below-normal rainfall and little flooding. Only the scientists with their T perspective maintained their concern over the possibility of another disastrous flood.

A local planner put it very plainly:

> Emergency planning is seasonal. It's ridiculous to emphasize flood prevention during the summer months. But on December 1 people start to listen. If you use the right timing, you can sell them on anything.

The familiar seasonal pattern of flood danger seemed to be the operative concern despite the nonseasonal nature of flooding caused by volcanic eruptions.

The Mt. St. Helens area clearly constitutes a long-term management problem: the geologic data prescribe continual dredging of the affected rivers. In the 1980s there were at least two obstacles: (1) the ideology of the Reagan administration, which militated against long-range funding of such local projects; and (2) the inappropriateness of federal legislation, that is, the inability of the Corps to purchase land for dredge spoils. We see organizational inertia, problem avoidance, fractionalization, and step-by-step problem solving in response to immediate crises. The county was weak in any confrontation with the federal government, and inequities resulted. In this case, we note that Mt. St.

Helens lies within federally owned land and that the problems it created were regional. Yet the burden of flood management responsibility was on local shoulders. Congress could, of course, declare the volcano a "continuing disaster" as a means to maintain the emergency funding flow, but there was no precedent. Furthermore, the affected parties did not have a well-established, effective lobby in Washington, DC.

Conclusion

The eruption acted as a powerful stimulant to the scientists. Mt. St. Helens suddenly became a living laboratory, a rich lode for research papers, and a justification for conferences. In these activities, the T perspective prevailed. However, effective mitigation demanded an O perspective. The frustrations in getting action can be traced to traditional organizational characteristics that inhibit action. One positive development was FEMA's formation of an interagency Hazard Mitigation Team. The Team cut across organizational boundaries and was problem focused. Representatives from eleven federal agencies examined coordination, funding arrangements, and action implementation. Subsequently, Cowlitz County formed an even more diverse group involving federal, state, and local officials, as well as scientists and private citizens, to aid in developing a floodplain management plan. Thus, multiple perspectives are swept into the planning process.

The following quotes simulate the spectrum of views:

- *T perspective:* "levee building is not a long-term cost-effective strategy"; "all we need is money and we can solve the flooding problem"; "I don't know why they want to rebuild in the floodplain given the risk."
- *T-O linkage:* "why should the county restrict building just because there was a mudflow 500 years ago?";
- *O perspective:* "even a massive eruption has not resulted in much change in floodplain ordinances";
- *O-P linkage:* "doesn't Reagan understand that we have a critical problem?"; "the county can't keep me from building; it's my land";
- *P perspective:* "well, it didn't flood the first year after the eruption"; "I just can't move back there after what I've been through."

Exploration of the cross-impacts among the perspectives is a formidable task, as suggested by the myriad of possible relationships.[2]

---

2. The use of digraphs for this purpose is discussed in the Appendix.

There are 16 major volcanoes in the Cascades, and two have erupted in the past 70 years. The prevalence of volcanoes near populated areas throughout the world, as well as the richness of insights drawn from the different perspectives, suggests that this approach can be quite useful in the formulation of disaster policy.

4.3 Denver International Airport (Szyliowicz and Goetz)

Szyliowicz and Goetz have undertaken a study of the decision making-process that guided the development of the new *Denver International Airport* (DIA) [20]. At a cost of nearly $5 billion, it represents the largest public works effort in Colorado's history. It covers 53 square miles and thus is currently the world's largest airport. It has been beset by many difficulties. The original cost estimate ($1.7 billion) nearly tripled and the opening date of October 1993 was postponed repeatedly due to baggage system problems. The original traffic estimates have proven to be excessively optimistic and the number of gates has been decreased from 120 to 88.

The Rational FAA Planning Process (T)

The key actors in U.S. airport planning are the *Federal Aviation Administration* (FAA), local or regional governments, and the major tenant airlines. The FAA has created a T-type master planning process that includes nine elements: (1) organization and preplanning, (2) inventory of existing conditions and issues, (3) aviation demand forecasts, (4) requirements analysis and demand forecasts, (5) airport site selection, (6) environmental procedures and analysis, (7) simulation, (8) airport plans, and (9) plan implementation. Information is collected, alternative solutions are evaluated, and the "optimal" alternative is selected. A single master decision maker acting with complete rationality is assumed.

The Actual Process ·

Denver's *Stapleton International Airport* (SIA) opened in 1929, was owned and operated by the City and County and periodically expanded. It is conveniently located but has proven increasingly inadequate to handle the growing traffic. By 1974 it was bounded on two sides by residential communities, on the third by commercial developments, and on the fourth by the Army Rocky Mountain Arsenal. Scheduled to be shut down, the Arsenal had become badly polluted as a result of its chemical weapon production. A consulting firm proposed in 1979 that SIA expand onto the Arsenal, which was located in Adams County. The

FAA agreed to pay 75% of a full-scale site study including all regional and local governments and concluded that, if the Arsenal cleanup costs were included, a new airport could be built for the same price as the expansion of SIA would cost. It recognized that the decision would be political, not technical; and in 1983 it voted for expansion (with Adams County in strong opposition).

Negotiations between the City of Denver and Adams County led to an agreement that Adams County would cede 50 square miles of uninhabited land east of the Arsenal to Denver and a new airport would be built on that land. The local business community was enthusiastic, the airlines unhappy. Airline deregulation in 1978 gave the airlines the freedom to schedule flights, create hubs, and abandon flights to small cities. Denver was now serving as a hub for United, Continental, and Frontier Airlines and experiencing rapidly rising traffic through the mid-1980s. This situation was the basis for the planners' projections. But, by the late 1980s, Continental was in serious difficulties and Frontier had disappeared. Therefore, both United and Continental felt the existing airport would be adequate. By 1987 tensions between the airlines and the City were high. A massive political campaign resulted in Adams County citizen approval of the deal, but objecting Denver residents were now also insisting on a vote. Again a strong political campaign saved the deal.

Congress agreed to provide $500 million and the City pressured the two hub airlines to support the new airport. In negotiations the airlines forced design changes and concessions. One of the conditions imposed by United was a fully automated, high-speed baggage system, which the City then decided to extend to the entire airport. Meanwhile, the cargo airlines did not like their proposed location and forced relocation of their facilities. Similar difficulties arose with the car rental agencies. All such changes added substantially to the costs.

The baggage system, planned to be the most sophisticated in the world— 700 bags a minute, 4000 individual carts, 17 miles of track, 150 computers, work stations, and communication servers—proved to be a disaster. A second shock was the decision by Continental to dismantle its Denver hub operations. Thus, three hub airlines were now reduced to one.

Conclusions

T: Key assumptions about air traffic growth and baggage system technology proved unreliable. The decisive importance of political factors is totally ignored in the rational model, which proves to be applicable only in cases where one agency is fully in control of the process and has widespread support (such as NASA's Apollo lunar landing project).

O: The primary organizational actors were the FAA, the City of Denver, Adams County, the tenant airlines, the Denver and Adams County electorate, and Congress. The City seriously underestimated the power of the airlines in the deregulation environment.

P: The principal individual actors were Denver Mayors Federico Pena and Wellington Webb, Colorado Governor Roy Romer, Department of Transportation Secretary Sam Skinner (also a key actor in the Exxon Valdez case; see Section 6.1), Richard Fleming of the Denver Chamber of Commerce, and the Adams County Commissioners. Their powerful influence—due to their negotiating skill, personality, flexibility, and leadership—was clearly not encompassed by the rational FAA planning model that was initially followed.

Other Planning Disasters

A look at other megaprojects shows that DIA echoed problems experienced elsewhere. The San Francisco *Bay Area Rapid Transit System* (BART) was based on hopelessly overoptimistic traffic forecasts. Originally estimated at $700 million, the cost had risen by 1974 to $1600 million.[3] The cost of the Sydney Opera House rose from $A 7 million to $A 102 million in 15 years; the Concorde went from £ 160 million to £ 1200 million in 14 years [21].

As with the DIA baggage system, advanced technology was involved in the Opera House design (novel dome structure) and BART (automatic train control and aircraft construction techniques). In the case of the Concorde the supersonic technology was not new but its commercialization presented unprecedented economic problems.

As with DIA, O and P factors played significant roles in other megaproject planning. To give just two examples:

- The planning of a third major London airport involved what could be called the London airports lobby (for example, airlines and British Airports Authority) and key politicians (like Labor's Anthony Crosland) favoring the existing airport Stansted, while Conservative politicians interested in urban containment and national prestige favored the Maplin location.
- The winning design of interlocking shells for the Sydney Opera House was that of a relatively unknown 38-year-old Danish architect, Jørn

could have easily worked.

---

3. The Los Angeles Metro Light Rail System has experienced similar problems. Neither has made a significant dent in Californians' love affair with the automobile.

Utzon. The selection committee included the famed architect Eero Saarinen who strongly advocated an adventurous solution. Utzon was an inexperienced, uncompromising perfectionist with a complete lack of knowledge of user requirements (such as acoustics, equipment, and catering). The final result is a visually spectacular center that has become the city's identifying image and tourist attraction but leaves much to be desired in functional terms.

Viewing such planning disasters, Hall classifies the "actors" as a "decision-making triangle":

1. *The bureaucracy:* interested in conservative policy maintenance and aggrandizement;
2. *The community:* a minority of activists and interest groups;
3. *The politicians:* maximizing votes by accommodating their demands to produce strategic coalitions close to the center of opinion.

4.4 Other Cultural Contexts

Following are a few glimpses that suggest the value of using multiple perspectives in cross-cultural system settings.

Environmental Problems in the Himalayas

Thompson and Warburton studied environmental degradation in the Himalayas and came to some striking conclusions:

> The classic development approach has been to sound the alarm and then, confident that the country's attention has been gained, to tell it what will have to be done if it is to avoid losing its resource base . . . [But] 'grand design' solutions are appropriate only when there is a shared understanding of 'the problem' and complete knowledge of the causes of 'the problem' . . . It has not worked [in the Himalayas]. It has not because it has ignored (as if it were some mere detail of implementation) the deep political, economic, and cultural structure that is, in fact, what determines the country's attention and lack of attention. What is needed is a more sensitive approach; an approach that places the 'mere details'—the institutions that constitute the deep structure—at the very center of the stage and relegates to the wings the alarm bellringers and their immaculate prescriptions . . . Though what

we have done is applied systems analysis, it may not look like it. There is, we concede, a fair-sized break between the traditional single-problem/single-solution approach and the one we have developed here. There are many ways to characterize this break but perhaps the best is in terms of the shift it makes from *product thinking* to *process thinking*. The systems frame is no longer a model of the problem but simply an evaluative mechanism. When the problem is to know what the problem is, we need more than one perspective. The approach by way of plural institutions and divergent perceptions meets this need. It gives us problems and solutions that are multiple but not infinite; certainties that are contradictory but not chaotic . . . In many ways, it seems to us, the institutions *are* the facts . . . Institutional accuracy [may be] more valuable (and more accessible) than factual accuracy [22].

The shift to process thinking is, of course, a characteristic of the O perspective (see Table 3.1).

Dam Building in China and Egypt

A gigantic dam construction program, the Three Gorges Dam, is proceeding in China. Zhu and Gu have examined this project and found that, until 2020, 19 counties will bear a direct impact. Some will benefit in terms of transportation and irrigation improvements; others will face serious ecological and social problems due to forced mass displacements of communities. Curiously, they found that:

some of the counties on the victim list acted as the most die-hard and active supporters of the Three Gorges Dam. The leader of one of the potential victim counties openly urged on a television program that the project should be approved and kicked off as soon as possible, the sooner, the better.

Later we [realized] the rationale behind such kind of behavior. If the project continued to remain in the feasibility [analysis] stage, hung in the air, the higher level authority . . . would not allocate any budget to the county. Those who were in charge . . . at the provincial level did not want to take the risk that the budget would be totally wasted [when the whole county would come under water. The leader reasoned that if the project [were approved] . . . at least the county would receive a large amount of migration money from the central Government, which was seriously needed for the immediate survival of its people, although in the long run [they] would face huge uncertainty, to say the least [23].

The leader was discounting the long-term consequences in favor of the immediate benefits, typical of O and P perspectives (see Table 3.1). Using the oriental version of a multiple perspective approach described in Section 3.8, Zhu and Gu saw this as an example of the significance of *renli* and the importance of the interplay of their three perspectives.

In applying the multiple perspective approach to agricultural development of the Wei Bei area of Shaanxi Province, Linstone et al. found that the O perspective tended to dominate T and P [24]. The centrality of the *danwei* or group was apparent; until recently a person's existence apart from his or her *danwei* was barely acknowledged. We found unique difficulties in drawing forth P perspectives that we have not encountered in work with Western cultures. The value placed on individualism in the West is foreign to Chinese culture, and this explains their discomfort when personal perspectives are sought.

The construction of the Aswan Dam in Egypt was studied by Rycroft and Szyliowicz. They too recognized the inadequacy of the rational T perspective:

> The role of the technological dimension varied markedly in the decision-making processes of Egypt, the World Bank, and the United States. None of the decisions examined in this study precisely fit the rational-choice model. Despite the highly technical nature of the project, Egyptian, World Bank, and U.S. decision makers consistently acted on the basis of extremely limited information, considered only a few policy alternatives, and made choices based on uncertain and often unquestioned assumptions. The decisions made by Egypt and the World Bank, examined in their entirety, correspond most closely to the organizational-process model, in which an effort toward satisficing is used to substitute for the rationalist optimizing standard . . . The study strongly reaffirms the primacy of politics; the technological dimension . . . was clearly secondary to political considerations for each of the participants in the High Dam drama. Only on the narrowest issues did technical concerns reign supreme [25].

4.5 Conclusion

We have sampled a wide spectrum of systems in the public sector, ranging from the rifle to the atomic bomb, involving environmental disasters from the United States to the Himalayas and planning disasters from the United States to Australia. In each case we found it exceedingly valuable to move beyond the technical perspective in understanding the complex system and clarifying the decision process. Next we turn to the private sector.

Acknowledgments

Quotations of Charles Peters, published by Addison Wesley Longman, © 1983, Charles Peters.

References

[1] Allison, G., *Essence of Decision: Explaining the Cuban Missile Crisis,* Boston, MA: Little, Brown & Co., 1971.

[2] Morison, E. E., *Men, Machines, and Modern Times,* Cambridge, MA: MIT Press, 1966.

[3] McNaugher, T. L., "Marksmanship. McNamara, and the M-16 Rifle: Innovation in Military Organizations," *Public Policy,* Vol. 28, No. 1, Winter 1980.

[4] Fallows, J., *National Defense,* New York: Random House, 1981.

[5] Davidson, J. W., and M. H. Lytle, *After the Fact: The Art of Historical Detection,* New York: A. A. Knopf, 1982, p. 351.

[6] Stimson, H. S., "The Decision to Use the Atomic Bomb," *Harper's,* Vol. 194, Feb. 1947, pp. 97–107.

[7] Amrine, M., *The Great Decision,* New York: Putnam's, 1959.

[8] Schoenberger, W. S., *Decision of Destiny,* Athens, OH: Ohio University Press, 1970.

[9] Morton, L. "The Decision to Use the Atomic Bomb," *Foreign Affairs,* Vol. 35, No. 2, Jan. 1957, p. 347.

[10] Peters, C., *How Washington Really Works,* Reading, MA: Addison-Wesley Publishing Co., 1981.

[11] Schwebs, D., Review of *How Washington Really Works* in *Technological Forecasting and Social Change,* Vol. 19, 1981, pp. 199–202.

[12] Kissinger, H., *Years of Upheaval,* Waltham, MA: Little, Brown & Co., 1982, p. 440.

[13] Kissinger, H., *The White House Years,* Waltham, MA: Little, Brown & Co., 1979, pp. 32–33.

[14] Ehrlichman, J., *Witness to Power: The Nixon Years,* New York: Simon & Schuster, 1982.

[15] Polmar, N., and T. B. Allen, *Rickover,* New York: Simon & Schuster, 1982.

[16] Borsting, J. R., "Decision-Making at the Top," *Management Science,* Vol. 28, 1982, pp. 341–351.

[17] White, G., *Strategies of American Water Management,* Ann Arbor, MI: University of Michigan Press, 1969.

[18] Crandall, D. R., et al., "Mt. St. Helens Volcano: Recent and Future Behavior," *Science,* Vol. 187, 1975, pp. 438–441.

[19] Board of County Commissioners of Cowlitz County, Cowlitz County Request for Special Legislation, Report to Federal and State Legislative Delegations, 1980.

[20] Szyliowicz, J. S., and A. R. Goetz, "Getting Realistic About Megaproject Planning: The Case of the Denver International Airport," *Policy Sciences,* Vol. 28, 1995, pp. 347–367.

[21] Hall, P., *Great Planning Disasters,* Berkeley, CA: University of California Press, 1982.

[22] Thompson, M., and M. Warburton, "Decision Making Under Contradictory Certainties: How to Save the Himalayas When You Can't Find Out What's Wrong With Them," *Journal of Applied Systems Analysis,* Vol. 12, 1985, pp. 6, 10, 11, 17, and 33.

[23] Zhu, Z., and Jifa Gu, "Evaluation Through the WSR Approach: The China Case," manuscript, Hull, UK: Centre for Systems Studies, University of Hull, 1997, p. 7.

[24] Linstone, H. A., et al., "Multiple Perspectives in Cross-Cultural Systems Analysis: The China Case," Report 87-2, Systems Science Ph.D. Program, Portland State University, Portland, OR, 1987.

[25] Rycroft, R. W., and J. S. Szyliowicz, "The Technological Dimension of Decision Making," *World Politics,* 1980, pp. 36–61.

5

Illustrations from the Private Sector

> You can't be rational in an irrational world. It isn't rational.
>
> J. Orton, *What the Butler Saw*

> The simple have something more than do learned doctors, who often become lost in their search for broad, general laws. The simple have a sense of the individual . . . The Franciscan teachers considered this problem. The great Bonaventure said that the wise must enhance conceptual clarity with the truth implicit in the actions of the simple.
>
> Umberto Eco, *The Name of the Rose*

In Chapter 4, we viewed the decision process in the public sector in terms of multiple perspectives. Now we turn to the private sector for illustrations, specifically the utility, electronics, and aircraft industries, as well as stock market trading.

The first corporate decision involves construction of a hydroelectric facility, the second an acquisition to develop applications of an advanced electronics component, and the third the manufacture of commercial wide-body trijet aircraft.

5.1 The Willamette Falls Hydroelectric Project (Hawke)

Portland General Electric is a medium-sized electric utility headquartered in Portland, Oregon, serving 700,000 customers in the northern portion of the Willamette River Valley. In the early 1980s, it proposed the construction of additional hydroelectric facilities at the Willamette Falls located 14 miles south of Portland in suburban Oregon City. The decision process began with the determination that a new generation was necessary to meet the rapid load growth and expanding economy of the time. The process established a template for those that followed, not just in the state but in the entire Pacific Northwest. The increased scope and sophistication of the process can best be evaluated using multiple perspectives.

Historical Background

Since the early days of pioneer settlement in Oregon's Willamette Valley, power from the natural waterfall on the Willamette River near Oregon City has been used for commercial purposes. Early industries at the Willamette Falls included a flour mill, saw mill, woolen mills, and a dry dock. In later years, these industries were replaced by paper mills.

River traffic to and from the upstream Willamette towns bypassed the falls overland until the construction of a large government lock was completed in 1874. In 1889, the Willamette Falls Electric Company tapped the falls for a hydroelectric power plant described as a "dynamo house" with rock-filled wooden bulkheads. This new plant generated 32.5 kW of power, which was then transmitted 14 miles to downtown Portland, where it powered lights to illuminate the city's streets. This was, interestingly enough, the first instance of long-distance transmission of electrical energy for commercial purposes in the United States. Known as "Station A," the plant is still in use today as part of a paper mill.

In 1892, the Willamette Falls Electric Company and several other small utilities merged into a new company, *Portland General Electric* (PGE). By that time, demand for energy from the Willamette Falls facility far exceeded its output. Consequently, as one of its first-generation ventures for generation facilities, the new PGE began construction of a larger plant at Willamette Falls, innovatively named "Station B." In 1894, three 400-kW alternating current generators were installed. Some of this plant's original equipment is currently on display at the Smithsonian Institute. In 1953, the plant was completely reconstructed and automated, and today it is known as the T. W. Sullivan Plant. Generating 15 MW of power, it is a contributing part of PGE's hydroelectric system.

Principal industries at Willamette Falls today continue to consist of paper mills. These companies' past use of water power in the wood-grinding process has now largely been replaced by purchased electric power as their technologies changed over time.

The T Perspective

To adequately understand PGE's "technical approach" to the Willamette Falls project, it helps to place it in the context of similar PGE decisions over the previous 80 years. In a company that had relied on large numbers of engineers and technical people for its ongoing growth and construction, most major decisions on generation followed well-defined guidelines. Land and water rights were secured, applications were made for permits, consultants were hired to design a facility, and contractors were hired to build it. There was comparatively little public interest in these projects because they were generally located in remote parts of the state.

The beginning of the latest Willamette Falls proposal was following the same track. It had been known since the early 1920s that additional generation capacity was available at the Willamette Falls site. In the late 1950s, the economics of the location became attractive. A list of the major studies since that time included:

- 1958, Bechtel: investigation of methods for increasing spillway height—broad analysis of the Station A/east-side site;
- 1971, Bechtel: broad analysis of using the existing paper mill site, update of the analysis on the Station A/east-side site—east-side channel excavation study;
- 1978, PGE: cost update of 1971 study—Stage II channel excavation study;
- 1979, Bechtel: cost update of 1978—fish facilities options investigated;
- 1980, Bechtel: broad analysis of west-side site—detailed analysis of turbine types.

Through these studies, the technical alternatives were reduced to four major possibilities:

1. Build a 60-MW facility on the Station A/east-side site.
2. Build a 60-MW facility on the west side by razing a portion of the existing paper mill facility.
3. Build a 75-MW facility on either the east or west side and close the T. W. Sullivan Plant. This would mitigate certain fisheries problems and the existing turbines could be sold advantageously on the market.
4. Install 20-MW additional capacity in the existing paper mill.

All of the options would involve an amendment to an existing federal license, which would simplify some of the permit applications. The water rights issue was clarified in a study done for PGE by a local legal firm in 1979 and resulted in PGE's filing for a preliminary water certificate. This assured priority status on the water usage should the project proceed. The fish issue was, and continues to be, extremely sensitive, and negotiations with various state agencies are an ongoing process. Recreational improvements were required under the licensing process, and these were coordinated with the appropriate local and regional governmental agencies.

Economic analyses of the technical options showed the 60-MW east-side option to be the most attractive. It would generate electricity for considerably less cost than new or planned thermal generation facilities. Unlike thermal facilities, a hydroelectric plant was at the time almost completely insensitive to rising fuel costs, transportation charges, and oil prices. A detailed cost-benefit analysis showed the benefits exceeding the costs by over $70 million over the first 20 years of the project.

In terms of financing, the planning and construction would extend over five years at a total cost of $70 to $100 million, depending on the cost of fisheries facilities. Long-term low-interest industrial revenue bonds could be sold for this type of hydroelectric project, and significant tax benefits could accrue. In the peak construction year, the project would represent no more than 10.5% of PGE's total construction budget.

At this point, with major studies completed, with favorable reports in most areas and with continuing negotiations with the fisheries people, PGE historically would have decided to proceed with the project. However, as will be discussed in the organizational perspective, the project did not proceed along the historical lines. Major additions to the process were made.

First, the PGE Public Affairs Department was consulted about the project's probable impact on the attitudes of the residents and elected officials in the Oregon City area. This was somewhat of a first for PGE—asking for public reaction in the initial planning process in order to make the program proactive rather than reactive. It reflected an increase in sensitivity to public input in major community decisions in general and to the Oregon City area's concerns in particular. A Citizens' Task Force was selected, based on the recommendations of a local consultant. It represented a cross section of community interests, and its input carried a majority of the weight in the decision on whether to build or not.

Additionally, a government coordination plan was worked out by the Public Affairs Department to assure that local, regional, and state officials were kept informed of developments on a timely basis. Informational packets were prepared for distribution to these officials and to the news media. In light of current planning processes, which in most cases legally require this kind of input, these additions seem terribly simplistic but at the time they were a radical departure, particularly for a regulated monopoly with almost 100 years of history in the local area.

In general, a change in the decision-making process had been made during the project. Still the traditional concerns had to be supplemented by additional considerations of public and political impacts and effects. The technical, economic, legal, financial, public relations, and political aspects were addressed by various organizational components, and the process proceeded in an orderly and rational manner. To see the impetus for the change in the process, however, one must view the underlying organizational and personal perspectives.

The O Perspective

At least three levels of organizational interactions were in play in the Willamette Falls Project: (1) PGE as an organization composed of many subunits that must interface with one another, (2) PGE as an organization interfacing with other organizations, and (3) PGE in a special organizational relationship with the local paper mills.

The O perspective is especially noteworthy in the Willamette Falls decision as it relates to the departmental subunits within PGE. Additionally in this case, the presence of strong leaders shows the relationships that can evolve between the O and P perspectives. Strong leaders can and should have significant impact and organizational characteristics. By the time the Willamette Falls project started, there had already been a long-established organizational structure for decision-making processes. Frank Warren, Chairman of PGE at that time, had been in control since the early 1950s and had established a fairly clearcut hierarchy for decision making. Under his leadership, the initial Bechtel studies were commissioned by the Generation Engineering Department, which also undertook the economic analyses with input from the Rate Department. Planning was done in each department as deemed appropriate.

By the mid-1970s, many changes took place that substantially changed the complexion of the company. The most significant of these was the retirement of Frank Warren. In addition, however, there were the expiration of long-term Bonneville Power Administration contracts and the replacement of this power with the construction of the Trojan nuclear facility, a drastic increase in oil prices and subsequent electric rate increases, and an accelerated public interest in all of these major decisions. The result was that organizational adjustments were made within PGE that were designed to reflect the increased importance of the large generation projects that began to dominate the company's efforts. Complexity increased dramatically.

Among the first changes were the formation, in 1977, of a Corporate Planning Department and the addition of a staff of 70 to support it. Although this new department did not abolish the older Generation Engineering Department, it did considerably diminish its original planning stature by assuming many of the responsibilities for resource and long-range planning, which the Generation Engineering Department had formerly held. In the beginning, then, cooperation between the Corporate Planning Department and some of the existing departments was not necessarily an easy task.

The new Corporate Planning Department was just one example; similar situations were occurring elsewhere in the company. Other new departments were being formed, and previously small departments were increasing in size to accommodate new external requirements and the new management's priorities. For example, as new, more sophisticated employee programs were added, the Human Resources Department staff increased in response. As the financial performance became a priority, new departments were formed to monitor, plan, and guide financial activities. In 1970, the company had about 1,800 employees; by 1980, the number exceeded 3,000.

Complexity was increasing, and interdepartmental relationships were constantly changing where once they had been stable. As a result, the imbedded decision process had to adjust to meet these new conditions. No longer could the simple hierarchical chain of command handle the decision making. The Willamette Falls Project, for example, was administratively set up to be run by a 12-member intercompany task force that would meet periodically to review progress and coordinate activities. This system would not necessarily have been considered when hierarchical decisions sufficed. In addition, an executive oversight committee was set up to provide general policy guidance and to handle high-level political contacts when necessary. The changes, the increased complexity, the distributed decision-making structure and processes, and the organizational rivalries, both healthy and otherwise, were natural occurrences that emerged when looking at the O perspective within the Company.

The general trend in the area of PGE interfacing with other organizations was also one of increasing complexity. Although legally the *Federal Energy Regulatory Commission* (FERC) had sole responsibility for approving the project, in practice it systematically brought other agencies into the process in ever-increasing numbers. As many as 16 individual state agencies and bureaus had to approve a project before FERC would consider the application. Many of these state bureaus deferred to input from several regional and/or local agencies. In the case of federal agencies, the company went through established procedures and worked on an informal level with the federal staffs. On state and local levels, PGE often devoted far greater planning and development resources to a decision than did the corresponding agencies. Informal rivalries often developed, based on the respective interest each group feels it represented. For example, fisheries was one area where federal and PGE staffs had far greater resources than the Oregon Department of Fisheries and Wildlife. (In general, these kinds of organizational relationships were further distorted nationally, where much larger, multistate facilities were matched against small state bureaus. As the public required additional input, the decision process and structures changed within these groups much the same way they had changed within PGE. Change, complexity, distributed decision-making structure and process, as well as organizational rivalries, were again emerging under the O perspective.)

A third organizational aspect emerged, which was peculiar to the Willamette Falls project, involving the relationships of PGE with the paper mills. A project at this location was attractive no matter who built it. In owning the land and filing for a preliminary water certificate, PGE put a lock on the ability to build from the start. But the relationships with large customers, particularly those in strong financial positions, do not lend themselves to clearcut decisions. When both became aware of the activity at the Falls, they expressed interest in joint participation. Discussions occurred over a year's time as to participation schemes that could prove financially beneficial to PGE and to the general rate payer and at the same time benefit the paper mills. With the high levels of return required in that market, the two conditions could apparently not be simultaneously achieved. The deference on the organizational and personal levels afforded customers of this size is a reality that cannot be ignored, and its impact on the decision process was tangible in terms of resources committed and time spent.

The P Perspective

In a project of this magnitude, there are numerous instances where distinct personalities influence the decision process. The Willamette Falls case presented two distinct generations of leadership.

Frank Warren was President and Chief Executive Officer (CEO) of PGE for 30 years. In the 1950s, 1960s, and 1970s, he personally made the final decision in the company on a wide range of issues. With comparatively few employees, his decision hierarchy was fairly flat. There was easy access from several levels below him. The Company promoted almost exclusively from within and was managed primarily by technical managers who had come up through the ranks. Under these conditions, the organization was stable, and the decisions followed orderly, well-established procedural guidelines, as discussed in the O perspective section.

In the 1970s, as the complexity increased on all fronts, changes also occurred in the leadership of the company. Robert Short was elected as Warren's replacement. His previous experience was in public relations and the political arena, with a solid background in finance. Under his influence, things changed appreciably.[1] William Lindblad was elected President at this time. Lindblad came to PGE in 1977 as a Vice-President from Pacific Gas and Electric in California. Short then chose three Senior Vice-Presidents. James Durham was previously Deputy Attorney General for the State of Oregon and had been with PGE since 1978. Ken Harrison was an officer with a major bank and had been with PGE since 1975. Chuck Heinrich, who had been with PGE since 1956, progressed through the Rate Department ranks.

In general terms, the upper management after Warren's departure was the opposite of that during his tenure. The newer executives were generally younger, had considerable nonutility experience, and were specialized in areas not necessarily specific to a power utility. Not surprisingly, these rapid changes created some uncomfortable feelings. Existing long-time middle managers perceived that not only were executive slots filled to which they otherwise might have aspired, but these positions were filled with individuals not likely to leave soon. Entire departments were being created and staffed with individuals with limited utility experience. The experience and decision base, which was once so solid, was changing almost daily.

The Willamette Falls project was of such a magnitude that an executive oversight committee was formed, which included Lindblad, Durham, and Harrison. As mentioned earlier, they were to provide policy guidelines and high-level political contacts in an effort to make an informed decision on a broader basis than technology alone. The group viewed the fisheries and public reaction as integral to that decision. In particular, they considered the fisheries negotiations as very sensitive and did not want to push the State Fisheries and Wildlife Department into making decisions at a speed not commensurate with its staffing. Finally, they wanted to be certain that appropriate attention was given to input from the paper mills—their leadership was influential in the community and they were personally known to the Steering Committee.

The project was considered by the broad-based 20-member Citizens' Task Force in the Oregon City area that had been established to gain citizen perspectives. Their input plus the final outcome of PGE's staff negotiations with the Oregon Department of Fisheries and Wildlife became pivotal points in the project. If input proved favorable, the project would have reverted to the traditional decision-making processes and standard operating procedures. If their input was not favorable, the project was to be cancelled or altered appreciably.

---

1. This change is quite typical. George Steiner recognized it in his 1981 article "The New Class of Chief Executive Officer": He is becoming "a public figure, a spokesman for both a company as well as the business institution."

Again, to the casual observer, the decision-making process appeared quite orderly and rational. Only when overlaying the organizational and the personal perspectives, can one gain appreciation for the behind-the-scenes motivations and impacts that influenced the Willamette Falls Project.

The Outcome

> *Anglers Concerned: PGE Hydroplant Plan Blasted (Headline)*
>
> We're acting like drug addicts in this panic over energy.
> > A member of Santiam Flycasters
>
> Positioning the powerhouse at the falls would be the worst place in the Willamette River to build.
> > A member of the Isaak Walton League
>
> Do we want to look like LA or like Oregon?
> > Another Santiam Flycaster
>
> *Source:* Article reporting Citizens' Task Force hearing [1].

The Citizens' Task Force was active for eight months. Numerous meetings and public input sessions were held as the Committee gathered facts and gained sensitivity to community opinion. Questionnaires were distributed to all customers by mail. A temporary office was opened in the community to supply speakers or information to local groups and citizens. Local, regional, and state community leaders and politicians were kept informed of developments. The end result of the process was a report from the Committee to PGE. In late 1980, two criteria had been established for project construction: (1) that the plant be economically justified and (2) that the Citizens' Advisory Committee confirm community acceptance and support. On March 3, 1981, PGE's Robert Short announced that the company would not build the Willamette Falls hydroelectric plant. The cost-effectiveness criterion was satisfied; the community support aspect was not. As Short stated to the Task Force:

> You pointed out that the project has little or no approval from either local or statewide fishermen, and the public just doesn't want any further development in this location that might disturb its present or its future. We determined our social and environmental responsibility must be given more weight in this particular project [2].

Editorial comment praised the decision:

Portland General Electric deserves praise for the process it used in deciding not to build a hydroelectric project at Willamette Falls . . . above all, PGE has demonstrated an environmental awareness and responsibility in using the citizens' committee to determine what people want. If other potentially controversial projects are proposed by corporations, PGE showed that the advisory committee is a good thermometer to take the public's temperature on how the project will be received [3].

While the Willamette Falls hydroelectric project will not see the light of day, the community participation process is expected to survive. The corporation appears committed to it at this time (paraphrased from [4]).

Over the next few years the load growth that originally motivated the proposal slowed dramatically and, when it re-emerged in the late 1980s, the industry was beginning to radically restructure. Smaller, low-cost gas combustion turbines changed the economic curves that had defined the industry for over 80 years. Smaller units could be built for lower per-unit cost than larger ones. This, in turn, redefined the organizational landscape as the industry began evolving from regulated monopoly status to competition. This is a transition still evolving in the country at this time. The personnel that defined the Willamette Falls case moved on. Short, Durham, and Lindblad all left in the 1980s, and Ken Harrison emerged as CEO. He led PGE through the first closure and decommissioning of a nuclear plant in the United States and through a recent merger with the international energy giant Enron.

As was evident in the Willamette Falls case, it is the combination of T, O, and P perspectives that led to a comprehensive understanding of the changes that occurred. The approach benefited from the insider's point of view in this case, and it was later used in a proactive sense as a project management tool in numerous applications. The multiple perspective concept added a richness to the events not possible with more traditional models and analyses.

5.2 Electronic System Market: Failure of a Strategy (Cook)

In the spring of 1977, the Manager of Business Development at the Data Reduction Group of Acousticon, Inc. proposed that Acousticon acquire Gramma Corporation, the third largest source of *Generalized Acoustic Survey* (GAS) Systems in the United States. Acousticon was Gramma's largest supplier, selling *surface acoustic wave* (SAW) filters to Gramma.[2]

2. The names of the product, companies, and individuals have been changed for obvious reasons.

(was this luck at could public opinion actually be a "good" forecaster of technological trends?

Much preparatory work and analysis led to negotiations that reached agreement on the conditions for the sale (including a price of approximately $12 million). The proposed deal was rejected by Acousticon's Board of Directors.

Gramma was sold to another company for $20 million in 1978 and resold to General Electric for $110 million in 1981. Acousticon entered the GAS market on its own in 1978. Two years and $6 million later, it withdrew.

We apply the T, O, and P perspectives to fathom a decision that seems difficult to explain on the basis of the T perspective alone.

Historical Background

Acoustic filters were invented in the mid-1950s as a way of discriminating the individual frequency components of the waves picked up by ground microphones, or geophones. These waveforms contain information that enables trained geophysicists to determine potential locations for oil exploration, but the information is difficult to extract. The filter permitted the user to look at specific narrow frequency bands from the wide range of noise returned when dynamite explosions were recorded through the geophones.

International Business Machines (IBM), working in conjunction with the Exxon Research Laboratory, introduced the 225 Geological Acoustic Survey System in 1958. Although Exxon used it in its pioneer GAS-1 system for automated data reduction, the product was a business failure for IBM. With a monthly rental of over $4,000, less than 500 were sold or leased.

The high cost of the early acoustic filters was due to their filtering technique, adapted from radar technology. The data had to be filtered using the nonlinearity of tetrode vacuum tube characteristic curves.

The result was that the monthly cost of a work station, which could generate the output of four to six manual analysts, was about $10,000, including the computer time to execute the analysis software. Because that cost in the late-1960s was equivalent to five fully burdened analysts, only the large oil companies had both the heavy analysis work load and the innovative attitude required to use computer GAS techniques.

In 1964, the Acoustic Device Research Department of Acousticon was trying to develop a technique for capturing low-level acoustic waveforms. Acousticon was (and is) the world's leading manufacturer of geophones, a device for capturing acoustic waveforms for recording on magnetic tape. By refining the SAW technology, Acousticon scientists discovered a technique that made it possible to record the various frequency domains independently, greatly simplifying the waveform analysis process.

The vision of a commercial market for the SAW acoustic filter outside geophony was the work of J. Crawford Pinkston, who headed a small group working on crystal structure analysis, determining faults in crystalline materials. When his optical input device failed to work, he took the acoustic filter to the market as the F5002, selling for $10,000. Pinkston later founded the very successful Digital Filter Systems, but his venture into acoustical analysis did not satisfy the business needs of Acousticon. He was replaced by Ralph Willsaw, a rapidly rising design engineer and manager who had recently completed a tour at Acousticon Holland. Willsaw recognized the need for a lower cost product and software to accompany it. He initiated a low-cost filter design program and hired an experienced software development manager.

The Acousticon 5010 was a major breakthrough when it was introduced in 1972. With a purchase price of $4000, and accompanied by the Accu-10 software package, it made possible an order-of-magnitude reduction in the cost of an analysis work station and opened up the acoustical survey market to a large number of applications. In addition to geophysical surveying, GAS analysis was found to be justifiable in testing the crystal structure of forgings, analyzing the internal operation of moving machinery, and forecasting the weather using GAS analysis techniques on satellite data.

The most successful analysis product in Acousticon's history was the 5015, follow-up to the 5010. It used a larger filter that could handle more discrete frequencies, permitting faster and more accurate analysis.

Two major application areas emerged: ultrasonic analysis of cast parts and immediate field evaluation of geophysical exploration results. For foundries, acoustical survey made it possible to detect flaws in the crystalline structure of cast parts before any of the cost of machining was incurred. In petroleum exploration, geophysicists in the field could evaluate the results of each shot before the equipment was moved and without sending the data back to corporate headquarters. Bad shots could then be repeated at once, reducing the cost of keeping the crew in the field. Quick to match up the new filter technology with a market need, a number of companies were formed to supply acoustic analysis systems. By 1976 there were four major contenders and numerous minor ones, as shown in Table 5.1.

The Situation in Spring 1977

At this time the Generalized Acoustic Survey Systems market seemed poised to explode. Numerous articles had appeared, documenting savings of 4:1 to 7:1 in manpower expenditure to accomplish a given analysis, and numerous specific applications had stable and proven software packages available. The GAS vendors, of course, were mounting major sales campaigns aimed at early and even late adopting organizations.

Table 5.1

Generalized Acoustic Survey Systems Market Shares (1976)

Vendor	Sales (millions of dollars)	Market share (%)	Orders for Acousticon filters (millions of dollars)*
E	16.0	24.6	1.78
F	13.0	20.0	1.72
G (Gramma)	10.0	15.4	0.82
H	8.0	12.3	1.21
J	4.0	6.2	–
K	4.0	6.2	1.49
L	3.0	4.6	–
M	1.5	2.3	0.55
N	1.5	2.3	0.72
P	1.0	1.5	0.10
Q	1.0	1.5	–
S	1.0	1.5	0.72
T	0.5	0.8	–
U	0.3	0.5	–
	0.2	0.3	
Totals	65.0	100.0	9.11

*Acousticon orders are not directly comparable with customer's sales because they reflect antici-pated growth. In some cases they are inflated to ensure delivery or to obtain greater discounts.

As can be seen from Table 5.1, Acousticon had been getting a significant proportion of the money expended even though it was only a supplier to, rather than a participant in, the GAS market. The costs of computers on a chip (microcomputers) and memory (RAM) had been coming down very rapidly. Several of the GAS vendors were now looking at building their own filters, based on digital *Fast Fourier Transform* (FFT) technology, rather than buying them from Acousticon. By doing so they could increase their own value added and offer lower priced work stations to their customers.

These filters had the unfortunate characteristic of being based on digital software FFT technology, with a series of narrow frequency ranges rather than the wide ranges available with the SAW filter. In addition, the data resolution was not as precise, and the time required to generate it was much longer. Some customers, it was felt, would continue to pay a premium for the higher quality of the SAW filter. The anticipation was that rapid growth in the market would lead to continued growth in sales of SAW filters to these vendors, for whom Acousticon was the sole source, although market share would be lost to the rapid growth of digital FFT filters.

The Acousticon *Acoustic Data Reduction Group* (ADR) was organized into three Divisions: Systems, *Original Equipment Manufacturers* (OEM), and Products (Figure 5.1). The operation was headed by Ralph Willsaw, who had been responsible for the growth rate of 45% per year since the introduction of the 4010. Willsaw had made the initial contacts with Gramma and felt strongly that the acquisition would greatly strengthen the position of ADR in the acoustic analysis market.

The *Information Display Systems* (IDS) division was responsible for two products that combined processing capability with filters and peripherals to make a functioning system. The IDS division was also responsible for investigating opportunities for Acousticon as a vendor of applications packages. The OEM division was responsible for sales to original equipment manufacturers of products to be built into their systems and resold. This division interfaced with the GAS vendors, including Gramma. It was headed by Jerry Grass, a former SAW design manager, who was open-minded about the acquisition but very concerned that it be handled in a way that would not jeopardize his relations with OEM customers.

The *Information Display Products* (IDP) division was responsible for the bulk of the product line: graphic terminals, hard-copy units, plotters, and peripherals that were nonintelligent (had no processing capability of their own). Many of the IDP customers were buying terminals as components for their own

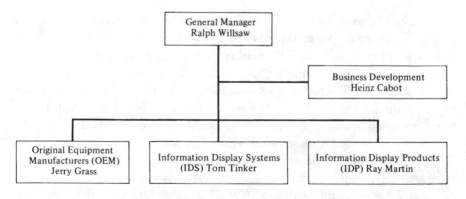

Figure 5.1 Acousticon Data Reduction Group organization.

in-house GAS systems or for use on time-sharing systems. Ray Martin, Manager of this organization, was not involved in planning for the acquisition.

The IDS division was headed by Tom Tinker, brought in from Honeywell by Ralph Willsaw to provide computer industry experience to the organization. Tinker was primarily an engineer and was finding his first experience with general management something of a problem: he lacked the vision and insight to plot a course for his group. His management style was to manage the ongoing business and let his subordinates generate the plans for the future of the division. As a result, a number of possible market venture products were under consideration, but none had caught the fancy of Ralph Willsaw, who had to approve them. He was interested in the acquisition of Gramma as a means of obtaining an established position in the market.

The strongest proponent and champion for the move was Heinz Cabot, recently brought in from Filcomp, the leading vendor of output plotters, where he had been Vice-President of Systems Development. Cabot was a business strategist who saw several strategic possibilities in the acquisition. The first was the one obvious to the other participants: establishing a direct marketing channel into the GAS market. Another was the idea of extending the market life of the acoustic filter by reducing Gramma's selling prices to the point where the storage tube volume would justify the new manufacturing facilities needed to produce a truly low-cost version of the device. The third was tapping Gramma's software expertise in acoustic analysis system design and using that to go into new markets. Above all, however, was the prospect of a major role in the management of the newly acquired business, which he viewed as a major career opportunity.

Gramma was a likely target for acquisition by someone. It was having trouble generating adequate cash flow to sustain the growth that was essential for retaining a market share in this rapidly growing market. Equity funding was almost nonexistent for companies such as Gramma, and its existing debt made further borrowing impractical. Its current position was marginally profitable, but its projections, based on adequate capitalization, were for good profits in the next several years.

Electrosight had initiated litigation against Gramma, claiming $25 million in damages and penalties for theft of trade secrets. Electrosight claimed that a group of programmers, who left to go to work for Gramma, took proprietary software with them. Gramma claimed that the group did original work that was not proprietary to Electrosight.

The U.S. Department of Justice guidelines indicated that the acquisition of Gramma by Acousticon would be viewed as a case of forward integration, in which a large vendor takes over a smaller customer. That move would have violated proposed new guidelines, but those currently in effect did not appear to prevent the acquisition. Adding to the concern was the fear that the newly appointed Carter administration officials showed signs of vindictiveness in their intent to prosecute mergers they opposed.

The Acquisition Decision

After extended negotiations, a tentative deal was struck. Acousticon would trade one share of Acousticon stock for every 3.25 shares of Gramma stock in a merger of interest acquisition. The effective sale price was $12.3 million, roughly equivalent to one year's sales. The principals of Gramma agreed to hold their stock for one year following the merger and to manage the company for that length of time. The basic tenor was friendly, and both sides assumed that the Gramma management would be integrated into Acousticon with little turmoil.

Gramma would be run independently of the ADR Group but would coordinate closely with it. It was the expressed intent of both parties to use Acousticon products in Gramma systems as a way to maintain the SAW filter as a major factor in the market.

An elaborate proposal was put together by the group working on the project. The acquisition was represented as an implementation of the XYZ Consulting Group Model, advocated by corporate planning, and a major business opportunity for Acousticon. The proposal concentrated on the technological perspective and ignored the position of Joe Towers, who had been instrumental in the decision making of the Board of Directors.

The proposal was rejected by the Acousticon Board of Directors on the basis of the contingent liability represented by the Electrosight lawsuit and because the ADR group was not sure that the acquisition could be integrated and managed properly. Indications were that the Board did not spend much effort on the merits of the business case, on understanding the GAS market, or on an XYZ-oriented portfolio-management consideration.

As a result of this decision, Tom Tinker was given the charter to build a petroleum exploration GAS system and take it to the marketplace. Rights to an existing software package were acquired from a software developer who failed to live up to his promises. After a few disastrous benchmark competitions, it was obvious that a great deal of further developmental work was needed to compete effectively. Additional software people were hired, and a VAX computer system was purchased from a leading computer manufacturer.

With an investment of somewhat more than $6 million and a product starting to win some of the competitive sales situations, a top management planning session came to the conclusion that Acousticon's share of the GAS market would not become substantial in the next few years. Following the business portfolio concepts of the XYZ group (which said the market leaders control a market and only participants with large market shares could be profitable), the group was shut down and the products removed from the product line.

The T Perspective

The acquisition made sense on the basis of objective consideration of both the technical and business aspects. Acousticon's products were already designed into the Gramma product line and had attained a good reception in the marketplace. The software supporting the system had been designed to make full use of the characteristics of the SAW filter and made an effective tool. Gramma's business was good, but growth was restricted by the availability of cash to fund the growth that would result from aggressive marketing. Acousticon, on the other hand, had a cash surplus without obvious business opportunities to pursue.

The SAW filter had not only been the basis for Acousticon's success in Generalized Acoustic Survey Systems; it had opened up the market, and made feasible an investment of hundreds of man-years in software development. But with the cost reduction of the semiconductor industry, digital filters could be designed by individual system vendors. This type of filter, in spite of its marginal resolution, is used because of its low cost and relatively high value added. In addition, the proliferation of home computers has given the industry a new low-end standard of "quick and dirty" filtering.

The SAW filters are made using commercial fused silica substrates in the form of ground and polished Vycor plates made from Corning 0120 glass. Because commercially available plates are used, they require a large amount of re-working. Because the typical volume of a glass plant is so high, glass companies are unwilling to entertain production runs of special plate types when a year's supply requires more set-up than run time. Several studies have shown that a substantial increase in plate volume is of enormous benefit to Acousticon, but the required market and pricing strategies have never been seriously entertained (Table 5.2).

The acquisition of Gramma has the potential for building the volume of SAW filters because at least one major GAS vendor will have the incentive to stay with that technology over the long run. If that volume could provide the incentive to invest in the special design and in *cathode ray tube* (CRT) production facility automation, the reduced price will keep other customers with the storage tube for the present.

On the business side, Acousticon had a good financial position, with the filter business generating a substantial amount of cash, and all major product lines profitable. Most investments for new product development and additions

Table 5.2
Plate Cost Versus Design Type

Design Type	Raw plate cost	Reworking cost	Total plate cost
Commercial	$18.00	$432.00	$450.00
Special*	67.00	113.00	180.00

*The special design involves $170,000 of tooling charges. Amortization over the first 100,000 plates (minimum order) is included in the raw plate cost.

to facilities are internally funded, although a line of bank credit has been negotiated to provide for future needs.

Gramma, on the other hand, is finding some difficulty in funding its growth. The GAS systems have the characteristic of requiring a significant investment in work in process because they contain major purchased components, including computers and filters, which have to be paid for long before the end customer's payment is received. Although absorbing cash, Gramma is profitable and is projecting growth rates of 35% to 45% for the next several years.

The Corporate Planning Group at Acousticon was a strong advocate of the philosophy of the XYZ Group, whom it retained as consultants. The XYZ Group holds that the business in which a corporation is involved should be managed as a portfolio of investments, where each opportunity is funded or dropped based on the merits of its market position. It further advocates division of the market into distinct market segments and holds that any business must be larger than the competitors and grow faster in order to control pricing in the market segments.

The XYZ Group suggests that growth can come from two sources: (1) taking the market share from competitors and (2) pre-empting their growth. The latter tactic is normally accomplished in rapidly growing markets by aggressive marketing and pre-emptive pricing. In this case Acousticon's financial strength would permit market strategies by which Gramma could overtake market leader E in three to five years of growth in the 45% to 55% range.

Based on the XYZ-oriented corporate investment strategy, the case for the Gramma acquisition is a favorable one.

Three major negative factors exist, which can be viewed as quantifiable risks in the technical perspective. One is that the move would require approval by either the Federal Trade Commission or the U.S. Department of Justice. There are no other producers of the SAW filter, but there is clearly a risk associated with a detailed review of this natural monopoly by either of those agencies.

The second is the litigation that has been filed by E. Acousticon planned to have an independent consultant look at the source code for both Gramma's and E's software packages and evaluate the degree of similarity at that level of detail. Common law doctrine states that a craftsman cannot be prohibited from practicing his craft, but the protection of trade secrets and proprietary information is critical to the computer business, where software cannot be patented. Working with the consultant, corporate attorneys can estimate the degree of risk associated with the lawsuit.

The third factor is the damage to relations with the existing customers because an Acousticon subsidiary would compete directly with them. Evaluation indicates that this point is moot because they will continue to use the acoustic filter displays if the cost-cutting strategy is pursued and will develop their own digital filters otherwise. Analysis indicates that the competition factor does not significantly change the GAS customers' probability of developing their own display, although it may have some effect on the timing.

The O Perspective

Acousticon was founded in Midland, Texas, shortly after World War II by a group of individuals who believed they could build a better geophone than any then available on the market. The SAW geophone is a device that detects sound waves and converts them to voltage waveforms with a high degree of accuracy. The excellence of their product, and their timing in catching the wave of geophone applications, led them to very rapid growth for the first decade of their existence.

During that decade, when it appeared that they could do no wrong, a number of organizational characteristics, which originated as ad hoc solutions to operational problems, developed into an immutable corporate culture, much of which exists today. Individual decisions made by managers to solve immediate operating problems quickly became "the way things are done at Acousticon."

On the boundary between the personal perspective and the organizational perspective is the operation of individuals in the nascent organization. In the process of managing the business, they take actions that evolve from solutions to precedents to practices, and finally mature as corporate policy. Although these policies may be actually inappropriate in the larger, more mature organization, changing them becomes difficult and requires the conscious effort of an individual. So the practice goes full circle, from the personal action of a founder to solve a problem, to corporate policy, to another individual operating under the motivational structure that drives individuals in organizations.

Acousticon was the result of the work of two men: Bill Hunt, a brilliant electrical engineer, and Jack Shaw, a talented businessman and humanitarian. Early in their efforts they hired Joe Towers, a conservative and risk-averse young lawyer, as corporate secretary.

From their efforts emerged a successful company with a unique culture; a culture that embodied several unusual characteristics, because the long period of strong growth permitted many practices to solidify into custom without the normal test of practicality and economic reality.

Among these characteristics are the following:

- *The concept of an "Acousticon Family":* no layoffs, no firings, very low turnover.
- *Profit sharing:* Employees are paid a base pay, and corporate profits are shared with employees as a percentage of base pay, usually around the 20% level. Employee cost consciousness is a result, leading to completely open stock rooms where employees help themselves to the supplies and equipment they need.
- *Decision making by consensus:* Most decisions are made in meetings where lengthy discussion of issues is much more the practice than is management fiat. Decisions take a long time to emerge and can be reopened at a later date by almost anyone.
- *Preference for building in-house rather than purchasing:* Acousticon winds its own transformers; forms its own sheet metal and plastic; wraps its own cable; and manufactures resistors, capacitors, and integrated circuits—components that most companies buy on the market. The general feeling is "we can do it better," which is often true, but does not take economics into account.
- *Reluctance to change:* The organization is slow to innovate in all areas except the technical ones. The way things are done is particularly slow to change, although new technical ideas are incorporated into products ahead of competitors. The company is totally unable to react quickly to changes in the market other than those it creates through product innovation.
- *Caution:* In any decision with legal implications, Acousticon will defer economic considerations to a conservative approach. Fear of litigation is a major concern of the corporation and affects its flexibility in pricing, acquisition consideration, factory operation, accounting, and a number of other operating areas. For years it preferred not to build

militarized products for the U.S. Government because of intrusive federal regulations such as the Renegotiation Act of 1951.

- *The "Acousticon window":* To be accepted by management a new product proposal had to fit the market characteristics of existing products. The selling price should be between $1000 and $10,000, and annual sales between 300 and 8000 units. Low-cost, high-volume items and big-ticket systems did not fit the manufacturing process, the sales practices of the field force, or the market understanding of management.

In this environment the proposal to acquire Gramma had a difficult path at best. Acousticon didn't buy things, it developed them. With one special exception, Acousticon had no operations other than field sales outside Midland. Top management had no "feel" for the Acoustic Survey System market, and GAS systems selling for $100,000 to $300,000 were outside the "Acousticon window." The pending lawsuit with E was frightening, as was the perceived threat by the antitrust forces.

So, despite the fact that the acquisition fit all the guidelines set by Corporate Planning's XYZ model—that the market prospects were very good for Gramma and that the strategy held great promise for extending the life of the acoustic filter—it was rejected by the Board of Directors. Joe Towers was the leading opponent of the move on the basis that the business opportunity, as he perceived it, was overshadowed by the risk involved.

The P Perspective

Five individuals were the prime actors in this situation.

Ralph Willsaw

Willsaw was a talented and multifaceted individual who had risen to the position of Group Vice-President in the upper management of Acousticon. He had a good sense of the market and an excellent set of managerial skills in addition to being an electronic engineer by training. He was the primary proponent of the acquisition because of the value he felt it would bring to Acousticon. He had confidence that the organization could be managed after it had been acquired and believed it was a good business decision. He was the most objective of the individuals involved, operating almost entirely on the basis of the technical perspective.

Heinz Cabot

Cabot had recently been brought in from Filcomp, where he was a Vice-President. Cabot was both a skilled negotiator and an intellectual. He had been chartered by Willsaw to find one or several acquisitions Acousticon could use to build on its base in acoustical survey to emulate the performance of Hewlett-Packard in the computer market. Cabot ran the day-to-day progress of the negotiations and generated a team spirit among the participants. He gave seminars on how to keep secrets, warned against IKBICTY (I know but I can't tell you) actions that might compromise the secrecy, and obtained a great deal of effort and cooperation from the group. He was motivated both by the potential business opportunity and by the prospect that he would be likely to play some management role in the new acquisition. Cabot was very astute in his consideration for all three perspectives, and he operated very effectively at organizational levels below Willsaw. Although he had no direct access to the Board of Directors, he and an associate did a great deal of research work with the outside corporate attorneys to investigate the potential impact of the pending lawsuit and the antitrust implications of the merger.

Tom Tinker

Tinker was a professional engineering manager brought in from General Electric by Willsaw to add experience to the organization. He functioned well in that role as long as the scope of the work to be done was well defined. In the unfamiliar role of General Manager, he was unable to develop techniques to test the validity of the recommendations made by his young and ambitious Marketing Manager. The result was that he operated with a short time horizon, concentrating on the accomplishment of existing goals rather than setting new ones. The Gramma situation appealed to him because it was in existence and could be evaluated using familiar management methods rather than the judgmental evaluation of future proposals, which he found difficult. When the acquisition was turned down, he proceeded to implement a development program to enter the market, depending largely on his marketing manager to provide direction. A number of major errors in management judgment were made by his organization, including underestimation of the competition, overestimation of the capabilities of the purchased software package, and expenditure of a great deal of money to take the product to the market with a major announcement rather than a slow entry to test the product's viability.

Jerry Grass

Grass, an excellent Manager, made clear the potential impact on his business of the acquisition but indicated that he could operate effectively either way. If

Acousticon came into the end-user market as a direct competitor, either through an acquisition or in-house development, it would hasten the conversion of the other OEM customers to digital FFT technology. His approach then was to open up new OEM markets where the SAW filter could still be effective and to emphasize OEM opportunities for other display group products, including copiers and desk-top computers. Grass occupied a key position because, from an organizational perspective, his group effectively had a veto on the proposal. His personal perspective was that new opportunities would open up as a result of the expected growth, and he had high personal regard for Cabot and the work he did. So rather than oppose the plan, his personal self-confidence led him to support Cabot. Grass now (1981) occupies the job then held by Willsaw as general manager of the whole organization.

Joe Towers

Towers was a very powerful individual who maintained a low profile. In an organization dedicated to open offices, he had the only office in the executive suite. A lawyer by profession, he approached all the corporate management decisions from a legal point of view. His impact on the culture was such that the organization was close to paranoid about potential violations of law or the prospect of lawsuits. It is impossible to estimate the impact of his decisions on the growth of the corporation over the years, but the relative growth of Acousticon and the competition indicate that Acousticon could now be twice as big as it is if it had been more aggressive. On the other hand, Towers' conservative policies have kept the company out of legal problems and remarkably free of direct government influence in light of the large volume of government business Acousticon does. Because he was an early and influential employee of the company, Towers has built an interesting position in the organization. He often finds it unnecessary to take personal action on decisions he opposes because he has had such a strong influence on the development of the corporate culture that subordinate organizations tend to follow policies that implement his views.

Implications

An advanced technology organization, like any other human organization, does not behave in a strictly "rational actor" mode. Hence the T perspective fails to describe its decision process adequately. The history of the corporation, its "family tradition," and its unique personnel mix are important determinants of its actions.

In the Acousticon case we have seen an example of a solid technological case rejected by the organization, with some individuals proponents of the move and others opponents.

impressive product
Environment of him

Several individuals were very interested in completion of the deal, since it would result in prestige for them and perhaps a career move to a position of responsibility in the new venture. The atmosphere of secrecy surrounding such a project carries its own aura of excitement, increasing the energy level of the participants. A great deal of work was done to substantiate the move, integrate the two companies, and prepare management presentations.

Opposed to the move were certain influential power agents at the top of the corporate hierarchy. Acting as curates of the corporate culture, they were concerned with federal antitrust implications, contingent liability from a trade secret theft suit by a litigious competitor, and integration problems with previous acquisitions. In addition, Acousticon had long pursued a "do-it-yourself" philosophy regarding technical development. There is no indication of ethical impropriety on either side, but the failure of the proposal has had a strong deterrent effect on other such technological opportunities that have been presented. It appears likely that this move, and one or two others like it, has had an inhibiting effect on Acousticon's long-term growth.

5.3 Commercial Aircraft: The Wide-Body Trijets[3]

The Competition

As John Newhouse so aptly put it, commercial aircraft manufacturing is a "sporty game" [5]. Since World War II, the U.S. aircraft industry has dominated the world's airliner business. Until the jet age, Douglas was the leader with its DC-3, DC-6, and DC-7. After World War II, the newly established U.S. Air Force chose its prime supplier of bombers, the Boeing Company, to develop a jet-powered tanker, the KC 135, in support of its jet bombers. Boeing had been out of the commercial aircraft business since 1950 when its clumsy, underpowered Stratocruiser failed. It was the KC-135 that brought Boeing back into the commercial aircraft business. This aircraft became the progenitor of the first successful commercial jet, the 707. The connection illustrates the impact of military developments on commercial product innovation. Douglas tried hard to catch Boeing with its own DC-8 but never quite succeeded. From 1957 to 1960 Douglas sold 42 DC-8s, compared with Boeing's sale of 170 707s. Lockheed, whose Constellation had been a worthy competitor to Douglas' DC-6, was convinced that there was room for another propeller-driven airliner (actually a prop-jet) before the jets took over com-

---

3. This illustration is based on the reports of Newhouse [4], Boulton [5], and Godson [6] as well as the author's own experience at Lockheed.

pletely. It produced the L-188 Electra, an efficient aircraft, also based on a military design, but a dismal failure. (Abnormal propeller rotation induced wing vibrations, causing a number of Electra crashes.)

Boeing soon surpassed its 707 success with the smaller three-engine 727 for the midrange market. Douglas went after the short-range market with its twin-engine DC-9 but had to suffer competition from Boeing's 737. The military once more set the stage with its competition for a gigantic cargo aircraft. Boeing and Lockheed competed fiercely and in 1965 Lockheed's C5A won.

Boeing shifted at once to the design of a commercial wide-body jet, the huge 747. The U.S.-lead airline was Pan Am, which had also been Boeing's supporter of the Stratocruiser. The 747 was a great achievement, but too large for its time; it became a status symbol as 66 airlines ordered it, three-fourths of them non-U.S. airlines. The airlines soon recognized the desirability of a smaller wide-body jet, analogous to the 727 in the narrow-body generation.

We shall now point out some highlights of the ensuing development of the wide-body trijet and note the relevance of the various perspectives.

T: American Airlines took the lead in 1966 and sent specifications for a twin-engine jumbo jet (250 passengers, 1860-mile range) to Boeing, Douglas, and Lockheed. At the time Boeing and Lockheed were still in competition for *supersonic transport* (SST). When Boeing won its pyrrhic victory, Lockheed immediately threw its engineering resources into the American Airlines proposal.

O: A major reason for Lockheed's supreme effort was pressure on its management to diversify and move away from its almost complete dependence on defense contracts. The proposed wide-body jet was now "the only game in town," that is, the only new commercial jet business in sight. It should also be noted that the three U.S. manufacturers were so intently competing with each other in the commercial aircraft business that they hardly noticed a spot on the horizon, the European Airbus Industrie consortium, which was also studying a twin-engine, wide-body jet under the brilliant leadership of the French engineer Roger Beteille. The year American Airlines initiated its proposal was also the year Douglas faced mounting difficulties. With bankruptcy looming, the company's bankers insisted on a merger.

P: Lockheed considered the merger opportunity, and its dynamic Chief Executive, Dan Haughton, later reflected:

> I didn't pursue it aggressively enough. We could have put the money together [5, p. 135].

He calls this failure one of the two biggest mistakes of his life. The smaller McDonnell Corporation, a military aircraft builder, did accomplish the merger in January 1967. Its founder, James McDonnell ("Mr. Mac"), was a strong willed and able man totally inexperienced in dealing with airlines.

O: The difficult adjustment of the Douglas "division" in Los Angeles to its new leadership in St. Louis, as well as the SST decision, gave Lockheed an initial advantage in its pursuit of the new wide-body jet. By summer, Mr. Mac had decided to compete, and the race was on. American Airlines was obviously not going to have its own way with the specifications because other airlines had to provide orders to make any new jet a reality. The range was extended and three engines, rather than two, were agreed upon. The key players in this game were now established: Lockheed's L-1011 and McDonnell-Douglas' DC-10 as proposed aircraft and the "Big Four" domestic U.S. airlines—American, United, TWA, and Eastern—as initial buyers.

T: A 1967 corporate analysis at Lockheed undertaken by the author considered the consequences of alternate L-1011 strategies, for example, a go-ahead on the basis of two (or three or four) Big Four orders totaling at least 60 (or 100) orders. A basic costing quantity of 350 units was used, with an average cost of $13.7 million. The analysis indicated the number of airlines that must be signed up at the time of the go-ahead decision to yield an adequate *discounted cash flow return on investment* (DCF ROI). It confirmed that a go-ahead with 60 sign-ups by two airlines had less than an even chance of achieving the desired earnings level at a $15 million unit price. The conclusion? Looking at the analysis from the airlines' point of view, the emerging strategy is evident: They should force the competing manufacturers into the lower prices to the point where the program would be barely profitable for one manufacturer with all Big Four airlines and then eliminate all but one manufacturer. Knowing this to be the airlines' strategy, the manufacturers could continue to underbid each other to this point and accept a break-even program on the assumption that all but one manufacturer will be eliminated. However, they run the risk of a very bad loss if the airlines split between two manufacturers. Unfortunately, this early analysis hit close to the mark!

T: As the competition progressed it became obvious that the differences between the two designs progressively shrank. The airlines' own engineers expressed a slight preference for the L-1011. Its third engine was mounted on the rear fuselage, whereas the DC-10's was perched on the vertical tail fin. The L-1011 had four hydraulic systems compared with the DC-10's reliance on three. The L-1011's hydraulic lines were positioned on the trailing edge of the wing, the DC-10's on the leading edge (with subsequent fatal results). The L-1011 also had the more advanced avionics and an all-weather landing capability. A crucial aspect of the competition centered on the choice of engine. Lockheed preferred the more sophisticated Rolls-Royce, whereas McDonnell-

Douglas offered both General Electric and Rolls-Royce engines. All in all, the L-1011 appeared to have an edge in terms of technology.

O: However, several key nonengineering executives made their judgments on the basis of confidence in the company rather than the design. This group included American and United Airlines, both having had decades of good experience with Douglas airliners. TWA, on the other hand, had a similarly long relationship with Lockheed (recall the popular Constellation). American Airlines had started the ball rolling two years earlier and now, in February 1968, wanted to be the first to order. As the deadline approached, the two bidders' supersalesmen, Dan Haughton of Lockheed and Jackson McGowen of McDonnell-Douglas, put on the "full-court press." Lockheed's price was slashed from $15 million to $14.4 million and then to $14.25 million.

P: C. R. Smith had been the driving force behind American Airlines since 1934. After being its Chief Executive for 34 years, he was asked by President Lyndon Johnson to be Secretary of Commerce, and George Spater replaced Smith at the airline's helm. Smith had developed a strong dislike of Mr. Mac and, according to Jackson McGowen, would have ordered the L-1011. But Spater was a different case; he had confidence in Douglas-built aircraft and was ready to announce an order for 25 DC-10s at $15.3 million each, confident that the other trunk airlines would have to follow suit and order the same aircraft.

O: When American's blow fell, the game took a surprising turn. The logic of the analysis and the similar realization of many participants in the game, that is, the importance of avoiding a destructive split by ordering both aircraft, went unheeded. TWA and Eastern announced orders on March 29 for 94 L-1011s. In addition, Haughton achieved a master stroke by obtaining an order for 50 L-1011s from the British Air Holdings organization. A few days later Delta Airlines ordered 24 L-1011s, so the total in this momentous week was 168 Lockheed trijets. American and McDonnell-Douglas seemed to be out on a limb.

P: When United Airlines' President George Keck called Haughton to ask whether he could have the L-1011 with the General Electric engine, Haughton made the second of the two biggest mistakes of his life: he answered no. As Newhouse reports, Haughton later admitted:

> We should have designed the airplane for alternative engines. We didn't do it, for financial reasons. The costs of developing a second engine would have been around $100 million dollars. But we'd have had enough orders to write off that money [5, p. 156].

O: United had a long-standing relationship with Douglas; therefore, it is uncertain whether a positive response to the engine question would have turned the tables. In any case United went for the DC-10 with an order of 60 and McDonnell-Douglas was back in the game. The 2/2 split of trunk airline orders was now a fact. And, as forecast, both companies lost substantial money on their programs. Lockheed, for example, garnered only another 76 orders in the years after that unforgettable week in Spring 1968!

The implications were serious indeed. Boeing remained the foremost aircraft manufacturer. Both McDonnell-Douglas and Lockheed lost their place in this market. We recall that American's original proposal in 1966 was for a two-engine medium- to short-range wide-body jet. While Lockheed and McDonnell-Douglas were battering each other, the European Airbus Industrie consortium moved in with its twin-engine A-300 Airbus and derivatives. With Asia now the fastest growing commercial aircraft market, the possibility of Asian aircraft manufacturing competition also looms on the horizon.

The Bankruptcy of Rolls-Royce

Lockheed began work on the largest jet aircraft ever designed, the C5A military transport, in 1965. To win the fierce competition with Boeing it had to propose a price that assumed the best of all engineering worlds, that is, a project in which everything goes right. This is standard procedure in contracting with the U.S. DOD. The hope is that the usual overruns can be later "taken care of" by claims and higher price follow-on orders. However, Secretary of Defense Robert McNamara instituted a *total package procurement* (TPP) system designed to improve the process. Under this concept, bidders were required to submit one bid covering research, development, and production. The winner's contract fixed the total price as well as specifications and delivery dates. In essence, the risks and uncertainties were shifted from the U.S. DOD to the manufacturer. The revolutionary C5A was the first major test of TPP; and Lockheed's inevitable overruns were now to be made good by the company, not the Pentagon. Further, the expected follow-on orders did not materialize in the wake of the Vietnam debacle. There was growing opposition to U.S. DOD requests, particularly huge transports designed to carry American troops to remote locations and facilitate U.S. involvement in distant conflicts, such as Vietnam.

O: The Company faced a $750 million claim by the U.S. DOD just at the time it was moving forward full force on the costly development of the L-1011. After prolonged discussions, Chairman Dan Haughton flew to Washington in January 1971 to settle the claim with Deputy Secretary of Defense David Packard. Haughton reluctantly agreed to accept a loss of $480 million. From Washington, DC, he flew on to London to meet with the Rolls-Royce management on progress and problems with their engine for the L-1011. Upon his arrival he was informed that Rolls-Royce would declare bankruptcy the next day. It was a terrible shock to the British public and to Dan Haughton. As a British government official put it, "the news of Rolls-Royce was like hearing that Westminster Abbey had become a brothel." Because Lockheed had selected the Rolls-Royce RB-211 jet engine (more advanced than that of General Electric) to power its L-1011, the implications for Lockheed were severe: the entire L-1011 program, a $1 billion investment, was placed in jeopardy. A switch to the General Electric engine at this late date would delay, and raise the cost of, the program. But so would salvation of the RB-211 program. And Lockheed was just made $480 million poorer by the settlement with the U.S. DOD.

It is interesting to speculate the effect if these two events, separated by a few days, had been reversed in time. If the U.S. government had had full knowledge of Lockheed's dilemma with Rolls-Royce prior to its meeting on the C5A with Haughton, a settlement more favorable to the company would have been a strong possibility.

P: At this point Haughton's brilliant management capability came into play.[4] He realized that the British government was willing to support Rolls-Royce's survival by providing a share of the needed funds. He had to keep the six airlines that ordered the L-1011 from bolting, and he had to satisfy the 24 American bankers who were increasingly nervous about their Lockheed loans. The British government was willing to advance $250 million to keep the RB-211 work going but wanted assurances that Lockheed would complete the L-1011 program; the U.S. government wanted its $480 million C5A reimbursement. Haughton persuaded each of his L-1011 customers to pay $640,000 more per airplane and the banks to extend their line of credit. But this was contingent on a $250 million government loan guarantee. The U.S. government had a justifiable concern in preventing the collapse of Lockheed, a prime DOD resource and a leader in aerospace technology. Its engineers believed deeply in the company slogan "Look to Lockheed for Leadership."[5] The Administration proposed the guarantee and Congress approved it by three votes in the House of Representatives and one vote in the Senate. In hindsight the guarantee was a complete success. The banks received their loan repayments and the U.S. Treasury collected $31 million in fees [8].

Much of the success of this cliff-hanger can be attributed to Dan Haughton himself. Born in 1911 to a poor Alabama farmer's wife, he started to

---

4. Chairman Courtland Gross had perceived Haughton's talent early: "I first met Dan Haughton in 1939, soon after he came to work for us. It was evident then that he had managerial and leadership qualities, loyalty, and very good judgment" [7].

5. The brilliance of just three technical achievements—the Polaris missile program led by Eugene Root and two "Skunk Works" projects, the YF-12 reconnaissance aircraft and the Stealth aircraft—amply support this claim.

supplement the family's income when he was eight. In school he was good in mathematics and graduated from the University of Alabama in accounting and business administration. His rise at Lockheed began with a $3300 per year job as a systems analyst in 1939. Ten years later he was president of two small Lockheed subsidiaries. John Newhouse, in his book *The Sporty Game,* gives this description of Haughton:

> Lockheed had a vivid style . . . In (Haughton's) day, it was a bold and exceptionally innovative company, more worldly than its competitors but somewhat less rigorously managed than Boeing or the engine manufacturers. Haughton is perhaps the most interesting figure his industry has produced. He is sometimes described as a red-clay aristocrat, both because he has a naturally gracious and modest manner and because his beginnings in rural Alabama were modest too. Yet he was also an inspirational leader, and was often said to be evangelical in promoting Lockheed's interests [5, pp. 49–50].

I, too, have been exposed to the Haughton style and have been similarly impressed. When he spoke, one was invariably reminded of his fellow Alabaman, Governor George Wallace. His complete dedication to his company was always in evidence. With regard to a controversial consultant, he once said, "I would hire the devil if it will do the company some good." He would typically spend a day at the Marietta, Georgia, plant, fly the company jet back to the Burbank headquarters at night, and be in his office at 5 a.m. It was general knowledge among his staff that the best time to see him was before 7 a.m.

The Grease Machine

O/P: Haughton not only drove himself mercilessly but also inspired remarkably intense levels of effort by his people. We recall that Haughton had garnered 168 L-1011 orders in the Spring of 1968, but this was still far below the break-even number of 250 (which itself kept rising inexorably). Haughton was determined to try for a miracle, to sell enough L-1011s to make the program profitable despite the market split. The key to overseas sales and marketing in most countries was a sporty game indeed. As Haughton's right-hand man, Lockheed's President Carl Kotchian, explained marketing expenses of $4.6 million in Japan in 1972:

> If you want to sell airplanes in Japan this is the way that you do it. It is a normal practice outside the United States. There are only certain countries where you do not have to make such payments: one is the United States

and another is England. In the rest of the world, generally speaking, you must practice this kind of thing in order to sell airplanes. You must have a man who has connections and give him money [6].

Two Japanese airlines were in the market for DC-10s or L-1011s: *Japan Airlines* (JAL) wanted 12 and *All Nippon* (ANA) wanted six. Of these, the ANA order was the more attractive because of follow-on potential. Kotchian was in charge of the Japanese marketing task. He recalls:

> If U.S. products were to be imported by Japan, the Nixon administration would be happiest if Japan purchased Lockheed planes. These were the plausible rumors that we were going to circulate. It was the main feature of our strategy [6, p. 240].

He knew that the procurement decision would be made by the Japanese government, not the airlines themselves. On August 21, 1972, Kotchian suggested to Lockheed's official representatives in Japan, Marubeni Corporation, that its head meet the new Prime Minister, Kakuei Tanaka. According to Boulton, the next day Marubeni's Managing Director proposed "a pledge to pay money to Prime Minister Tanaka." Kotchian asked, "How much?" The reply: "The customary amount to ask for a favor in connection with a major transaction is 500 million yen." If Lockheed could come up with the cash, Marubeni associate Toshiharu Okubo would look after arrangements for transferring the cash because he was "very close to Mr. Enomoto" (Tanaka's secretary). "It was at this point," says Kotchian, "that I was convinced that the money was going to the office of Japan's Prime Minister."

Kotchian then went to see Lockheed's influential agent Yoshio Kodama and there meet Kenji Osano, the single biggest private stockholder of both airlines and an old confidant of the Prime Minister. He also needed 500 million yen. Kotchian:

> In the morning I was made by Mr. Okubo to promise 500 million yen intended for Mr. Tanaka and in the afternoon I was asked by Mr. Kodama to pay an additional 500 million to Mr. Osano. It occurred to me that 500 million yen seemed to be a figure frequently used in Japan [6, p. 240].

Thus, in one day, Lockheed's President had committed the corporation to $3.5 million in payoffs. Subsequent disclosures indicate that the competition was also making "questionable payments" in Japan.

This was not the end. To clinch the ANA order Okubo needed another 120 million yen in cash for ANA President Wakasa and six Japanese politicians. Okubo:

> If you ready the money first thing tomorrow morning, we can formally get the ANA order during tomorrow without fail. I would like to have the whole sum ready by 10 a.m. [6, p. 249].

The timetable was too tight, but 30 million yen was delivered before 10 a.m. Six hours later, Kotchian was asked to be at ANA's head office at 6 p.m. There Wakasa told him:

> Congratulations, Mr. Kotchian, your company has got our company's contract [6, p. 249–250].

Kotchian:

> If, in a situation where high government officials have influence on matters pertinent to a private company, money is requested as payoffs for those officials, can that private foreign company, which wants its products to be bought at all costs, realistically decline the request on the grounds that it is not a good thing from the ethical point of view [6, p. 252]?

The Senate Subcommittee investigating the payoffs found that Lockheed had paid out $22 to 24 million to spur overseas sales of its L-1011, Starfighter, and C-130 transport between 1961 and 1972 [9].

P: Few Lockheed employees voiced criticism when these revelations hit them through the media coverage [10].

Barbara Alexander, Senior Secretary:

> Everybody's doing it. That's the name of the game; that's the way business is done all over the world these days. Why do they have to pick on Lockheed?

George Crozier, hydraulic specialist, with the company nearly 40 years:

> Everybody else does it—not just in aerospace, but throughout business . . . Mr. Haughton's been responsible for keeping this company on its feet; we need him; it's too bad he has to be the scapegoat.

Mae Woods, Secretary:

We're not angry; we're scared. I told [my 14-year-old idealistic son] that what the company did wasn't right, but that it had no choice. And he said: "How could you say that?" I told him that "you wouldn't be asking me these questions if you were 44 and had to pay bills."

It should be noted that the avalanche of scandal revelations involving business and Japanese government since the Lockheed affair has finally led to public outrage, indictments of high officials and company executives, as well as some modest systemic reform steps.

The DC-10 Cargo Door Case

Marketing is certainly not the only industry activity for which the O and P perspectives shed insights. An engineering problem may also require these perspectives for more than superficial understanding.

T: On June 11, 1972, an American Airlines DC-10 enroute from Detroit to Buffalo experienced an explosive decompression over Windsor, Ontario. Although most control cables were disabled, it landed safely at Detroit. The trouble was quickly traced to a rear cargo compartment door that was not properly locked and had blown off. This was, in fact, not a new problem. In 1969, Nicholas Schipper of the Dutch Civil Aviation Authority had voiced his concern to the FAA over possible loss of control of the DC-10 if a collapse of the floor between passenger and cargo levels occurred. In April 1970 the subcontractor for the cargo door, Convair, recognized that the cargo door locks were inadequate and conducted a "fault analysis" of the problem. This analysis also showed that, following a cargo door blowout, the floor of the passenger cabin would collapse. A month later in the standard pressure vessel test of the DC-10 at McDonnell-Douglas, the forward cargo door exploded open and part of the floor buckled. An engineering fix was made: venting between the passenger compartment and forward cargo hold [7].

O: The FAA has at its disposal two means of effecting change in aircraft systems: (1) issuance of recommendations incorporated in the manufacturer's service bulletins and (2) issuance of air worthiness directives. The former are advisory, the latter have the force of law. Manufacturers inherently dislike directives and strongly prefer to deal through service bulletins.

O: Within five days of the American Airlines incident, the Los Angeles office of the FAA had prepared a directive ordering a fix of the cargo door locking system. The Washington FAA office promptly released the directive on June 16, 1972.

P: Douglas Division President McGowen contacted FAA Administrator Shaffer personally immediately after the incident and reached a "gentleman's agreement" to go the Service bulletin route.

O: The Los Angeles and Washington offices were not aware of the agreement when the directive was issued. On June 19 an order went out from the FAA to its regional offices to destroy the directive. In its stead McDonnell-Douglas issued Service Bulletin A52-35, which strongly recommended a quick fix: a viewing window in the cargo door so that the cargo loading crew could check whether the door was properly locked (using a flashlight to peer in if needed).

O: The *National Transportation Safety Board* (NTSB), an agency independent of the FAA, is charged with investigation of accidents. It makes recommendations to the FAA on the basis of its examinations. The existence of two such organizations has inevitably generated bureaucratic animosity between them. The NTSB claimed at one point (1970) that it had made 121 recommendations for correction and improvement based on its accident investigations, yet only 45 were either "complied with" or "essentially compiled with." In response the FAA insisted that it had received 115 recommendations from the NTSB and complied with 105, rejecting only 10.[6]

By June 23, the NTSB had prepared its recommendations (A-72-97, A-72-98) with respect to the DC-10 cargo door problem: (1) an effective locking mechanism and (2) venting between passenger and aft cargo compartments. The FAA ignored these recommendations, and no directive was issued. The FAA merely told the NTSB that "additional modifications are being considered."

P: On June 27, Dan Applegate of Convair wrote a remarkable memorandum in which he noted the design weaknesses, not merely the cargo door but also the susceptibility for catastrophic failure of the cabin floor [11]. But Convair was a subcontractor and its management did not feel it could press Douglas on this point. Besides, the feeling was that most of Applegate's assertions must be known to the Douglas engineers.

O: On July 3, a more substantial modification in the locking mechanism was recommended in Manufacturer's Service Bulletin 52-37 by McDonnell-Douglas. The airlines made the modification gradually (for example, United

---

6. Significantly, the same organizational animus still persisted years later. In the case of the B-737 Air Florida jet crash into Washington's 14th Street Bridge on January 13, 1982, NTSB recommended on-ground wing deicers or an increase in take-off speed. By November, the FAA concluded that it was premature to order either change. In January 1983, NTSB went public with a response letter rejecting the FAA conclusion and urging immediate action.

averaged 90 days for its DC-10s and American Airlines, 268 days). Presumably the corrective measure was also incorporated in DC-10s not yet completed or delivered to the airlines.

In fact, not all DC-10s received the modification. On March 3, 1974, 20 months after the issuance of the service bulletin, a Turkish THY DC-10 rose from Paris on its way to London, lost the rear cargo door 12 minutes later, and crashed with a loss of 346 lives. The correction had never been made on this aircraft. As in the American Airlines case the passenger floor collapsed into the cargo area below and crippled the flight control system, severing the cables embedded in the floor.

McDonnell-Douglas records showed that the modifications stipulated in Service Bulletin 52-37 had been made on this aircraft prior to delivery to the airline (and on another found subsequently to be defective). Apparently the quality-control records were inaccurate [7, p. 238].

The DC-10 has experienced other accidents that raise questions about the design and engineering of the aircraft. In 1979 a wing engine fell off following takeoff in Chicago and in 1989 explosive disintegration of the fin-mounted tail engine near Sioux City, Iowa, caused loss of control. The human toll of the Paris, Chicago, and Sioux City crashes was 730 lives! In all three cases inadequately protected control systems were responsible. Did management at Douglas believe it could get by with fewer defenses against failure than were installed on the L-1011 and the Boeing 747? Did knowledgable engineers lack the courage to confront their ethical or moral responsibility vis-á-vis management?

Summing Up

It should be apparent that the O and P perspectives illuminate facets that are central to the decision-making process in the commercial aircraft business.

The O perspective tells us:

- Headquarters management may be inclined to weight the O more heavily than the T perspective and override engineering advice. Engineers were overriden at both airline (on aircraft purchase preferences) and manufacturer (on safety concerns).

- Rational analysis may easily succumb to other deep-seated corporate needs. The disastrous effect of splitting the market and building two similar trijets was recognized in advance; there is almost an aura of Greek tragedy to the game.

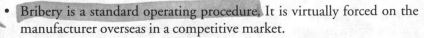

- Bribery is a standard operating procedure. It is virtually forced on the manufacturer overseas in a competitive market.
- The pervasive organizational reaction "don't rock the boat" can have deadly long-term impact. The DC-10 cargo door could have been a minor matter if handled forcefully at the outset by all concerned. (The automobile industry has shown a similar tendency.)

The P perspective suggests:

- One person's leadership, charisma, and negotiating skill can save an organization. The Rolls-Royce bankruptcy involved Lockheed, 24 U.S. banks, and two governments in an incredibly complex situation. Dan Haughton personally was the key to its successful resolution and saved Lockheed.
- Matching a leader to a situation (or P to O) is crucial. Mr. Mac had been an outstanding aircraft industry pioneer, but his lack of familiarity with the commercial side of the business had a serious impact on the organization at crucial moments.

In general, such insights can be developed prior to the decision point, albeit not by confining ourselves to the traditional T-oriented "analysis." Indeed, recognition of the implications of such insights may be used to good advantage. Two examples: (1) pointing up a specific need to match the key person (P) to the situation (T/O) and (2) raising vital ethical issues that are not the focus of T or O.

However, we also are made acutely aware, from both O and P perspectives, that unforeseeable events can prove critical. The selection of C. R. Smith by President Johnson to become Secretary of Commerce may have been pivotal to American Airlines' choice of the DC-10. A reversal of appointment days for Dan Haughton to settle the C5A claim with the Pentagon and fly to London to meet with Rolls-Royce might have substantially helped Lockheed.

5.4 Trading: The Stock Market

Finally, even the stock market can readily be seen in terms of our perspectives. In *The Mind of the Market*, Charles Smith observes:

Why is the [stock] market so contradictory? The most important roots of these contradictions are the conflicting perspectives different persons have of the market and the different interpretations of market events that these varying perspectives generate . . . Different assumptions regarding the underlying structure generate very different accounts of 'what' is happening [12, pp. 20–21].

He identifies four professional perspectives:

1. *The Fundamentalist:* Market values reflect local, national, and global economic conditions. The *New York Times, Wall Street Journal,* and *Barron's* are avidly read. The general attitude is that of a conservative financial advisor.

2. *The Cyclist/Chartist:* There are underlying patterns and rhythms to be grasped, a transcendent order to be discovered.

3. *The Insider:* Institutional influences and social relationships are the key. Contacts are nourished and "the boys with the money" are watched to draw forth inside information. People are more important than reports as sources.

4. *The Trader:* The market is a sporting game in which intuition and chance are important. There must be a "feel for the market." Psychology is appreciated: some companies catch the imagination of the street while others do not. We also have the spectacle of the brokerage house "groupies" trailing with pencil and paper the current in-house guru who has a hot streak picking stocks to buy and sell.

In our terms of reference 1 and 2 are oriented toward T (the former data-focused, the latter theory-focused), 3 is dominated by O, and 4 by P. Smith notes, however, that few professionals are pure, that is, true believers who rely solely on one perspective. Usually their perspective is more fuzzy; the balance or mix is apt to be influenced by the immediate objective, for example, selling stocks or newsletters. Not surprisingly the result for the consumer is often confusion. Smith concludes:

What our analysis of the market indicates is that it is useless to attempt to select one orientation, one logic or one purpose, and ignore the others; it indicates that the mind is inherently multifaceted and any attempt to deny this will only lead to an incomplete picture of whatever subject is being studied [12, p. 153].

5.5 Conclusion

As in the case of the public sector, we find that in the private sector multiple perspectives prove very useful in clarifying the issues for decision making. The technical perspective simply cannot grapple with all the significant aspects that must inform the decision process. Whether we deal with electronic equipment or commercial aircraft, utilities or the stock market, each perspective draws forth vital considerations. For the successful executive this is hardly a revelation; for the technologist sheltered from the messy realities of life, it well may be.

Acknowledgments

Quotations of Charles Peters in Section 4.1 reprinted with permission from *How Washington Really Works* by Charles Peters, published by Addison Wesley Longman, © 1983 Charles Peters.

References

[1] *Oregonian,* Jan. 15, 1981.

[2] *Oregonian,* Nov. 4, 1981, p. B3.

[3] *Oregon Journal,* March 18, 1981.

[4] *Sunday Oregonian,* March 8, 1981.

[5] Newhouse, J., *The Sporty Game,* New York: A. A. Knopf, 1982.

[6] Boulton, D., *The Grease Machine,* New York: Harper & Row, 1978.

[7] Godson, J., *The Rise and Fall of the DC-10,* New York: D. McKay Co, 1975.

[8] Meyers, H. B., "For Lockheed, Everything's Coming Up Unk-Unks," *Fortune,* Vol. 80, Aug. 1, 1969, pp. 76–81 and 131–134.

[9] *Time,* Feb. 23, 1976.

[10] *New York Times,* Feb. 17, 1976.

[11] Fielder, J. H., and D. Birsch (eds.), *The DC-10 Case,* Albany, NY: The State University of New York Press, 1992.

[12] Smith, C. W., *The Mind of the Market,* Totowa, NJ: Rowman and Littlefield, 1981.

6

Technology: Risk and Assessment

There are more things in heaven and earth, Horatio,
Than are dreamt of in your philosophy.

William Shakespeare, *Hamlet*

I had other things to do.

Lawrence Rawl, chairman of Exxon,
explaining his failure to visit the scene of the Alaska oil spill

6.1 Perspectives on Risk

Physical hazards have always been a feature of life. Until the twentieth century, the primary hazards were natural ones, such as storms and earthquakes. In addition, living organisms such as viruses, animals, and fellow human beings posed major threats.[1] In modern times a new set of threats has been added: explosions, chemical and oil spills, drugs, pollution, radioactive material, and network failures, to name just a few. The combination of an ever-exploding global population and ever more powerful technologies has become deadly. Population growth not only multiplies the need for energy and materials, which industry is striving to fill, but it also places many more people in harm's way. Thus, in the twenty-first century we should anticipate a growing number of industrial accidents with catastrophic consequences. The Three Mile Island and Chernobyl

---

1. For new threats from living organisms, see Section 6.5.

nuclear accidents and the chemical explosion at Bhopal, India, give us a fore-taste of the intensifying challenge to the management of technology.

Analyses of such hazards and their consequences have traditionally in-volved engineers and scientists who have calculated probabilities of equipment failure, mapped fault trees, and sought "objective" T-type measures to quantify human life and "acceptable risks" for a society. But traditional forms of analysis do not capture vital aspects that are inherent in such problems. They fail to recognize that the determination of risk constitutes an inherently ill-structured problem. All such disasters involve a series of complex relationships between humans, private and/or public organizations, as well as the technologies them-selves.

Risk is in the mind of the beholder. It is highly subjective, a perception embedded in our psyche (P) and our social setting (O). Given a particular haz-ard, different parties "see" inherently different risks.

Nevertheless, analysts have striven to develop "objective" measures to ex-press "acceptable risks" for a society. Starr [1] attempted to determine the cost-benefit of risk using fatalities per person per hour of exposure and average amount of money spent by an individual participant or average contribution the activity makes to an individual's annual income. Inhaber compared the risks of various energy systems on the basis of occupational and public deaths per megawatt-year net output over the lifetime of the systems [2]. Hohenemser [3] used "quantitative measures of hazard consequences that are conveniently ex-pressed as mortality or injury probabilities," and Litai et al. [4] focused on actu-arial analysis to develop risk conversion factors. The results of such endeavors have not proven very satisfactory. Government agencies use a crazy quilt of quantitative life valuations: OSHA $2 to $5 million, EPA $1 to $7.5 million, and FAA $650,000 [5].

However, we also observe that a very different path has been taken by other analysts in recent years.

- Tversky and Kahneman cite many biases that inexorably dominate in-dividual perceptions of risk and ignore the scientist's model of risk [6].

- Fischhoff concludes that people's risk perceptions are colored by their own prejudices as well as the way the risks are presented to them [7, 8].

- Turner finds that organizational responses to hazard cannot be treated as purely technical problems [9].

- Covello is concerned that little attempt has been made to analyze the effects of organizational and social structural variables on risk percep-tions. "With relatively few exceptions researchers have not adopted an organizational or social structural perspective" [10].

- Douglas and Wildavsky insist that the selection of risk is a matter of social organization and its management an organizational problem [11].

- Thompson goes further, pointing out that

different people may perceive risks differently and . . . . may vary quite considerably in the level they deem to be acceptable [12]. An adequate theory of risk-handling style will have to go below the institutional level and take account of socially induced variations in individual perceptions of risk and in individual strategies toward risk [13].

The recent risk analyses of the siting of *liquified natural gas* (LNG) facilities in four countries focuses on the organizational process rather than the technical aspects (see Appendix A2). Kunreuther et al. [14] find that risk analysis cannot be separated from political processes. Ascher and Overholt [15] see the organizational perspective as "the central metaphor" in dealing with such processes.

Fischhoff et al. [7] present seven criteria for evaluating the acceptability of approaches to risk decision making and they clearly reflect quite different perspectives:

- logically sound   → technical perspective;
- open to evaluation   → technical perspective;
- practical   → organizational perspective;
- politically acceptable   → organizational perspective;
- compatible with institutions   → organizational perspective;
- conducive to learning   → personal perspective;
- comprehensive   → technical/organizational/personal perspectives.

In this chapter we will consider using multiple perspectives to shed light on technological risk management and impact assessment. Table 6.1 is an adaptation of Table 3.1 to the area of risk.

6.2 The Alaska Oil Spill[2]

At 12:04 a.m. on March 24, 1989, in calm seas, the tanker *Exxon Valdez* struck Bligh Reef in Prince William Sound, Alaska. Eight of the eleven cargo

Table 6.1
Risk Concerns Seen in Perspectives

Technical (T)	Organizational (O)	Personal (P)
One definition of risk for all	Definition customized to organization or group	Individualized definition
Compartmentalizing problem by discipline	Compartmentalizing problem by organization slot	Ability to cope with only a few alternatives
Data and model focus	Perpetuation of entity is the foremost goal	Time for consequences to materialize (discounting of long-term effects)
Probabilistic analysis; expected value calculations	Compatibility with standard operating procedures (SOP)	Perceived horrors (cancer, AIDS, Hiroshima)
Statistical inference	Avoidance of blame; responsibility spread	Personal experience
Actuarial analysis	Inertia; warnings ignored	Influenced by media coverage of risk (The China Syndrome)
Fault trees	Fear exposure by media; attempt stonewalling	Peer esteem (drugs)
Margin of safety design; fail-safe principle	Financial consequences; threat to product line	Economic cost (job loss)
Quantitative life valuations, cost-benefit	Threat to organizational power	Freedom to take voluntary risks
Validation and replicability of analysis	Litigious societal ethic	Salvation; excommunication
Failure to grasp "normal accidents" [16]	Reliance on experts and precedent	Influence of culture
Intolerance of "nonscientific" risk views	Suppression of uncertainties	Ingrained views; filter out conflicting input
Claim of objectivity in risk analysis		Opportunity to gain respect, fame

tanks were punctured and the result was the largest oil spill in U.S. history. Of the 53 million gallons (or 1.26 million barrels) of crude oil carried, 21% spilled (10.8 million gallons). Almost all of the spill (10.1 million gallons) oc-

---

2. An early version of this work was prepared for the State of Alaska Oil Spill Commission at its request in September 1989. However, this material should not be construed as reflecting the opinions or recommendations of the Commission.

curred in the first five hours after the accident. The oil spread over 3000 square miles in Prince William Sound and the Gulf of Alaska. The ship was under the command of Captain Joseph Hazelwood. A sobriety test was given to him ten hours after the accident and showed a .06% blood alcohol level, which is above the *U.S. Coast Guard* (USCG) limit of .04% but below the state's .10% limit.

Capt. Hazelwood notified the USCG 22 minutes after the grounding. The on-scene USCG coordinator notified the National Response Center, the State of Alaska, and Alyeska, the petroleum service company responsible for pipeline and Valdez port operations, within one hour of the accident. Alyeska's response was delayed over twelve hours after notification, far beyond the five hours stipulated in its official contingency plan. Within 24 hours, the *Exxon Baton Rouge* was positioned alongside the *Exxon Valdez* to transfer the nearly 80% of oil still in the tanks of the grounded ship. On the second day Exxon Shipping Company assumed responsibility for the cleanup. Estimates of the shoreline contaminated by oil ranged from 730 to 1245 miles. Figures for sea bird deaths climbed from 28,000 in 1989, to 90,000 to 270,000 in 1990, to 580,000 in 1991. Estimates of sea otter casualties ranged from 872 in 1989 to 5500 in 1991. There was a loss of at least $12 million in herring fishery, while 30% of the salmon spawning grounds were threatened.

The Technical Perspectives

We shall focus on the engineering aspect and leave aside, except in passing, other important technical perspectives such as the economic one.

The State of the Technology

It had been found in earlier spills that clean-up efforts may actually compound the original damage and create a double disaster. After the *Torrey Canyon* oil spill, some 2 million gallons of detergents were used to treat an estimated 13,000 tons of oil on Cornish coasts and another 0.5 million gallons were sprayed at sea. Scientists found that the detergents did much more harm to shellfish than the original oil spilled. In addition, some of the aromatic hydrocarbons used to dissolve the detergents and to aid in mixing the oil also caused much damage to wildlife [17]. In the case of the *Exxon Valdez* spill, high-pressure hot-water cleaning sterilized the beaches and made them more inhospitable to life [18]. These events already suggest the state of the art of clean-up technology.

Oil spill clean-up methods can be divided into two kinds and both were used in this case: (1) oil containment and recovery and (2) oil degradation and removal. The most striking revelation of the T perspective is the inadequate state of the available methods. In their report to the President, Transportation

Secretary Samuel Skinner and Environmental Protection Agency Administrator William Reilly concluded that "oil spill clean-up procedures and technologies are primitive" [19, p. 169]. *General Accounting Office* (GAO) data imply that no more than 10% to 15% of oil lost in a major spill is ever recovered by human effort. The reasons are apparent:

- Manual removal along the shore is labor intensive and inefficient. No evidence for the primitive state of the art is more compelling than the pictures on television news of thousands of Exxon workers in the summer of 1989 wiping off oiled rocks on the beaches with paper towels. Cleaning oiled beaches with high-pressure jets of very hot water sterilized the areas treated. The *National Oceanic and Atmospheric Administration* (NOAA) studies years later showed that uncleaned beaches were healthier than cleaned ones.

- Chairman Lawrence Rawl of Exxon admitted that "with a large spill like this one, you can't get booms around it" [20]. The fishermen helping with the booms complained about "the low-quality boom . . . [which] continually broke, fractured, and pulled apart as the oil gushed" [21].

- Skimmers were used with some success in conjunction with the booms, "but long periods of inactivity resulted when they became disabled . . . only about 10% of the designed recovery rate could be achieved." Clogging was a continuing problem [22].

- Dispersants may work when there is some water turbulence, but very little testing has been done in the last decade. There is much uncertainty about their effectiveness and the possible harm they may do to fish. No clear governmental policy directives on their use were in effect prior to the accident, and the resulting confusion delayed decisions.

- Burning in-situ may be suitable in calm-sea conditions and was tried, but there was disagreement between Exxon and the State of Alaska about its effectiveness and nothing of any significance was accomplished. Burning produces toxic chemicals, including carcinogens and acid rain.

- The spill triggered some experiments with bioremediation. This process involves the use of microbes to biodegrade spilled hydrocarbon molecules. The concept appears environmentally attractive and relatively inexpensive, but much research remains to be done.

The prevention of oil spills has focused on improving the design of tankers, for example, use of double hulls. There is dispute about their effectiveness. They add about $15 to $20 million to the tanker construction cost.

It is characteristic of systemic disasters that the impact is difficult to measure. Even definitions present serious difficulties. Foremost in this case is the question: How do you define "clean up"? How clean is "clean"? By 1991 Exxon declared that its studies showed that a "healthy" biological community existed in the area. But it may be quite different from the one before the spill.

A Truly Complex System

The twenty-first century will feature increasingly powerful technology, creating an ever larger potential for accidents that have unprecedented impacts. We are thus forced to examine complex industry-based systems in a new light. One such group comprises systems characterized by the combination of (1) very low likelihood of disastrous failure and (2) catastrophic consequence if such failure does occur (see the comments on probability later in this section (pages 172–173). Supertankers have transformed the oil-shipping system into just such a type.

In complex systems virtually everything interacts with everything. In our case, oil shipping from Alaska has connections at one level with the Alaskan economy, the Alaskan ecology, Alaskan lifestyle, oil prices in the United States, the U.S. economy, U.S. Mideast policy, the global air and ocean environment, the oil industry, and alternative energy development. At another level, we must deal with the actors directly involved: Exxon, Alyeska, the State of Alaska, the Federal government (Department of Transportation, Environmental Protection Agency, NOAA, Department of Justice, Department of the Interior), Valdez and other communities, the Coast Guard, the fishing industry, the insurance industry, United Nations International Maritime (Consultative) Organization, and environmental groups. On a third level the system includes (1) on the high seas: the ship itself, radio communications, and weather; and (2) in Prince William Sound: the terminal, other ships, the Vessel Traffic System, shipping lanes, and ice.

Marine accidents have involved an astounding array of factors: "radar assisted collisions," supertankers negotiating channels only two feet deeper than they are, tugboats blocking radio channels by playing music, monumental storms, captains playing "chicken" in sea lanes with 40 ships about, and in this case a captain with a history of alcoholism and a revoked driver's license in charge of a supertanker. The appalling condition of many tankers in operation is another factor. Typical deficiencies include 20-year-old navigation charts, unlicensed engineers, inoperative anticollision radar, a hopeless fire-control plan, and manuals written in a language foreign to the crew.

There is a multitude of ways that a series of very low likelihood events can interact to create an unexpected, disastrous system failure. In the case of the *Exxon Valdez*, we can list many such events. If any one of them had not occurred, the spill might well have been averted or minimized. For example,

- If Capt. Hazelwood had stayed on the bridge and not turned over control of the ship to Third Mate Cousins at 11:50 p.m.;
- If the ship had kept its speed down to permit safe movement through the small ice flows present in the traffic channel (broken off from Columbia Glacier); its increasing speed made departure from the ice-strewn channel necessary;
- If Helmsman Kagan had quickly followed the simple turn command given by Cousins;
- If the Coast Guard had monitored the ship's movement through Prince William Sound;
- If Alyeska had been in the status prescribed by its own contingency plan;
- If Exxon had followed its existing policy and dismissed Capt. Hazelwood after the first drink he had subsequent to his alcohol rehabilitation (suggested by Exxon Chairman Rawl in an interview) [20, p. 50].

The pattern is typical for complex systems. Unfortunately, it is still not widely understood. The pattern obviously makes the establishment of liability exceedingly difficult. Each of the accused parties or stakeholders can convincingly spread the blame.

It is easy to neglect interactions among the many possible subsets of a system and to miss important feedback loops. It is useful to distinguish between two kinds of interactions, simple ones and intricate (Table 6.2), and two kinds of coupling, loose and tight (Table 6.3). Examples of the four combinations of interactions and couplings abound:

1. Simple interactions + tight coupling: dams, some drug processing plants;
2. Simple interactions + loose coupling: post office, most manufacturing;
3. Intricate interactions + tight coupling: nuclear power plant, space mission;
4. Intricate interactions + loose coupling: universities, R&D facilities.

Table 6.2
Comparison of Interactions in Systems

	Simple	Intricate
Equipment	Spread out	Tightly spaced
Common-mode connections	Few	Many
Subsystems	Segregated	Interconnected
Parts substitutability	Easy	Limited
Feedback loops	Few	Many (often subtle)
Controls	Single purpose	Multiple, interacting
Information	Direct, on-line	Indirect or inferential
Understanding	Extensive (expected interactions)	Limited (surprising unplanned interactions)

[Reprinted with permission of Charles Perrow from his book *Normal Accidents,* published by Basic Books, Inc., pp. 88, 96, © 1984.]

Table 6.3
Comparison of Couplings in Systems

	Loose	Tight
Process delays	Possible	Not possible
Order of sequences	Changeable	Invariant
Alternative methods	Available	Not available
Slack in resources	Possible	Little slack allowed
Buffers, redundancies	Can be improvised	Must be designed in
Substitutions	Available	Must be designed in

[Reprinted with permission of Charles Perrow from his book *Normal Accidents,* published by Basic Books, Inc., pp. 88, 96, © 1984.]

It seems obvious that systems of type 1 are best managed in a centralized manner while those of type 4 operate best in a decentralized way. For type 2 either centralization or decentralization usually works, but type 3 presents a real dilemma. For tightly coupled systems centralization is desirable, but for intricate interactions decentralization is preferable. As we move into the twenty-first century, type 3 must be expected to become a more common occurrence.

Fortunately, the information technology of the new century should be able to deal with simultaneous centralization and decentralization as never before (see Section 3.7).

Examples of these couplings and interactions can be found in the marine transportation system:

- *Tight coupling:* Modern tankers have very restricted maneuverability due to the large size combined with single screws and modest engines; it takes over 20 minutes to stop a 250,000 tonner doing 16 knots. Often the ships operate with minimal clearance between their hulls and the channel bottom. Owners create a tight coupling of another kind by pressuring captains to maintain tight schedules. Another example is the traditional authoritarian hierarchy on board ship.

- *Loose coupling:* the tenuous connection between insurance rates and a shipper's operational performance, the loose enforcement of regulations by the underbudgeted and understaffed Coast Guard.

- *Simple or expected interactions:* the visible and planned operations that comprise oil shipping, such as the terminal-tanker oil transfer relation, the tanker navigation-designated shipping lane relation, interactions in the boiler subsystem resulting in breakdowns, and failures of radar and satellite communications.

- *Intricate or subtle interactions:* the connection between tank cleaning and gas vapor explosions, liquified natural gas leakage and vapor cloud flammability, detergent use and ecological damage.

The marine transport system evidently has aspects of both tight and loose coupling, as well as both uncomplicated/expected and intricate/unexpected interactions. A critical question: How should the system be modified or redesigned by altering the interactions and coupling to improve its operation?

We hasten to point out that even elimination of unexpected interactions would not mean that the system is *fail-safe*. By this we refer to an ability to design the system so that catastrophic consequences cannot occur. In the case of oil shipping, this means designing the shipping system so that no large spills can occur. Engineers traditionally aim for fail-safe design, and this is a sound approach for relatively simple systems such as bridges and buildings. However, complex human-machine systems cannot be made fail-safe, no matter how much redundancy and control is built into them. Anticipation that some "solution," some combination of preventive steps, can eliminate the possibility of serious tanker accidents, is not realistic.

A more reasonable objective is to make the complex system *safe-fail.* This approach trades avoidance of failure for survival of failure. It minimizes the cost of failure rather than the likelihood of failure. This is, incidentally, the design principle of advanced living systems, including human beings and ecosystems.

After seven years of scientific studies of the region following the accident, we have to admit that "nobody actually knows much about anything in the Sound—or in any such complicated ecosystem" [18]. Since Prince William Sound's ecosystem was not subjected to detailed analysis before the accident, comparisons with the current state are difficult. Indeed, even if it has changed significantly, it is hard to determine if the change is detrimental. With complex systems, where everything interacts with everything, the usual reductionist approaches of science will not suffice—and the past seven years of scientists' efforts in Prince William Sound prove the point.

An Error-Inducing System

A curious feature of the marine transport system is that it is an error-inducing system. In such a system, the configuration of its components induces errors and defeats attempts at error reduction [16]. As such it contrasts with the air transport system, which is safety-reinforcing. Table 6.4 displays some key distinctions.

Nearly half of the 3250 transoceanic tankers, many of them more than 20 years old, are registered under five "flags of convenience" (Panama, Liberia, Greece, Bahamas, and Malta). They are characterized by particularly weak registration standards. The poor safety record of ships—15% of the world's ships have some kind of collision each year—thus becomes less puzzling: it is an integral characteristic of the system.

In an error-inducing system some aspects are too loosely coupled and others are too tightly coupled; some interactions are too simplistic, others too intricate. Increased electronic gear and automation are characteristic of the new tankers and the technology is assumed to reduce human error. But the effect can be perverse: it easily leads to more carelessness and a willingness to take risks previously avoided. In such a system, the more complicated the equipment, the more likely it is to be out of order or operated improperly. The combination of (1) nonoccurrence of crises over a period of years and (2) the existence of contingency plans and equipment (ignoring partial dismantlement and current inoperable status) creates great confidence that nothing can happen.

It is typical of error-inducing systems that operator error is a prominently given explanation for an accident. But this argument is misleading. For example, exhaustion due to excessive work hours and routing short cuts to avoid the anger of superiors in the home office in case of late arrival may easily lead to human navigation decisions resulting in catastrophic accidents. Yet it would be

Table 6.4
Comparison of Safety-Reinforcing and Error-Inducing Systems

Air transport*	Marine transport
Co-pilot shares responsibility, teamwork	Authoritarian captain, little sharing of responsibility
Moderate productivity pressure: captains can cancel flights	Severe productivity pressure: owners force tight schedules
Ground controller shares responsibility, ATC** mandatory: ATC can override captains	No equivalent of ground control: *Vessel Traffic System* (VTS) is only advisory
Federal presence large: tough standards and enforcement; FAA has central responsibility	Federal presence minor: lax standards and enforcement (U.S. ranks only 14th in ship safety); VTS only small part of USCG duties; no FAA equivalent
Strong international cooperation	Weak international cooperation: "flags of convenience" provide weak regulation; toothless UN International Maritime Organization
Attractive work conditions: strict limits on work hours	Debilitating work conditions: overwork common
Neutral physical environment: storms avoidable, alternate airfields and delays acceptable	Hostile physical environment: storms not avoidable, alternate ports unacceptable
Accidents get high visibility: extensive media coverage	Accidents get low visibility unless vast environmental side effects
Victims of accidents identifiable: airlines carry people whose support and business they need	Victims of accidents anonymous: e.g., foreign seamen, fishermen, wildlife; no significant customer effect at the gas pump, even with sharp price rise after disaster

*In industrialized nations generally (except Russia)

**Air Traffic Control

totally inaccurate to simply state the cause as "human error." Rather, it is a system error, that is, an error of the whole system, not of any one of its parts.

Implications

Based on the T perspective, we find that the oil-shipping system can be improved in at least three ways:

- *Heightened prevention:* better understanding of system coupling and interactions to institute changes that will make the system less error-inducing and more safety-reinforcing;

- *More effective response:* upgrading of crisis management plans and procedures;

- *More effective response:* major effort directed toward the development of improved cleanup technology.

However, in the final analysis, natural processes are likely to continue as the primary agent of oil spill clean-up in the coming decade.

The Organizational Perspectives

The principal organizations involved with the Alaska oil spill crisis include Exxon and Alyeska Corporations; the *Alaska Dept. of Environmental Conservation* (ADEC); Alaskan towns such as Valdez and Cordoba; Native Indian communities; Federal government agencies such as the Depts. of Justice, Interior, and Transportation, the *Environmental Protection Agency* (EPA); the NOAA; and the USCG. In addition, there are the Alaskan fishing industry, environmental groups, and insurers. Each has its own view of the problem and its own agenda. Their perspectives not only differ from each other but from the technical perspective discussed in the preceding section.

The stakes in the Alaskan oil fields have been high indeed. From 1977 to 1987 it is estimated that the after-tax oil company profits were $40 billion, the revenues for the State of Alaska $24 billion, and the revenues for the federal government $19 billion. The flow of oil constituted a financial gusher amounting to $400,000 per hour. From the outset, environmental concerns were answered by the industry with firm assurances that the pipeline would not endanger wildlife in Alaska, that operations in Prince William Sound would be the safest in the world, and that the industry could deal promptly and effectively with any oil spill, resulting in minimal effects on the environment.

Exxon Corporation

As owner of the *Exxon Valdez* and a major partner in one of the most powerful industries in the world, the role of Exxon Corporation in this crisis is the central one. To the profound relief of the governmental actors, both federal and state, Exxon at once took on responsibility for the clean-up. It is safe to assume that the most important objective of this top "Fortune 500" corporation is to maximize its profits from oil drilling and marketing operations. The dangers it faced as a consequence of the Valdez incident and public outrage included:

- Heavy clean-up costs;
- Expensive litigation instituted by the affected parties;
- Constrictive changes in operating rules that add to the oil-shipping costs;
- Denial of future oil exploration permits;
- Pressure to reduce favorable federal and state oil industry tax breaks;
- Boycotting of Exxon gas stations by motorists;
- Disinvestment in Exxon stocks by individuals and funds;
- Impetus to accelerate development of nonfossil fuel energy sources such as solar and nuclear energy as well as electric batteries for cars.

Only the first three have proven significant. The perceived dangers appeared serious enough to justify a major effort at damage control, specifically a sizeable dollar expenditure. The addition to the $2.5 billion spent on the clean-up, another $900 million has been paid to the Trustees for "restoration." In other words, the disaster has thus far cost Exxon at least $3.4 billion [23].

Damage control clearly was the foremost near-term strategy. The primary components of this strategy appeared to include the following:

- *Mobilizing vast resources to clean up the oil spill:* 31 hours after the grounding, Don Cornett, the top Exxon official in Alaska, said that it "doesn't matter if they are really picking up a hell of a lot of oil, at this point—it makes a real bad impression with the public, without any activity going on." The level of personnel in Alaska associated with the Valdez operations quickly reached a figure of 11,000.
- *Focusing the blame on Capt. Hazelwood of the Exxon Valdez:* Capt. Hazelwood was publicly fired by Exxon within days of the accident for violating company policies, specifically, not being on the bridge and consuming alcohol within four hours of boarding the ship [24].
- *Shifting the blame away from Exxon to other organizations:* ADEC was blamed for advising Exxon that the proposed dispersant could be toxic, and the USCG was blamed for not immediately giving a go-ahead to fly sorties to spread the dispersant [20, p. 52].
- *Communicating the impression that the clean-up operation is effective:* Exxon data provided by its Valdez manager Otto Harrison indicated

that, as of July 31, 1989, 197 miles of Prince William Sound and 508 miles of the Gulf of Alaska shore had been treated. Exxon's May 24 estimate of impacted shoreline mileage was 209 in Prince William Sound and 521 miles in the Gulf of Alaska area. Thus it appears that 94% of the impacted beach in Prince William Sound and 98% in the Gulf of Alaska shoreline were already taken care of, leaving every expectation that the job would be completed by September 15, 1989. It is natural for the public to assume "treated" means "cleaned up."

- *Announcing new operational procedures that will presumably prevent a recurrence of this crisis:* On August 1, 1989, Alyeska presented a Tanker Spill Prevention and Response Plan for Prince William Sound. Its innovative features are the creation of Community Response Centers and an Incident Command System organization for the Alyeska spill response team.

Public relations (PR) are clearly a key to the effective pursuit of such a strategy. However, despite its impressive show of action, Exxon stumbled badly. It failed to manage the PR aspects of the crisis well. A contributing factor, for which Exxon management bears no responsibility, is the nature of the spill as a media subject. In contrast to a nuclear power accident or the national debt, it is easily understood and visually communicated. We cannot "see" nuclear radiation or a trillion dollars, but we can certainly see dead otters and birds, gooey rocks, and oil floating on the water surface. Close-up images of an otter or seal fighting for its life tears at the heart of television viewers. An accident of this sort becomes a mega-media event, in other words, show business. Television newsman Dan Rather was able to show the spill to the East Coast on the national evening news before the response team had arrived on the scene at Bligh Reef, just 28 miles from its Valdez base!!

A further critical factor underlying Exxon's perspective is its corporate culture. Great entrepreneurial and technical skills have transformed the major oil companies from daring industrial pioneers to global giants. However, until recently they never were in the position where accidents in their operations could have impacts that would be widely perceived as catastrophic. In this regard the oil industry is in a position somewhat analogous to that of the utility industry.

Electricity generation became a commercial enterprise early in the twentieth century, as did oil production. Although the complexity of power generation and transmission steadily increased, the utility industry was not prepared for the level of complexity presented by nuclear energy. The Rogovin Report labeled the Three Mile Island accident a "management problem." The Kemeny Commission found that "[the utility] did not have sufficient knowledge, expertise, and personnel to operate the plant or maintain it adequately" [25]. There was no adaptation in management to either the knowledge-intensive character of the new technology or the potential for catastrophe. Stringent minimization of error-tolerance in internal operations and the criticality of external effects were not perceived as central. The utility companies' corporate culture contrasted sharply with the U.S. Navy's nuclear program as personified by Admiral Hyman Rickover. The differences between the Navy and utility industry in approach to construction and operations were startling.

In the oil industry, a corporate organization in an era of 18,000 ton deadweight tankers in World War II cannot be expected to be appropriate for the 200,000+-ton DW supertankers of today. A tenfold increase in size creates an entirely new presence: the possibility of low-likelihood/severe-consequence incidents. It is hardly surprising that a well-established, highly successful corporation failed to recognize for a long time that it was engaged in a new ball game that called for a new style of management.

Profitable operation must be of foremost concern to any oil company and is aided significantly by rigorously minimizing costs. In 1986, when oil prices sagged, Exxon's flattened income and lagging stock price led the company to undertake a major internal restructuring. But it was designed to prop up profits and stock prices, not to create a management control system as sophisticated as its technology now demanded. The result was a drop of 28% in worldwide employment and implementation of many other cost-cutting measures. The work force was stretched thin and morale declined as a result [26]. With the help of automation, sharp cuts were made in ship crews—from as many as 40 in the late 1960s (for smaller ships) to the Exxon Valdez's 24 in 1986 and 19 in 1989 [27]. This was in line with Exxon's aim for a 16-man crew on fully automated, Diesel-powered tankers by 1990 [19, p. 12]. The result was longer work hours, overworked seamen, and lower morale. It is a situation not uncommon in industry.

There is great pressure on ship captains to maintain tight time schedules. Shell has determined that, for its fleet of tankers, cutting one hour in port saves a total of $5 million annually. Tanker captains often take risky shortcuts to make up time; this was the case for the *Torrey Canyon* traversing the hazardous Scilly Islands with the result of dumping 100,000 tons of oil on the British and French coastlines [16, p. 183]. At other times, they avoid the use of expensive tugs in harbors and bays.

Alaska Oil Spill Commission Chairman Walter Parker pointed to a common industry policy decision, not a captain's choice, to operate its tankers at sea speed in Alaskan waters for the same economic reason. Not surprisingly, the traffic lanes in Prince William Sound were increasingly ignored. The ice breaking off Columbia Glacier and entering the traffic lanes does not pose any danger to tankers provided they move slowly, say, at 5-knot speed; they can pose a danger at high speed. The *Exxon Valdez* was accelerating to sea speed and moving outside the traffic channel after dropping off the harbor pilot, thus seeking to avoid the ice and clear the Sound more rapidly [27].

The advantages of Exxon as a large and tightly coupled organization have come to the fore most effectively in mounting the very large clean-up operation. As soon as it took over from Alyeska, things began to happen. This was demonstrated by the rapid deployment of the *Exxon Baton Rouge* to transfer most of the oil from the stricken ship, its rapid manpower mobilization, and effective installation of a communications center in the spill area. The local airstrip, which had handled about 10 flights per day prior to March 24, was soon handling 750 to 1000 flights a day. Exxon's capability was again demonstrated in the case of the Arthur Kill spill when Exxon's mop-up team quickly recovered about one quarter of the oil.

To outsiders, the power of Exxon and, more generally, the oil industry, appears awesome. Historically, the companies have been linked together not only through industry associations and a large number of joint venture arrangements but through interlocking directorates by way of common directorates in commercial banks. And it is reasonable to assume that, in recent years, former oil man George Bush has been a valuable, sympathetic contact in Washington. In the 1990–92 period, oil companies gave $1.3 million to the Republican National Committee and other Republican groups (and only $733,000 to the Democrats). Globally, the oil industry is able to dominate the United Nations *International Maritime Organization* (IMO). For example, the industry lobbied successfully against an IMO proposal to require double hulls [28].

However, inside the corporation the power of its opponents is seen as onerous. The management sees itself constantly under pressure to defend its operations from ever more strident energy conservation, environmental, and other anti-industry groups that exploit legal processes and the media to impede their operations. The insiders are bitter about the extraordinary amount of time they must now devote to compliance with increasingly burdensome rules. They see themselves being chased offshore by the climbing costs of operation foisted on them in the United States.

Alyeska Pipeline Service Company

This company, charged with the operation of the Trans Alaska pipeline and Valdez port complex, is owned by a consortium of oil companies. The three largest shareholders are British Petroleum with 50.01% share, Arco 21.35%, and Exxon 20.34%. The State of Alaska insists that the oil companies control Alyeska's budget to a degree that makes them responsible for Alyeska's performance in the spill.

In 1971 hearings before the Interior Department, L. R. Beynon of British Petroleum testified for Alyeska that its proposed plan would deal "promptly and effectively with any oil spill that may occur, so that its effect on the environment will be minimal . . . operations at Port Valdez and in Prince William Sound [will be] the safest in the world " [29]. However, the initial 1976 Alyeska contingency plan was already considered inadequate. The ADEC regional supervisor for Prince William Sound opened his comments on the Plan to the DEC Deputy Commissioner on December 13, 1976, as follows:

Alyeska's Valdez Terminal Oil Spill Contingency Plan, in almost every major facet, contains mistakes and inadequacies, demonstrates microscopic thinking, and worse, omits major functions that are necessary. In addition to the following general critique of major shortcomings, certain expletives are penciled in the margin of the Plan. The initial Plan is so bad, the Department should consider prosecution for violation of Solid Waste regulations and anyone who reviews this Plan should get hour-for-hour comp[ensation] time as sick leave [19, p. 39].

In view of the huge cost overrun, subsequent cost-cutting efforts in the operations of the consortium are hardly surprising.

A whistle-blower, former oil broker Charles Hamel, has provided much information about the pipeline safety and environmental problems to state and federal authorities. Alyeska hired a security firm, the Wackenhut Corporation, to mount an extensive undercover operation to find the sources of the leaks (in information, not in the pipeline). The elaborate sting set up a phony environmental organization to win Mr. Hamel's confidence. Former employees of the security firm admitted that Hamel's garbage was stolen and his telephone records were analyzed [30].

An investigation by the *Wall Street Journal,* which can in no way be called "anti-business," painted a grim picture of the company [31]. It reported that many oil spill safeguards were quietly scrapped, promised ones were never implemented, and new regulatory controls were vigorously fought. According to this source, employees admitted they sometimes fabricated environmental records and doctored test results. Defenses against a major accident were allowed to fall into disrepair. A dedicated emergency 12-man spill response team was disbanded in 1982.

In 1988 Alyeska tried to control state inspections of the terminal by requiring advance notice of inspection visits and refusing to permit the DEC to bring video cameras [28]. Alyeska also ignored state law in failing to notify

Lawn, as head of the Valdez office, that some clean-up equipment was not operational as specified in the contingency plan [32].

Alyeska demonstrates the power of the oil industry:

> When individual regulators do lean on Alyeska, its response can be fierce. Dan Lawn, the state's top Alyeska inspector, was thrown off Alyeska's premises one day in 1986 . . . Alyeska . . . tried to get him fired and attempted to limit his access to the terminal . . . Says Mr. Lawn: "I would characterize their attitude toward regulators as utter contempt" [31].

The GAO found in 1991 that

> Alyeska's ability to clean up a major oil spill is in doubt because the company has never conducted a full test drill. The oil companies are opposed to such a drill, the audit said, because it would require temporarily shutting down the pipeline. The drills have been limited to such practices as hiding a piece of black plastic, which is supposed to simulate oil, and then ending the drill once the plastic is found [33].

After the Exxon Valdez oil spill, it took three times as long for Alyeska to respond as its contingency plan had postulated. The barge assigned to the response had been damaged by a windstorm several weeks earlier and was being repaired. President Nelson insisted that the contingency plan did not require that the barge be loaded. He pointed out that the readiness factor was not relevant in this case since the response team would only have been able to handle a 2000-barrel leak even if it had been stationed at Bligh Reef.

No effort was made to boom off the tanker immediately after the spill. One ex-Alyeska employee explained that the USCG prevented placement of the booms around the ship for fear oil fumes might create an incendiary gas bubble. Alyeska subsequently contended that key parts of the plan were mere "guidelines . . . that cannot really be extrapolated to the real world." Even Exxon Chairman Lawrence Rawl agreed that "Alyeska was not equipped to handle an unfortunate incident like this one" [20, p. 52].

Significant changes have been initiated since the accident. In addition to changing its top leadership, $1 billion is being devoted to improving response capability. For example, Alyeska has converted three ships to *emergency response vessels* (ERVs). They now escort tankers in the Valdez area and are outfitted with skimmers, boom, and cranes for immediate use in case of spill. A fully manned skimmer barge has also been placed on constant standby alert in Prince William Sound [34].

U.S. Coast Guard

The USCG is a chronically overcommitted and underfunded, quasi-military service organization. With 37,000 people, it is minuscule by comparison with the DOD; in fact, the USCG is comparable in size to the combined staffs of the Congress and the White House (34,000). Illegal immigration and drug traffic soaring in recent decades and the barrage of environmental legislation have greatly strained its resources. In the case of the Valdez incident, the USCG failed to monitor the tanker after it veered outside the normal shipping lanes and did not communicate with the ship until after the grounding, about an hour after Capt. Hazelwood's last radio transmission announcing his detour to avoid ice (11:25 p.m.). Surprisingly, the tanker was not then tracked by radar but only spotted after it ran aground. (The USCG maintains that it was not required to track ships as far as Bligh Reef.)

For the Valdez oil spill, the role of the Coast Guard was a central one: it provided the *on-scene coordinator* (OSC) in the person of Vice Admiral Harold Robbins. In this role, he had to approve the clean-up plans of Exxon. The relation between the Coast Guard and Exxon is itself complex. In organizational terms, we have noted the enormous power of the oil industry and the weakness of the Coast Guard. An example of the relative power is the alacrity with which the Coast Guard bowed to industry pressure to reopen Prince William Sound to oil shipping days after the spill. It is, of course, fairly common in our system to find regulating agencies bending to the will of those whom they are mandated to regulate. Furthermore, recalling the "revolving door" between the U.S. military and the defense industry, we should not be surprised that senior retired USCG personnel find second careers with the oil companies.

Thus, the industry's new Marine Spill Response Corporation is headed by retired Coast Guard Vice Admiral John D. Costello. The Alaska Oil Spill Commission Report gave the Coast Guard's "unduly friendly relationship with industry" as one reason for its failure to provide proper oversight of the country's oil transportation system [19, p. 150]. Recent actions by the Coast Guard to improve its operations include wider radar coverage and establishment of a round-the-clock watch supervisor position in Valdez [35].

The Federal Government

At the time of the spill, the Federal government was headed by a former oil man, George Bush. The U.S. Department of Justice, a key actor in the drama, had been transformed into arguably the most politicized one in an Administration that was strongly pro-business.

On February 27, 1990, the Department indicted Exxon on five criminal counts. This followed months of negotiation to effect a plea bargain under which Exxon would have paid $150 million into an environmental restoration fund, possibly adding $350 million later. The company would have retained veto power over how the money was spent. Under the proposed settlement, the federal government would also have agreed to drop any civil suits for damages against Exxon [36]. The draft minutes of the March 2, 1990, meeting between state and federal officials suggest that the Justice Department was less than wholehearted in its dedication to prosecute Exxon. In the minutes, Justice Department representatives appear to characterize the public's mood as unreasonably vindictive toward Exxon, saying

> the public would not be satisfied unless Exxon's assets were essentially depleted and all board members put in jail . . . [37].

The Federal government was clearly eager to settle. Furthermore, the President and Governor Hickel of Alaska were anxious to open the *Arctic National Wildlife Refuge* (ANWR) to oil exploration. Although increasing the average fuel economy standard for new cars from 27.5 to 34 miles per gallon by 2001 would save more oil than could ever be pumped from the refuge, President Bush announced that he would veto any energy bill that did not lift the restrictions on Arctic oil development [38].

Under the leadership of Department of Transportation Secretary Samuel K. Skinner, a $1.1 billion settlement of the federal and state civil and criminal cases was hammered out. On April 24, 1991, Alaska Federal District Judge H. R. Holland rejected the agreement, deciding that the proposed fines were inadequate and would send the wrong message, suggesting that spills are a cost of business that can be absorbed. In view of Exxon Chairman Rawl's boast that the settlement would "not have a significant effect on our earnings," the judge's action is understandable [39]. Five days later, Judge Sporkin announced that he was not satisfied that the rights of the native Alaskan villages were protected by the settlement [40]. Next, the Alaska House of Representatives rejected the settlement. The second phase ended when Governor Hickel and Exxon formally withdrew their approval of the settlement and Exxon withdrew its guilty plea.

On September 30, 1991, a renegotiated settlement was announced by Governor Hickel, with Exxon committed to pay a slightly higher amount over a ten-year period—$1.125 billion rather than $1.1 billion as called for in the original settlement.

The State of Alaska

The state receives 85% of its revenue from oil and each of its permanent residents receives an annual check from the oil fund. In 1991 this amounted to

$931.34, or $3725.36 for a family of four. These facts inevitably weigh heavily in the relationship between the state and the oil industry. Not surprisingly, there is much popular support for this source of Alaskan wealth. Indeed, there is hope that opening the ANWR to oil drilling will prolong the flow of money to the citizens. The oil companies contribute substantially to the legislature, and the state gives large tax breaks to oil companies [41]. On the other side, an oil industry view is that the state taxes the industry too heavily and raises its taxes whenever it needs money.

Local Communities

Many communities were affected by the oil spill. Within a week of the spill, Valdez saw its population more than double. By summer 1989, it swelled to more than five times its normal size. The town's economy became totally disoriented, with some raking in windfall profits and others finding the sudden rise in living costs disastrous.

In Cordova there were bitter complaints by the *Cordova District Fishermen United* (CDFU) about the poor response of Exxon to early offers of concerned, knowledgable, and willing Cordova fishermen to help promptly to deploy booms. The fishermen felt the urgent need to secure the five fish hatcheries in Prince William Sound and went on a worldwide search for boom. Many foreign and domestic companies called back to say, to their surprise, that Exxon had told them they did not need any more boom at this time. Nevertheless the fishermen proceeded to obtain boom equipment to secure the hatcheries.

The Alyeska plan of August 1, 1989, suggested that the oil companies appeared to have learned a lesson from this experience. Alyeska's new Regional Citizens Advisory Committee was designed to avoid a repetition of the non-involvement on the part of the local population during the crisis, the basis for much anger against Alyeska.

In Tatitlek and other native villages, there was confusion as to what subsistence food sources were poisoned by the spill. In Chenega Bay there was panic as the oil-laden waves rolled in. In Seldovia, nearly all residents volunteered to design, build, and deploy their own log booms. When Exxon ignored their effort, the frustrated community became resentful. In Homer there was anger when Exxon sent a public relations man. In Kodiak the domestic violence rate tripled and the caseload for the Mental Health Department rose 700% during the first few months [19].

The natives were particularly incensed that they were hurting economically while Lawrence Rawl boasted that Exxon was not hurt at all by the settlement. They felt that they were alone and abandoned as usual [42].

Other Groups and Organizations

There were, of course, many other organizations involved with the oil spill crisis. Examples are environmental groups: The Cousteau Society, the National Resources Defense Council, and the Wildlife Federation. Indirect participants include the insurers and Exxon stockholders. There are also the international organizations that are concerned with oil spills. The UN International Maritime Organization has promulgated worldwide tanker standards and safety regulations but has no power to enforce them. "Flags of convenience" are used by owners to register their ships in countries such as Panama, Malta, and Cyprus, which have low taxes and minimal regulations. In 1992 seven of these countries accounted for more than half the ships lost. The worldwide tanker situation is worse than that prevailing in U.S. waters. It is estimated that 20% of the world's tankers are unsafe. The Institute of London Underwriters refused to insure 85% of the 133 ships it inspected in 1992 [43].

Summary

Many in the oil industry would argue that a spill in which there was not a single human casualty hardly constitutes a catastrophe. Exxon, the central and most powerful actor, responded immediately and massively. Its tight coupling and enormous resources gave it great leverage. However, the task of alleviating the disastrous effects in Prince William Sound was hampered by the less than satisfactory coordination among the various organizational actors, each bent on protecting its own back and avoiding blame. Damage control was clearly the foremost concern of organizational thinking.

Although Exxon's clean-up costs ultimately exceeded $3 billion, this amount did not constitute a major financial burden for a company of Exxon's enormous size. The effectiveness of the clean-up is another matter entirely: it remains technologically far beyond the industry's current capability and an uncertain prospect for the future. Furthermore, the profoundly changed level of technological sophistication and risk accompanying the supertanker era has not been reflected in the industry's management style.

Alyeska's actions raise serious questions about its ethical standards and its ability to perform emergency response, one of its stipulated missions. Constant overcommitment and underfunding reflect the absence of any constituency in Washington for the Coast Guard. Its weakness makes it difficult for the Coast Guard to stand up to industry pressures.

The judicial system's problem lies in the inherent nature of complex systems. It is impossible to pin responsibility on any one participant. The accident would not have occurred if any one of at least six minor failures would not have happened. These failures involved the captain, the crew, Alyeska, and the Coast Guard, as well as Exxon.

The scientific understanding of the Prince William Sound ecosystem is quite inadequate. The system is extremely complex and in the courtroom each side can marshal analyses to prove its point. One juror at the punitive trial later observed:

> You got a guy with four Ph.D.s saying no fish were hurt, then you got a guy with four Ph.D.s saying, yeah, a lot of fish were hurt [18].

The studies that Exxon and the State of Alaska did were largely kept secret until legal settlements were reached, resulting in lack of data sharing and duplication of effort.

The State of Alaska also has problems facing up to the industry in view of its almost total dependence on oil revenues. Its support for oversight and control of oil operations has been quite limited until recently. It has a difficult task standing up to both Exxon and the federal government with their enormous resources. The fishing communities were badly hurt, but their voice, although articulate, is a small one among the organizational power players and easily drowned out.

A pervasive dilemma is the creeping routinization of organizational activities. In its early years, the Alyeska operation appears to have been well managed and there was a serious attitude toward spill response. Even minute spills were cleaned up promptly and completely. The Coast Guard also exercised firm control. Only a single tanker at a time was allowed in the Valdez Narrows, traffic lanes were observed, and three ship traffic control operators were on duty at all times: a supervisor, a radio operator, and a radar watch person. Later the Alyeska operation deteriorated and the Coast Guard saw itself as being only a "provider of information."

How can an organization responsible for systems that may experience catastrophic failure, albeit with very low likelihood, maintain its initial high effectiveness over a long period of time? We shall address this question later in this section.

Creeping bureaucratization is also glaringly apparent in the disposition of the $1.125 billion that was to be provided by Exxon in the renegotiated settlement. For four years following the spill, the main beneficiaries were the throngs of attorneys and consultants.

Personal Perspectives

Human Beings and Probabilities

Human beings do not deal with probabilities as would mathematically programmed computers. A consultant study done by Woodward-Clyde for Exxon calculated the "most likely" oil spill size to be in the range of 1000 to 2000 barrels, while an "unlikely" 200,000+ barrel catastrophic spill would probabilistically occur only once in 241 years [27]. Since the Alaskan pipeline life span is about 30 years, Alyeska felt comfortable in using a 2000-barrel spill as a goal for clean-up capability in its 1987 contingency plan. This is like reasoning that the most probable auto accident is a fender bender and car safety design should be based on this possibility. The reality is that the very low probability of a catastrophic spill—once every 241 years—by no means negates the possibility that another such spill may occur in the next 12 months.

Human beings also have difficulty grasping very low probabilities. We are comfortable discussing probabilities of 50%, 20%, and 10%. We have trouble dealing with probabilities such as 0.0056—the probability of losing a ship in the year 1979 (400 ships lost in a worldwide fleet of 71,129)—and 0.00004—the percent of load spilled by Valdez tankers from 1977 to 1989 (based on 8700 loaded tankers departing from Valdez).

Recalling that past events fade in our mind, it is inevitable that the *Exxon Valdez* disaster is discounted as time moves on (also see Section 7.1). It has disappeared from front pages, television screens, and most peoples' consciousness. In the same way the environmental effects (for example, disappearance of a species) are typically long term and, hence, discounted relative to the near-term economic impacts (for example, loss of jobs).

In cases of low-likelihood events where the consequence of their occurrence is catastrophic, probabilities do not offer a basis for planning.

Exxon's Top Executives

When a Japan Airlines DC-8 crashed in Tokyo Bay as a result of pilot error, the president of the airline resigned. A heightened sense of personal responsibility is uncommon in American corporations. When the Union Carbide industrial accident occurred in Bhopal, India, Warren Anderson, CEO of Union Carbide, flew to the scene of the disaster. Lawrence Rawl, Exxon's chairman, stayed out of public view for nearly a week after the disaster and let others take the heat. He defended himself in a *Time* interview:

> We had concluded that there was simply too much for me to coordinate from New York . . . I went on TV and said I was sorry. I said a dozen times that we're going to clean it up. But people keep saying that I don't commit. I don't know what the hell that means. What do you do when you commit? Do you hang yourself . . . ?[44]

Rawl's remarks one year after the accident did not shift.

On not going to Valdez: "It wouldn't have made any difference if I showed up and made a speech in the town forum. I wasn't going to spend the summer there . . ."

On being charged with arrogance: "That bothers the hell out of me. Maybe 'big' is just arrogant. Or maybe I just get emotional and that's arrogant. Or maybe I say things people don't like to hear. Is that arrogance? You tell me" [44].

The photo of the chairman that accompanied the article vividly, if unintentionally, exuded an aura of defiance.

Hours after the $1.1 billion Phase 2 agreement engineered by Secretary Skinner was announced, Mr. Rawl still expressed little regret over the spill, allowing in a news conference that, in the two years since the spill, his most painful moments were usually caused by bad publicity. In the words of the general counsel of the National Audubon Society, "Mr. Rawl's comments were incredibly arrogant" [39].

When Alyeska's top executive in Valdez, Chuck O'Donnell, was awakened at 12:30 a.m. by a call from the terminal informing him of the accident, he ordered a subordinate to head to the terminal and went back to sleep. A company spokesman insists that this was "in accordance with accepted consortium procedures for dealing with possible disasters" [31]. The failure of the supervisor to follow the plant operating guide in the Arthur Kill oil spill was similarly explained as being "consistent with customary field practice" [45].

The Exxon executive who was, in a sense, the eye of the storm was Exxon Shipping Company president Frank Iarossi. He strove intensively to bring all available resources to bear, only to find himself frustrated at every turn by his own corporate superiors, as well as the bureaucratic behavior of key Coast Guard and State of Alaska individuals.

Capt. Hazelwood

As captain of the *Exxon Valdez*, Joseph Hazelwood was inevitably thrust overnight from obscurity into the limelight. It was never clearly established in the subsequent trial that the captain was drunk at the time of the accident. An alcohol test was administered 10 hours later and his actions immediately after the grounding were not characterized by those present as those usually associated with drunk behavior. However, Hazelwood's two earlier arrests for drunk driving, the repeated revocation of his driving license, his involvement in an alcohol rehabilitation program, and his admission of drinking before sailing on March 23, 1989, weighed heavily against him in the public eye. Polls showed that 70% of the populace believed Hazelwood "was guilty for sure" of some wrongdoing [46].

With the trial behind him, Hazelwood reflected that, like the tragic figure in *Les Miserables,*

> It seemed like I was Jean Valjean with about a hundred inspectors chasing me around the sewers of Paris [47].

Exactly one year after setting out on the fatal voyage, Hazelwood was convicted of the misdemeanor charge of negligent discharge of oil and sentenced by Alaska's Judge Karl Johnstone, himself a commercial fisherman in Prince William Sound until 1988, to spend 1000 hours helping to clean up the beaches and to pay the state a token restitution of $50,000. The judge lectured the defendant:

> I think Capt. Hazelwood knows the buck stops with him and he has to take responsibility [46].

However, the Clean Water Act of 1972 grants immunity to those who report oil spills to the authorities. Although this provision was meant to uncover minor spills, it was the basis for a reversal of the Hazelwood verdict by the Alaska Court of Appeals in July 1992. Capt. Hazelwood had promptly notified the Coast Guard after the grounding and was thus not considered legally negligent [48].

The inherent nature of complex industrial systems that are subject to accidents involving very low probability plus very severe consequences poses an unprecedented legal challenge to the judicial system. How is liability to be assigned in "normal accidents," where inherently many actors or none can be held responsible [16]?

National Leadership

The possibility of serious problems was recognized before the Alaska pipeline was authorized. In the period 1969 to 1973 there were intensive debates between the oil companies and the environmentalists about the safety of the proposed oil transportation system. However, the 1973 oil crisis led to a quick resolution of the debate. Congress approved, and President Nixon signed the bill authorizing construction of the pipeline and terminal. Even the White House signing ceremony gave inadvertent recognition to the situation.

Two weeks after the Alaska oil spill (April 7, 1989), President Bush held a press conference in which he, like Exxon Chairman Lawrence Rawl, focused on the "alleged human error of a pilot" as the cause of this "aberration." Although he campaigned in 1988 as "an environmentalist" and manifested righteous wrath at the pollution in Boston harbor, he took only mild interest in the largest spill in American history. He did not visit the scene of the disaster.

The key player at the national level proved to be Department of Transportation Secretary Samuel K. Skinner (see also his role in the Denver International Airport case, Section 4.3). On his role in the Phase 2 settlement negotiations, he observed:

> I viewed my job as a facilitator. You had a huge amount of egos and interests that had to be blended together. In my experience I've found that if the principals don't want to settle they look for an opportunity to get out. In this case everybody wanted a deal because they knew the alternatives didn't make sense [47].

He believed that a successful negotiation was possible only if it was conducted at the Cabinet level.

The Chief Judge for the U.S. District of Alaska who rejected the Phase 2 agreement, H. Russel Holland, is described by long-time acquaintances as an "ultimate professional," "a decent man," and "totally honorable." A Reagan appointee to the Federal bench, he was neither strongly environmentalist nor pro-development. His decision was clearly influenced by the many letters he received criticizing the paltry size of a penalty that did not "adequately punish the defendant for the crime for which guilty pleas are offered" [39].

Alaska's Dan Lawn

Dan Lawn was hired by the *Alaska Department of Environmental Conservation* (ADEC) in 1979 and became an acknowledged expert on the Alyeska operations in Valdez. His outspoken criticism of Alyeska in the 1980s became a thorn in the company's side until Alyeska President Nelson finally tried to have Lawn's superiors remove this "troublemaker." He complained about the unwillingness of Alyeska to spend money, of cutting back manpower, and letting the system deteriorate. In a 1984 memo to ADEC he warned:

> we can no longer ignore the routine monitoring of Alyeska unless we do not care if a major catastrophic event occurs [27].

With Alaska's oil revenues declining in consequence of the oil price collapse, monitoring was a badly underfunded activity and, according to Lawn, served as a signal to Alyeska that it could reduce its response capability with impunity.

A state test of the emergency response procedures was conducted in the winter of 1986. It involved the spill of 60 barrels of oil (simulated by a spill of oranges). The company had failed a similar test in 1984. Lawn judged their performance in 1986 as less than passing.

Lawn was on the scene of the *Exxon Valdez* spill within three hours of the grounding, at 3 a.m. on March 24. Nine hours later he was still wondering "where the hell's the response equipment?" However, his superiors saw Lawn as a "loose cannon" and subsequently demoted him for "lack of objectivity and professional manner toward those we regulate." He filed a grievance case and won but was understandably bitter: his many warnings had gone unheeded until it was too late. To Lawn, neither the federal government nor the oil companies kept their early promises that any spill could be contained.

Governor Walter J. Hickel

Alaska's Governor Hickel played a significant role before and after the oil spill. Serving as second governor of the new state from 1966 to 1968, he was an early and ardent champion of the exploitation of Alaska's natural resources, in general, and oil, in particular. He promoted drilling in Prudhoe Bay, proudly recalling even now:

> I told them to drill right there. I told them there was 40 billion barrels down there [50].

After several unsuccessful political campaigns, this self-made millionaire was re-elected governor in 1990 and once again championed exploitation of Alaska's natural wealth: oil exploration from wildlife refuge areas, timber from national forests, a natural gas pipeline, a water pipeline, and gold mining. He is intent on freeing Alaska from federal land use and environmental restraints. Hickel's effort to obtain a quick cash settlement of the oil spill was predictable for a man whose motto is "big projects define a civilization" [50].

Cordova Fishermen

The local fishery people showed the most emotional reaction, at times stunningly articulate. An example is Michelle Hahn O'Leary of Cordova, representing the CDFU. Cordova is totally dependent on fishing. Her testimony:

> Our lifestyle is ruled by the tides and the fish that inhabit Prince William Sound, instead of by a clock . . . 1989 is the 100th aniversary of commercial fishing in Prince William Sound. What a sad, destructive, and pathetic situation fishermen and all the members of the Sound face in this historic 100th year. . . .
>
> We cohabit daily with land otters, sea otters, seals, eagles, Canada geese, and many species of water fowl and shore birds that feed and haul

out on the beach in front of the house. These are our companions and friends . . . We find ourselves crying as we harvest oil-coated dead sea otters and deck load our boats with birds doomed because they ingested toxic oil as they attempted to free their wings from the black goo [21].

She subsequently served as secretary of the new Regional Citizens' Advisory Council of Prince William Sound.

Jeff and Claire Bailey fulfilled a life dream in moving from Massachusetts to Cordova. Jeff (32) crewed on fishing boats from April to September, while Claire (30) ran the Killer Whale, a combination deli and café. In December she shut down the restaurant and filled in as an X-ray technicican in Cordova's Community Hospital. They lived comfortably on a $60,000 income. In their leisure time, he hunted moose and bear and they went clam digging, hiking, and kayaking.

On March 24, 1989, their life changed. The State cancelled the herring season, although Exxon reimbursed the fishermen for their losses. Oil pollution cancelled his plans to harvest kelp from the bottom of Prince William Sound. Claire's café lost customers and help because two-thirds of the townspeople were off working on the clean-up. Exxon paid Claire $2000, but the café continued to lose $500 a week. Conscience did not permit Jeff to go to work for Exxon—a costly decision. Jeff became politically active as he battled to obtain compensation from Exxon for the "indirect" losses the café suffered [51].

There were long compensation delays because Exxon used complicated and debatable formulas to determine the fishermen's compensation for lost catches. The company wanted to base compensation on past catches; the fishermen preferred an average share of available catches. Despite the spill, fishermen netted 23.8 million salmon from Prince William Sound in 1989, more than the 10-year average of 20 million but less than half of the 48 million fish anticipated before the spill [52]. In 1990 they took in 43 million, and in 1991 the salmon runs were again expected to be of record proportions [53].

The lavish clean-up effort poured large sums of money into the fishing villages, for example, $53 million worth of purchases and salaries into Valdez, a town of 3500 population. Local "spillionaires" were created while the influx of transients created problems ranging from crime to sewage. There are today many Alaskans who would not mind another large oil spill to generate economic largesse. Greed remains one of the most powerful human motivating drives.

At the other end of the social spectrum, the local Native Americans were seriously hurt and the divorce rate in the general population rose. In Cordova alcohol and drug use increased by 28% [35]. According to Jean-Michel

Cousteau, the social chaos created in the affected area by the spill are as significant as the ecological problems [54].

Summary

The human tendency to weigh the near term more strongly than the more distant past or future means that there will be a steady lessening of interest in the oil spill as time moves on.

Exxon and consortium executives have intense loyalty to their companies, but a sense of personal responsibility for the oil spill is associated solely with Capt. Hazelwood. The nature of complex systems confounds both pinpointing of responsibility and determination of losses, resulting in a legal quagmire. A "tough, get-out-of-my-way" attitude seems to radiate from the top of the corporation [55]. However, the company made a sizeable clean-up effort and compensated the fishermen and the towns for losses and problems resulting from the spill.

A self-styled "environmentalist," President Bush showed little personal interest in the crisis; he had Secretary of Transportation Samuel K. Skinner take on a key negotiating role.

ADEC's Valdez inspector Dan Lawn became an unpopular Cassandra with his outspoken criticisms of Alyeska and early warnings of a potential catastrophe. Governor Walter J. Hickel, himself a former Presidential Cabinet Secretary, was motivated primarily by concerns for the Alaskan economy to offer the basic settlement proposal soon after his election.

Among the people whose lifestyle was sorely affected by the spill, the fishermen spoke out with surprisingly articulate voices, but their political power was modest.

Overall, two points stand out. First, the accident at Bligh Reef is seen in strikingly different ways through different eyes. To Lawrence Rawl it appeared to be an annoying diversion of attention from running Exxon's business. To President Bush, Governor Hickel, and other oil industry executives, it represented a threat to the opening up of the Arctic National Wildlife Refuge for oil exploration. To the Coast Guard's Admiral Yost, it was an overblown minor incident since no one was killed. To Alaska's Dan Lawn, it was an outrage because much of the damage was the result of inexcusably sloppy Alyeska operations. To environmentalists it was an unprecedented ecological catastrophe, and to the native fishermen it was a horrendous threat to their way of life.

Second, the reflexive pattern of organizations to protect themselves by pinpointing individual scapegoats is perceived in both public and private sectors. Exxon focused its glare on Capt. Hazelwood, while ADEC left Dan Lawn "twisting in the wind."

Implications

Important Lessons

We shall now consider some implications of our analysis to date from T, O, and P perspectives. In effect, we offer our integration of the various perspectives. Others, examining the same perspectives, may well use different weighting factors and arrive at different implications.

As a starting point, we must recognize that the system we have examined is open and dynamic, requiring continued monitoring and periodic re-examination. The long-term effects of a large oil spill, the achievement of significant improvements in clean-up technology, and the ability to adapt the organizational culture and style to the demands of potentially dangerous technologies will not be known for many years. A decade after the accident, we are still uncertain about the damage to the ecosystem and the desirability of well-meaning human intervention. Environmentalists have focused on short-term impacts and have not addressed the question of whether a change in the ecosystem necessarily equates with deterioration over the long-term. We have been repeatedly surprised by the resilience of the ecosystem. Thus, we are facing a nonterminating task (Guideline 5 in Section 9.1).

The knowledge about the effects of oil pollution, as well as the means to clean it up, is totally inadequate. It is indicative that we lack an unambiguous definition of the meaning of "clean up." We cannot expect that sudden discoveries will resolve the uncertainties. As with the discovery of cancer-causing materials, vital impacts of oil pollution on the exceedingly complex ecological system in Prince William Sound, as well as the Alaskan social system, may require many decades of careful field observation and laboratory research.

An illustration of the time dimension of impacts is provided by the case of the Welland Canal. The building of the waterway to connect the St. Lawrence River to the Great Lakes in 1829 made it possible for lampreys to bypass the natural barrier of Niagara Falls and gain entry into Lake Erie. It took 110 years for them to enter the lake and decimate fishing there [17]!

In the long term, natural processes prove far more effective than any human intervention attempted to date. But human concern is focused on the near term and a sense of frustration is shared by all parties. Exxon, which had responsibility for the clean-up, learned that throwing massive resources of money and manpower at the problem could not solve it. It is doubtful whether a takeover of the clean-up operation by the federal government would have done any better; indeed, it might have done worse.

Let us step back and consider the basic options.

The Fail-Safe Approach

There are several alternatives.

1. Extend the Alaska pipeline through Canada to the United States, thus obviating the need for shipping oil by sea. This possibility was seriously raised in the 1960s and dropped for debatable, if not spurious, national security reasons. The oil companies view a pipeline to the contiguous U.S. border as undesirably restricting their oil distribution options.

2. Have the actual clean-up capability determine acceptable tanker size. This would mean drastic reduction of tanker size and greatly increased tanker traffic. It would require a vastly improved and empowered marine traffic control system. It would also result in unacceptably inferior cost effectiveness in oil-shipping operations. It is therefore another unrealistic approach.

3. Stop Alaska oil shipping and shift to other fuels. The high level of *carbon dioxide* (CO_2) emissions produced by oil (and coal) may play a major role in raising the atmospheric temperature (the greenhouse effect) and contribute heavily to stratospheric ozone depletion. A shift to less CO_2-producing natural gas would help to reduce the likelihood of a climatic crisis in the next century. Even more desirable would be a shift away from fossil fuels entirely. Nuclear and solar energy produce no greenhouse gases at all, but current nuclear energy systems also have a potential for catastrophe. This leaves solar energy and nuclear fusion as attractive options at some time in the twenty-first century. Finally, taking into account the huge investment of the oil and automobile industries in current fuel technology, it is obvious that this option is unrealistic until an environmental crisis is widely perceived to be imminent.

The Safe-Fail Approach

The system can certainly be made less error-inducing and more safety-reinforcing. Research and development efforts may make the clean-up technology less primitive. Significant technical improvements in prevention and in response capability appear feasible. The proposal of the the American Petroleum Institute for a new industry response organization has been implemented with the creation of the *Marine Spill Response Corporation* (MSRC). Additional steps have been proposed and, in some cases, partially implemented by the private and public sector organizations. Consider the following examples.

- *Alyeska:* Escort vessels for all laden tankers in Prince William Sound, fully manned skimmer barge on constant standby in Prince William Sound, establishment of a Regional Citizens Advisory Council to draw the local population actively into Alyeska operations, and creation of Community Response Centers to help local residents with equipment to protect their shorelines. Significantly, an escort tug was at hand and may have helped to avert the potentially disastrous grounding of the disabled tanker *Kenai* in Prince William Sound in October 1992 by pushing the bow of the ship away from Middle Rock with only 100 yards to spare. The tanker was carrying 35 million gallons of Alaskan crude oil.

- *The Coast Guard:* Expanded marine traffic control (full, state-of-the-art radar coverage of Prince William Sound, manning for effective monitoring), strengthened licensing requirements and enforcement, alcohol testing of captains prior to departure, close examination of ship crew fatigue induced by manpower reductions and promulgation of new regulations, limiting work hours.

- *The science and engineering communities:* Research on vessel configuration (for example, use of bow thrusters or twin screws for improved navigational capability), alarm systems for automatic pilots, bioremediation, and chemical dispersants.

- *The State of Alaska:* Closer tanker and terminal inspection, stricter spill response requirements, and increased civil penalties for spills.

- *The Department of Transportation:* Improved National Contingency Plan.

- *The U.S. Congress:* Requirement for double hull tanker construction, oil spill liability, and compensation legislation.

Many other steps can be taken to make the system less error-inducing and more safety-reinforcing; for example:

- Alter the marine insurance system to provide more incentives for shippers to operate safely;

- Provide meaningful penalties for shippers who are found to have inadequate crews (undertrained, understaffed);

- Tighten up Coast Guard enforcement by providing specific budgets for inspectors and giving the service more incentives for effective inspection programs (patterned after the FAA).

These steps certainly move the system in the right direction, but in a real-world setting we must draw on the organizational and personal perspectives to penetrate more deeply.

Organizational Rethinking

We recognize that most organizations are motivated to make major changes in their structure only when they are in a state of crisis, and the oil industry is hardly in such a state. The federal government has the resources but not the motivation; the State of Alaska has the motivation but not the resources. Thus, organizational rethinking presents a major challenge.

Recognizing the weakness in clean-up technology, such rethinking must concern itself with both spill prevention and clean-up. There must be a match between technical and organizational capabilities in both areas. The possibility of very low likelihood accident and very severe consequence requires unique standards of human technical and management abilities as well as a strong sense of individual responsibility on the part of those involved in shipping-related operations. Consider two examples:

- *Prevention:* Normal operations must be imbued with a sense of intolerance for noncatastrophic errors. The individual at all levels must see detection of, and alerting to, a problem and potential failure as a personal duty. Cover-up must be punished.

- *Response:* The response teams must maintain a continual high state of readiness. They must be able to resist the normal tendency of creeping complacency and routinization after public interest and concern diminishes as the *Exxon Valdez* accident recedes in the mind.

However, the error-inducing quality (see Table 6.4) may still bedevil the system after technical improvements are in place.

- The improvements may create such an aura of improved security that control of the ship is more often left to lower rank crew members—"with these improvements, anybody can run the ship." (See Section 6.5 on "risk homeostasis.")

- The added costs to the oil companies of paying for the improvements may lead them to cost-cutting measures elsewhere, for example, further crew reduction and design economies effected in new ship orders that increase risk of ship failure.

Also, accelerated research is likely to move in a vacuum unless there is a close linkage established with a knowledge-intensive operational organization.

The bits-and-pieces approach offered by the various proposed improvements does not per se leave us with an organization that ensures effective integration of improvements and long-term maintenance of a high state of readiness and capability. Nor does it give us a high degree of knowledge about all aspects of the system's operating characteristics and environment. There are many ways sources of failure can fall between the cracks. We can never eliminate them all, but we can do better than the present compartmentalized approach to safety in complex systems. With the present approach, is anyone authorized to examine the system couplings and interactions for weaknesses and take action? For example, should productivity pressures on ship captains be loosened to reduce their need to take imprudent risks? Who can order the requisite changes?

For both prevention and clean-up, the concept of the *high-reliability organization* with superbly motivated and trained personnel deserves serious consideration. In the area of prevention this means that it has the authority to stop tanker operations or override captains and terminal managers in pursuing safety concerns. It has the autonomy to practice readiness and to order drills. It has a very high level of system knowledge and is able to monitor research, propose, and test new technological developments. We refer to an organization that can shift from routine to crisis management easily, that is, one whose organizational hierarchy is flattened instantaneously. In the area of response such an organization has frequent drills that are held to very strict standards and evaluations. In both prevention and response, the organizational culture reflects an uncommon sense of personal responsibility [56, 57].

We find examples of high reliability organizations in both public and private domains:

- In the private sector: some utilities (electric, telephone), some airlines, some medical organizations;
- In the public sector: the nuclear submarine, the nuclear aircraft carrier, the national air traffic control system, the Los Angeles County Fire Dept.

A particularly interesting example is the Strategic Air Command, which was kept on an effective high state of alert continuously for many years to be ready in minutes for the unlikely event of a Soviet nuclear attack. A Command Post was kept airborne at all times.

LaPorte recounts an interesting observation on an aircraft carrier during practice take-offs and landings. A sailor on the deck suddenly waved off incoming aircraft. Upon being summoned to the bridge, he explained to the captain his reason: he had misplaced some tools on the deck and was afraid an aircraft could suffer damage upon landing. Instead of scolding him, the captain praised him for recognizing his personal responsibility. For an instant the organizational pyramid was flattened. Note the striking difference between this approach and that of Alyeska described earlier. Some distinctive characteristics of high reliability organizations are summarized in Table 6.5.

Such an organization in our context will exhibit a balance of tight coupling and loose coupling (Table 6.3) that transforms oil shipping from an error-inducing into a safety-reinforcing system. Examples include tighter coupling in forced adherence to strict rules and looser coupling in the organizational flexibility to shift rapidly from hierarchical (vertical) to nonhierarchical (horizontal) type. With the organizational perspective, there is a practical question always close to the surface: Where are the appropriate points of leverage for implementing recommendations for change? In view of the stature of the oil industry, it would appear to have very strong leverage in comparison to other organizational actors. Therefore, a private organization emanating from the American Petroleum Institute could be a driving force in creating high-reliability organizations.

Table 6.5
Characteristics Exhibited by High-Reliability Organizations [57]

1. Complex and demanding tasks performed under considerable time pressure with near-zero error rate and almost total absence of catastrophic failure.

2. A strong, clear sense of the primary mission, operational goals, and technical means to achieve them.

3. Powerful, knowledge-intensive systems well understood.

4. System mechanisms and processes nearly completely specified.

5. Production units complex, linked into large operating networks.

6. Capacity of networks to adjust to surprise.

7. Consequences of failure perceived to be great.

8. Near-failure almost as difficult to tolerate as actual failure.

9. Error regimes specified as deviation from norms and basis for identification and alert.

10. Wide agreement in society on events to be avoided.

11. Monitoring capability to detect external effects of operations.

12. Error-absorption and damage containment capabilities.

13. Abillty to shift from hierarchical to flat organization instantaneously.

The previous joint industry operation, Alyeska, must be kept clearly in mind as a nightmarish example of what not to do. We recall:

- Alyeska experienced a deterioration of operational capability over time.
- Alyeska appears to have had little autonomy.
- Alyeska practiced cover-ups.
- Alyeska was not managed and staffed by a breed of personnel characteristic of high reliability organizations.

Let us now consider the organizational aspect of *research and development* (R&D). A crisis often initiates a burst of research and experimentation. The *Torrey Canyon* disaster prompted work on detergent toxicity. It is expected that bioremediation will command more attention now because of the Alaskan oil spill. There is agreement on the part of industry and the government that research in clean-up technology is needed. The API Report and the Report to the President both stress this point.

What is missing here is any sense of an industry-institute/university working partnership. If a high-reliability organization is to function, the level of technical knowledge throughout the organization must be on a higher plane than has been acceptable in the industry in the past. Close, sustained interaction between operations and the research/engineering effort is highly desirable. Current personnel rotation and economic constraints must, and can, be lifted to make it possible. This interaction would specifically facilitate the transfer of technology, usually the weak link in the technological innovation process.

There is, of course, the option of a federal program. The federal government has the experience and funds to undertake a strong R&D program. But the motivation is lacking.

- There is no Sputnik orbiting the earth, (mis)interpreted by the public as an ominous sign of a Soviet military threat, loosening the federal purse strings.
- The military-industrial establishment has strong political leverage even following the end of the Cold War, as reflected in ballistic missile defense R&D appropriations. The medical-industrial complex also has political leverage in R&D. Strangely, the oil industry's undoubted political power has not been effectively asserted in a similar way to strengthen federal R&D in oil transportation and spill-related technology.

- Oil transportation and spill-related technology does not have the glamor in the science/engineering community as does information or space technology.

Alaska's small population does not translate into high leverage in Congress. An Advanced Technology Center in this field does not appear a realistic option for Alaska. A coalition of states including Alaska also does not appear feasible; the only other west-coast state for whom R&D in this field should be of major concern is California, site of the Santa Barbara and Huntington Beach spills. The two states are probably too dissimilar in resources needed for such R&D to permit consideration of such a union.

Individual Attitudes

Profound organizational changes of the kind indicated here are likely to succeed only if there is also a corresponding change in individual attitudes. Each individual has his own perception of risk. The CEO of Exxon, the tanker crew, and the Cordova fisherman clearly have very different perceptions of the Alaska oil spill. Similarly, the traditional oil-shipping organization and the high reliability organization discussed in the preceding section have disparate perceptions of desirable operating styles.

Improvements in technology and organization can reduce the frequency of catastrophic spills and mitigate their impact. But the effectiveness of an organization depends on its individual members. A high-reliability organization cannot be expected to succeed if the participants do not share its perspective. Ideally, a corporate leader with a vision of an ethical shipping system can communicate that vision to his associates and sweep them along, that is, have their individual perspectives coalesce with his organizational one. The reality is that the myopia determining the short planning horizon of most corporate managers, stockholders, politicians, and citizens generally threatens to make the farsighted leader appear a Don Quixote fighting windmills. The benign neglect of Presidents Reagan and Bush in matters of environmental protection and corporate ethics has also had its effect.

The importance of individual ethics is seen when we realize that the world's oceans are being constantly damaged by oil (and other substances) dumped surreptitiously. For example, vessel tanks are cleaned and residue is quietly slipped into the water. The publicized oil spills pale in comparison with the quantity of oil slowly and insidiously converting the ocean into a convenient garbage dump through wreckless human action. Away from the coast, it is physically impossible for any organization, governmental or private, to effectively police such behavior on the part of ship crews. Only individual ethics can ultimately prevent marine environmental deterioration.

Our aim has been to show the value multiple perspectives in dealing with the complex, low-risk/severe-consequence system of shipping oil from Alaska. Each perspective draws forth significant insights not obtained by the others. We observed, for example, the primitive nature of clean-up technology (T), the need for high-reliability organizations (O), and the influence of key actors like Lawrence Rawl and Samuel Skinner (P).

It is a daunting challenge to bring the oil transportation system close to a safe-fail status. Technological changes without organizational changes are not likely to be very effective. Neither will organizational changes without changes in individual attitudes—at both senior management and ship crew levels.

6.3 The Bhopal Chemical Accident (Bowonder and Linstone)

We began this discussion with some general observations of the proliferation of physical hazards in a world of expanding population and technology (Section 6.1). We now examine the Bhopal accident, an industrial event quite different from the Alaska oil spill but exhibiting distinct commonalities in terms of the perspectives.[3]

The Accident

Union Carbide Corporation's (UCC) subsidiary *Union Carbide India, Ltd.* (UCIL), established an Agricultural Products Division in Bhopal, India, in 1966. A decade later it decided to manufacture Carbamate pesticides, specifically carbaryl, there and production began in 1979. Such pesticides are based on *methylisocyanate* (MIC), a highly reactive chemical that polymerizes easily.

Bhopal is the capital of a fairly underdeveloped Indian state, Madhya Pradesh, with only a limited number of industries. In the period 1971 to 1981 it experienced 74% population growth and with it a proliferation of squatter settlements, many close to the UCIL plant.

UCC's safety manual clearly indicates that precautions are necessary for its storage.

---

3. This section is based on papers by B. Bowonder [58] and by B. Bowonder and H. Linstone [59] in *Technological Forecasting and Social Change.*

- MIC must be stored only in stainless-steel tanks.
- MIC tanks must be filled only to the half level, or another empty tank must be kept for evacuation in case of an emergency.
- Only a nonreactive fluid may be used as a refrigerant.
- Above the MIC an inert atmosphere of nitrogen must be provided.
- The MIC storage tank must be refrigerated and kept at close to 0°C.
- There must be a scrubber (alkali spraying) for neutralizing MIC, in case there is any escape.

In addition, to deal with the accidental release of MIC directly into the atmosphere, four safety measures were provided:

- A vent gas scrubber for neutralizing MIC in case of a leak;
- A water spray for neutralizing MIC;
- A flare tower for burning the vent gases;
- A public siren to warn residents.

There were six accidents at the plant between 1979 and 1983, three of them serious spills. In July 1979 a safety auditor from UCC indicated that safety was being neglected at UCIL. On December 9, 1980, the UCC management asked UCIL to draw up a disaster-cum-evacuation plan. On December 24, 1981, one worker died at the plant due to a toxic leak. In February 1982, 24 workers were hospitalized following another accident. In May 1982, a safety team from UCC reported poor safety management practices at UCIL and gave specific examples. On October 5, 1983, there was another serious accident, but no fatalities.

In November 1984, a plant modification was made, interconnecting *relief valve vent header* (RVVH) and *process vent header* (PVH) through a jumper line. A standby line would vent MIC when the RVVH and PVH were shut down. On Sunday, December 2, 1984, the production superintendent gave orders to MIC plant operators to clean the pipelines and four filter pressure safety valves. Due to a faulty valve, water started accumulating in the pipelines and entered an MIC tank, initiating a violent reaction. (If there had not been the jumper line connection, no water could have leaked into the tank.)

The first leakage was reported about 45 min after a shift change at 10:45 p.m., and the MIC started leaking into the atmosphere. The MIC plant supervisor was new to the MIC unit and the incoming shift, seeing the pressure in the tank rise, assumed it had been pressurized in the preceding shift to transfer MIC into the process plant. The crew experienced some eye irritation and the washing of the pipelines was stopped at 12:20 a.m. At 1 a.m. the warning siren was switched on for 1 minute. The police called UCIL but could not get any positive information. Three hours after the leak, the siren was restarted. Slowly a gas cloud consisting of methylisocyanate, its decomposition and reaction products, began to settle down in areas close to the factory. By the morning of December 3 about 12,000 people had gone to the Hamidia Hospital. The next night the MIC cloud recondensed over the city and by the morning of December 4 about 55,000 people came to the hospital. By official estimates, about 2,500 people died; unofficial estimates put this number at 5,000 to 8,000.

T Perspectives

Analysis showed that technical errors included:

- *Bad structural design:* inadequate vent gas scrubber and water sprays;
- *Use of wrong materials:* cast iron pipes were used when stainless-steel pipes were specified for MIC;
- Large-scale MIC storage without a proper safety system (11 times the normal level);
- *Defective instrument:* pressure gauge read 10 psi when actual pressure exceeded 40 psi;
- *Removal of freon coolant:* manual called for cooling below 15°C;
- *Poor instrumentation:* no on-line system for monitoring contents of MIC tank, no automatic initiation of water spray in case of leak.

System errors included:

- MIC pipelines and valves not regularly checked;
- Poor implementation of safety audit recommendations;
- Inadequate operational procedures to examine valves when MIC tank fails to be pressurized;
- Absence of emergency management plan and hot lines for communication.

Human errors included:

- *Operational errors:* washing MIC lines at night, disconnecting the flare tower for maintenance;

- *Error in recognition:* operator did not recognize entry of water into the MIC tank during cleaning of lines; the earlier failure to get the MIC tank pressurized was not perceived as a consequence of a leak somewhere;

- *Errors in communication:* new shift not informed of pressure increase in MIC tank, plant supervisor did not inform the works manager when the leak was detected.

For more technical details, the reader is referred to [58].

O Perspectives—The Corporation

Proprietary Information

Much information on MIC was considered proprietary by UCIL. In particular, there was inadequate dissemination of data on its toxicity. According to the medical journal *Lancet,* nothing appeared in the medical literature during the seven years prior to the accident that would have provided insights on the effects of large-scale exposure of humans to MIC. U.S. Occupational Health Guidelines [60] for MIC indicated that MIC vapor is an intense lacrimator; it irritates the eyes, mucous membranes, and skin. Exposure to high concentrations can cause cough, dyspnoea, and chest pain. Other studies indicate that MIC can cause permanent eye damage and is dangerous when inhaled even in greatly diluted form [61]. It appears that UCIL provided little indication of MIC toxicity when it applied for a license for production of carbaryl pesticide and for expansion of its Bhopal facilities in 1976. The state director of public health knew nothing about the MIC handled at the plant—neither did the mayor, who was a physician, nor the chief administrative officer responsible for Bhopal disaster contingency plans.

A result of the lack of detailed clinical information was a medical controversy after the accident about the efficacy of using sodium thiosulfate as an antidote. The Head of Toxicology of Bhopal Medical College advocated the use of sodium thiosulfate injections [62] while the Madhya Pradesh Department of Public Health opposed this treatment. Some toxicologists [63] thought that MIC decomposes to hydrogen cyanide at temperatures above 200°C and were concerned about combined exposure to MIC and hydrogen cyanide.

Stonewalling

The first organizational reaction to a technological disaster is almost always the same. The O perspective sees an industrial disaster as a threat to the organization. Therefore, there is a desire to suppress information and effect a cover-up. H. J. Heinz stonewalled when the rancid tuna crisis erupted; Metropolitan Edison Company stonewalled when Three Mile Island took place; the Soviet government stonewalled when the Chernobyl news broke. It is almost an automatic reflex action, an SOP, to circle the wagons when a threat looms. This reaction itself creates serious undesirable consequences. In the case of Chernobyl, it caused health concerns, if not panic, in Sweden, Poland, Romania, and Austria.

In the case of Bhopal, the possibility of cyanide poisoning was first denied, alarms were delayed, and thousands received unnecessary exposure to the MIC cloud. In its "investigative report" UCC asserted that 1000 to 2000 pounds of water would have been required to account for the chemistry of the residue left in the tank after the accident. It still insisted that the source of the water was unknown [64].

Contingency Planning

It was clearly known that MIC reacts violently with water and that water was a commonly used liquid in the plant. The possibility of an unintentional mixing was unlikely, but not impossible. This is an example of the low likelihood + severe consequence combination discussed earlier. Traditional corporate planning tends to ignore such a remote possibility. In their reliance on the T perspective, corporate analysts accept econometric models without probing core assumptions and accept technological risk models that shun "normal accidents." In both areas uncertainty is anathema. It is either dismissed as being unmanageable or replaced by probability-type risk.

However, some corporations have learned a lesson from the military: do enough "what-if" exercises to develop a capability to handle surprises (see "Crisis Management" in Section 8.4). They not only examine several alternative future environments but develop a hedging strategy [65]. Beyond this, they are learning the art of "crisis management" [66]. H. J. Heinz learned from its rancid tuna shipping incident and set up its own emergency-management team. Some firms no longer wait for a disaster to strike; they develop detailed contingency plans to cope with such surprises. United Airlines has a crisis team prepared to take charge in the event of a major airline disaster; Dow Chemical has produced a 20-page program to communicate with the public during a disaster; it even includes such particulars as who runs the copy machines. There are consulting firms to train corporate officials and provide expert crisis managers. Existence of a trained crisis team at UCIL could have limited the extent of the disaster with far smaller loss of life.

Management Inertia

The safety audit in 1982 pointed to the failure to use slip blinds before washing the pipe lines. Nevertheless, the workers continued the practice without corrective action. Early warning signals are commonly ignored. One analysis of hazard-warning structures has found that major hazards usually involve a series of small accidents prior to the occurrence of a major catastrophe [67]. The series of early warning signals noted earlier did not move the UCIL management to take adequate action [68–70].

A UCIL worker on monitoring the tank temperature:

> For a very long time we have not watched the temperature. There was no column to record it in the log books [71].

Companies use public relations to calm (or lull) the citizens. U.S. utility industry reactions to Chernobyl included PR statements that such an accident cannot happen here because "defense-in-depth" design makes "our nuclear plants among the safest in the world" [72]. Such statements are true but irrelevant: "safest in the world" may be unacceptable if the consequence of an accident occurrence is seen as catastrophic.

Some transnational companies maintain different standards for U.S. and overseas facilities or operations. Often this is done with approval of the government. For example, in November 1986, President Reagan gave approval for the export of drugs that had not been approved by the Federal Drug Administration for U.S. sale [73]. Similarly, cigarette manufacturers are not inhibited today from exporting their potentially deadly products.

Blind Technology Transfer

Technology is not transferable in isolation. It takes place from one societal/cultural setting to another. In the case of the United States and India, there are vast differences between these settings and they affect the success of the transfer. The T perspective does not capture the differences; we must turn to O.

Human error appears to be a major causative factor of "normal" disasters. Human societies have unique cultural characteristics. We have seen that American technology transferred to Japan develops in a unique way: Japanese manufacturing operations differ from American ones. American engineers designing a system for American use rarely consider foreign applications in their work. Commonly it is an afterthought introduced by the marketing staff.

American technology transferred to India must develop in a unique way. Therefore, application to an Indian facility of safety rules and procedures developed for American use is naive. For example, preventive maintenance is not natural to many Third World cultures. Workers are often assigned to jobs without understanding how to respond to nonroutine situations. It is often not clear to the workers that safety is as much a function of the human participants as of the mechanical system [74]. It is an important concern, therefore, that organizations and individuals in India act and react differently than those in Union Carbide's Institute, West Virginia, facility. Nevertheless, Union Carbide executives testified that the same safety standards were used in both facilities [75].

The tendency to assume other cultures are similar to the American and have the same values still seems to be a widely held misconception in the United States. The American military leadership failed to understand the Vietnamese communists; Americans cannot comprehend why the most devout Moslems do not consider democracy as the ideal system. The relative importance of O and P perspectives in China differs drastically from that in America and Western Europe. This situation becomes a dilemma when an American corporation effects technology transfer that carries with it the possibility of accidents considered unacceptable in the host country. The T-focused technical audits of the Union Carbide staff failed to consider vital aspects of Indian culture, such as attitudes toward preventive maintenance and precise adherence to rules of operation. In sum, we see a corporate imbalance of T and O perspectives as well as a failure to integrate them for technology transfer.

Management Short-Term View on Staffing

The losses being sustained by UCIL motivated the company to take money-saving steps. The decision to stop refrigerating the MIC storage tank helped, as did staff reductions among operating personnel. Prior to the accident the size of the production staff was reduced from 12 to 6 and maintenance staff from 6 to 2. One week before the accident the maintenance supervisor position on the second and third shifts was also removed and the responsibility added to those of the general production supervisor [63, 76]. The MIC control station had only a single person, although the manual specified the required number as 2.

The production supervisor (with the newly added maintenance responsibility) who was on duty the night of December 2–3, 1984, had been transferred from a carbide battery plant only one month earlier and could hardly have had an in-depth familiarity with the operating and newly transferred maintenance procedures [63].

The T perspective concern for safety is often in conflict with the O perspective concern for profit. The shorter planning horizon of the O perspective dominates the longer horizon of the T perspective with the result that longer term consequences are discounted (see Section 7.1).

In both military and industry, job rotation is considered desirable to develop able managers and executives. They should be familiar with all aspects of an organization. In a high-tech environment this modus operandi raises serious difficulties. The rotation does not facilitate deep familiarity with a complex operation. By the time the person has learned the details of the operation and its pitfalls, he is transferred to another job. At UCIL a technical manager especially trained at the Union Carbide Institute plant was transferred by UCIL to a non-MIC unit at Madras.

The U.S. military establishment has recognized this dilemma in some exceptional situations. It is exemplified by Admiral Rickover's long association with the Navy's nuclear submarine program. The striking contrast between the Navy and the utility industry nuclear programs thus comes as no surprise.

Organizational Linkages

Hamidia Hospital in Bhopal had very close linkages with UCIL. The company had contributed a wing with sophisticated equipment to the hospital. Many of the doctors have close connections with UCIL executives. This muted criticisms of UCIL procedures.

O Perspectives—The Government

Enforcement of worker safety and environmental rules is the responsibility of state governments. The department of labor in Madhya Pradesh State employed 15 factory inspectors to monitor more than 8,000 plants. Inspectors in some offices lacked typewriters and telephones; they had to travel by public bus and train. The Bhopal office had two inspectors, both mechanical engineers with little knowledge of chemical hazards [77]. Even so, some safety lapses were reported to the chief inspector of factories, but he renewed the license annually without acting on them.

The Bhopal development plan, issued August 25, 1975, specifically required plants manufacturing pesticides to be relocated to an industrial zone 15 miles away, yet the existing UCIL plant received an MIC license just two months later.

The Labor Minister opposed moving the plant because it is an Rs. 250 million investment and the trade union was against any move. Here there is a conflict-of-interest characteristic of different O perspectives: the safety of the nearby public versus the welfare of the labor force. It is reminiscent of the arguments in the United States on nuclear power plants—environmental versus economic concerns.

MIC was not a normal factory emission and, therefore, was not even monitored by the pollution control board. The provincial Labor Minister admitted that the state's industrial and environmental safeguards were deficient [77].

P Perspectives

A Human Limitation: *Ceteris Paribus* Projections

The human mind has difficulty in dealing with systems involving multiple interactions simultaneously. This is illustrated in forecasting. We easily focus on one technology and one variable or a few; we then study some of its impacts. Engineers project the evolution of microelectronics and assess future computer capabilities. Demographers forecast future population and look at urban crowding and potential food shortages. But forecasts tend to ignore the reality that everything changes simultaneously. This *ceteris paribus* habit, changing one parameter but assuming the rest remain unchanged, reflects a limitation of the human mind and is facilitated by the compartmentalization of problems. It is further justified by the fact that the joint probability of occurrence of two unlikely events is even less than their already low separate probabilities.

The *ceteris paribus* limitation accounts for the inability of otherwise able analysts to develop meaningful scenarios for the future, and it is a source of problems in risk management. An interconnected global village does not operate *ceteris paribus*. It has been noted elsewhere that we tend to ignore feedback loops. Kane [78] and Hardin [79] have demonstrated that "you can never merely do one thing." As has been shown earlier, the many interactions possible between system elements boggle the mind (see Section 2.3).

In risk analysis we similarly face a reality of complex systems with which the mind cannot cope. The usual solution is to ignore most interactions and concentrate on one hazard at a time and some of its presumably most significant risk implications.

Another Human Limitation: Misapplying Personal Experience

The human mind's integration of its own experiences is a ready source of distortion and error. We focus on two apparently contrary tendencies.

Discounting the Distant Past and Future

It has long been recognized that we tend to discount the future; that is, the further an event lies in the future, the less we weight its importance. The same applies to the past: events in the more distant past are discounted relative to events in the recent past. We shall return to this subject in Section 7.1.

Filtering Out Input Conflicting with Ingrained Views

Perhaps the most powerful barrier to new input is created by our existing mind-set. Upbringing and education implant a mindset that proves very resistant to change. Kuhn's *Structure of Scientific Revolutions* dealt with this in the hard sciences. Similarly, a person with strong technical training may be unable to do justice to multiple perspectives. The tendency to filter out images inconsistent with past experience is one of the descriptors of the P perspective (Table 3.1). New evidence is accepted if it is consistent with one's beliefs (developed through education and/or experience), rejected if it contradicts previously held perceptions. There is no active search for information that contradicts accepted beliefs.

The effect of such biases is reflected in the Bhopal case. Personal physical experience with a hazard tends to magnify its effects in the mind, while nonexperience tends to minimize its potential effects. As an old saw has it, "what I don't know can't hurt me."

In an interview after the accident, the Works Manager at UCIL was asked whether he did not know that even in fairly low concentrations exposure to MIC could be fatal. He gave "my view, the company's view":

> We do not know of any fatalities either in our plant or in other carbide plants due to MIC. We know that, at 20-ppm concentration, some people found it intolerable, unpleasant to stand around [80].

Once a hazard is recognized, the nature of its physical manifestation contributes to distortions. Human beings are more fearful of known dangers they cannot readily sense than of those they can easily detect. There is the well-known fear of the dark. The Works Manager at UCIL:

> You see, about phosgene, it is much less perceptible than MIC; the symptoms appear after eight hours. So our view is that phosgene is potentially more dangerous [80].

These comments also remind us of a problem often encountered with the O and P perspectives: they may be difficult to separate without much more in-depth interviews. That is, we cannot be sure, based on the interview, whether the Works Manager gave his own or his company views.

In most societies distortions are also caused by the media. In the West sensational news is amplified and unexciting news is downplayed. As a result the individual overestimates the likelihood of being murdered and underestimates dying of asthma and stroke [7, 81].

A Worker's Perspective

Human reaction to a fearsome occurrence is intuitive. Suman Dey, a UCIL worker, has recounted the event:

> There was a tremendous sound, a messy boiling sound, underneath the slab, like a cauldron. The whole slab was vibrating. [He started to run away, heard a loud noise behind him, saw the concrete crack and gas shoot out of a tall stack connected to the tank.] I panicked . . . [When the plant superintendent arrived] he came in pretty much of a panic. He said, 'What should we do?' [71].

With no senior supervisory personnel on site Sunday night, the operators did not activate the alarm for hours, fearing censure for creating public panic. The operator washing the MIC line did not know about the seepage of water into the MIC tank. Not surprisingly, the empty tank that was kept for pressure relief in case of excess pressure was never used.

The fractionalization of job responsibilities is another characteristic problem, particularly in areas where the work force has limited training and education. It may be tolerable in a system with loose coupling, but it is dangerous when the coupling in the system is tight.

Ignorance of Outsiders

The residents of nearby squatter settlements were poor and often illiterate. They knew nothing about the plant and its alarm system or MIC and its toxicity. We should stress that even the Bhopal chief administrative officer revealed that "I have never heard of a compound called MIC," while a factory doctor insisted that the gas is not lethal and only causes eye and lung irritation [77]. Many residents ran toward the plant when the alarm sounded.

An Exception: A Well-Trained Professional

In an adjacent plant, Straw Products Ltd., the General Manager evacuated about 1400 workers in five buses as soon as the MIC leak was detected. Almost all lives in this plant were saved. This executive had been a Brigadier in the Indian army and his military training provided the needed crisis management capability.

The requirements placed on an operator in an emergency situation are in some sense the inverse of those faced in normal working conditions. He is expected to make correct inferences and decisions about complex phenomena in a short time under great stress [82]. It is a situation quite familiar to a military establishment. A peacetime army's leadership is very different from that needed in wartime (see Section 4.1).

The Vast Opportunities for Human Error

The opportunities for human error increase exponentially as the system size and complexity grows. The description of the events surrounding the accident under the T perspective suggests some of the realities of the situation. Human errors may be (1) unintentional or (2) intentional. The following are illustrative of the experiences throughout the world:

1. Poor alertness, confusion, illness (mental or physical), drug-caused debilitation, ignorance, misunderstanding (possibly due to language problems), overwork, laziness;

2. Hostility (for example, revenge against a superior), bribery or pay-off (for example, to sign-off on procedure even if not followed, to accept defective equipment).

There is no way to eliminate these causes even if a large part of the operation is automated.

Integration of T + O + P

The three types of perspective influence each other. A case in point was the design of the processing equipment at Bhopal. It was a product of the technologists (T perspective) with some recognition of the U.S. operating environment, that is, the organizational setting O for such plants in the United States. In addition, human factors were taken into account in the design as well as the instruction manuals (perspectives of American workers and American supervisors). Even for American installations the integration of such a set of perspectives does not prevent problems. We find:

- Overconfidence in current technical knowledge;
- Failure to recognize interactions among system components that have been designed relatively independently;
- Failure to anticipate people problems and human responses in crises;
- Failure to anticipate the combinations of low-likelihood errors with severe consequences (Perrow's "normal accidents" [16]).

When such a system is transferred into another culture, such as India, we have to consider Indian O and P perspectives. It is unreasonable to expect the integration of the U.S. perspectives to be similar to that of the Indian ones. And this suggests a striking weakness in the decision process of multinational corporations.

We see reflections of this situation in other settings. The marketing failures of American products in Japan is well known. General Motors (unlike BMW) for many years exhibited a corporate blindness to Japanese concern with quality, size, and product prestige, not to mention the need for right-hand drive, thus failing miserably in marketing its products in Japan. Johnson & Johnson learned that Japanese consumers pay much more attention to the packaging of a product than do American consumers. It therefore repackaged its products for the Japanese market and has been successful.

6.4 On the Nuclear Accidents

Three Mile Island and Chernobyl have become identified with industrial nuclear power accidents. We shall comment on them briefly and point to commonalities with the accidents already discussed in some detail.

At Three Mile Island the errors included inadequate training of the utility company operators and supervisors, toleration of poor control room practices, and failure of the construction engineers (Babcock & Wilcox) to inform their nuclear reactor customers of persistent failures of pilot operated relief valves. The President's Commission concluded

> . . . the fundamental problems are people-related problems and not equip-
> ment problems . . . wherever we looked, we found problems with the hu-
> man beings who operate the plant, with the management that runs the key
> organization, and with the agency that is charged with assuring the safety of
> nuclear power plants [25, p. 8].

At Chernobyl a mishap on April 26, 1986, occurred in the context of a turbine test. Faulty actions caused a loss of the water that continuously cools the uranium fuel rods in the reactor's core. This led to a partial core meltdown. As of August 1986, 31 fatalities were noted and over 200 were hospitalized with radiation sickness. A total of 135,000 people had to be evacuated and the long-term effect is estimated at 5,000 to 24,000 additional cancer deaths in the Soviet Union over the next 70 years [83]. While Westerners have pointed to technical flaws in the reactor design [84], the Soviet report to the International Atomic Energy Agency focused on a series of human errors, mistakes that violated safety regulations and, in some cases, common sense. Andronik Petrosyants, head of the State Committee for the Use of Atomic Energy, said:

> For almost 12 hours the reactor was functioning with the emergency cooling system switched off . . . It is quite possible that the [previous] smooth operations brought on complacency and that this led to irresponsibility, negligence, lack of discipline and caused grave consequences [85].

Valeri Legasov, first deputy director of the principal Soviet atomic research institute, added:

> If at least one violation of the six would be removed, the accident would not have happened. The engineers psychologically did not believe that such a sequence of improper actions would be committed. Such a sequence of human actions was so unlikely that the engineer did not include [it] in the project. Is that human or technical [85]?

The six errors are:

1. *The crucial error:* The operational reactivity margin at the reactor core was dropped substantially below the permissible level (6 to 8 rods equivalent instead of 30); result: ineffectiveness of the emergency protection system.

2. The power of the reactor was allowed to drop below the 700-MW level prescribed for the tests; result: reactor difficult to control.

3. During the experiment all eight main circulation pumps were switched on, individual pump discharges exceeding specified limits; result: lowered water levels, coolant temperature in main circulation circuit approaching saturation temperature.

4. Automatic blocking devices were shut off in an attempt to prevent the reactor from shutting down (so the testing could be continued); result: no automatic reactor shutdown capability.

5. Defense systems controlling water level and steam pressure were blocked off; result: reactor protection systems cut off.

6. The emergency cooling system was shut off over a 24-hr period in violation of regulations; result: inability to reduce the scale of the accident [86].

In both Three Mile Island and Chernobyl the engineers had focused on the T perspective while neglecting the O and P perspectives, which deal with people. The designs had specifically considered technical failures resulting in large-scale consequences but underestimated the significance of nontechnical failures, precipitating a chain of events inducing compound technical failures with similar large-scale consequences. It should also be noted that proposals to correct problems made by technologists nearly always involve "technological fixes." They usually add to the complexity of the system and create new sources of failure. The more complex the system, the more unpredictable it becomes [87]. In a large computer program we see that each correction of errors introduces new ones. No general program exists that can correct the errors of any program.

The Chernobyl experience also teaches some unique organizational lessons that carry over to other accidents [88]. First, existing government and industry have neither the competence nor the credibility to do what is needed. A new organization, the Pripet Research Industrial Association, was established to manage decontamination and research on the Chernobyl site; it has 6,000 employees. Second, the scope of the accident was such that it is difficult to imagine how one can meaningfully prepare for it. A million cubic meters of soil have been moved so far and the scope of the water supply problem is staggering. Third, such an organization must have longevity to deal with both acute and chronic problems with high effectiveness for decades. For example, it must monitor the sarcophagus around the damaged reactor for decades. How will the Russian political transformation affect this ability? There are fifteen Chernobyl-type reactors still operating in the former Soviet Union. Another accident, fortunately minor, occurred in March 1992.

Another recent examination of the Three Mile Island, Bhopal, and Chernobyl accidents focuses on deficiencies in the four generic system control structures:

- *Inherent controls:* original design to ensure a stable system that is easy to control (T type);
- *Engineered controls:* procedures designed in to maintain stability and automatically carry out certain transitions and protective functions (T type);
- *Societal controls:* laws, regulations, norms, and practices (O type);
- *Personnel controls:* operational instructions, work practices (O/P types).

Each of these industrial systems exhibited deficiencies in each of the four kinds of control structures. For example, personnel control failures are exemplified by operators at the plant unaware of problems with a failed open pressure relief valve (Three Mile Island), lax management attitudes regarding obvious deficiencies in safety (Bhopal), and major plant tests initiated without reactor safety clearance (Chernobyl). Engineered control failures include misleading indication of pressure relief valve position (Three Mile Island), unavailable safety systems at the plant (Bhopal), and the possibility of disconnecting crucial safety systems (Chernobyl).

The control structures are, of course, interrelated: tightening one often leads to loosening another. The study observes:

> It is a relatively recent recognition that organization and management can have an influence on the safety of technical systems . . . a complex system will require many different views, depending on the control task under consideration . . . The complexity of the technologies can be managed only with a consideration of multiple perspectives (technical, organizational, personal) . . . [89].

Several systemic T, O, and P contradictions that are at the root of such industrial accidents are cited by Shrivastava.

- T: efficiency versus flexibility in design, size versus communication/ control capability, and automation versus reliability;
- O/P: competing stakeholder demands, productivity versus safety, opposing political pressures, and work experience versus vigilance [90].

Another aspect of uncertainty is confusion under pressure. In military terms we have "the fog of battle." Communications break down; human beings operating at great stress make unwarranted assumptions. The crisis period in Europe preceding World War I is a classic example [91]. In looking at today's sophisticated strategic command and control system, the State Department's George Ball reminds us:

> The decisions of politicians and ultimately military commanders are never—and will never be—made in a sterile environment or dictated solely by mathematical possibilities. They will reflect the probability of overhasty, poorly calculated, responses; the pressure of alarmed and uninformed public opinion inflamed by propaganda and factual error; the fears, ambitions, frustrations, and anger of military and political leaders playing by quite different rules, acting and reacting on the basis of rumor and misinformation [92].

At Three Mile Island, communications between the Nuclear Regulatory Commission and Three Mile Island were less than satisfactory from the beginning. Harold Collins, the assistant director for emergency preparedness in the Office of State Programs, testified:

> I think there was uncertainty in the operations center as to precisely what was going on at the facility and the question was being raised in the minds of many as to whether or not those people up there would do the right thing at the right time [25, p. 118].

The operators in the plant's control room were unaware for hours that a critical valve was stuck open and draining cooling water out of the reactor. Joseph Hendrie, the Chairman of the Nuclear Regulatory Commission, and Governor Richard Thornburg of Pennsylvania were unsure whether to evacuate the area.

> His information is ambiguous, mine is nonexistent and—I don't know, it's like a couple of blind men staggering around making decisions [93].

Before leaving the subject of nuclear energy management, we note that the reader may also find the multiple perspective examination of the Nuclear Waste Policy Act of 1982 by Clary insightful [94]. By 1973, when a radioactive waste leak occurred at the Hanford, WA, installation, the issue of nuclear waste disposal and its impact on the environment was becoming a serious public concern. Congressional action was the outgrowth of the interplay between available scientific information, the organizational capacity of federal agencies, and the fragile and fleeting political consensus forged by the nuclear industry, the states, environmental groups, and the Department of Energy. On the technical side, many scientific aspects of waste disposal were not fully understood. On the organizational side, the nuclear industry was anxious to shift the political risks of disposal to the government and thus became a major force behind the proposed Act. The environmentalists played a surprisingly minor role, supporting the legislation but reluctant to see it result in potential benefits to the utility industry. The states and Indian tribes were concerned about community costs and health and sought an effective role in site selection. The Department of Energy welcomed the Act but found the balancing of the long-term scientific and short-term political considerations difficult; inevitably it succumbed to the latter.

Implementation of the Act brought to the forefront formidable obstacles, leading to its amendment in 1987. The focus now was on just one location, the State of Nevada. The dominance of the nuclear industry was still evident and the changes did not resolve the conflicts of the various interests. Clearly, the Congressional decision-making process in this technical area remains badly flawed.

6.5 Implications and Prospects

The technological fix will not suffice. The first lesson is that we cannot eliminate the possibility of catastrophic failure in complex systems that involve human operators. Bhopal is neither the first nor the last accident to demonstrate human error as a key factor. Three Mile Island and Chernobyl show a similar pattern on the part of the two superpowers. It is, in our opinion, counterproductive for engineers to look invariably to technological fixes. This instills in management the illusion that more technology can solve their problems. There are multitudes of combinations of unlikely accident factors; and, as noted earlier, systematic attack to eliminate them totally is unrealistic. For example, added controls and monitoring systems increase complexity and add entirely new sources of error. Therefore, the first option that should always be considered focuses on reducing the complexity by reorganization or modification of the system.

- **Level 1: Seek Means to Reduce the Likelihood of Catastrophic Consequences with the Given System**

Some obvious steps may be deduced from an examination of the several perspectives.

- T: Try to make the system "safe-fail" by decoupling subsystems so that an accident can be bounded or limited to one subsystem.
- O/P: Transform instruction manuals to allow for cultural differences, resulting in effective equivalence in practice rather than merely literal equivalence in language; bring in individuals in the early stages of planning overseas operations who have the necessary perspectives to balance the likely dominance of T and U.S.-oriented O perspectives.
- O: Insist on crisis management training for all managerial personnel or create a special crisis management team, as is done in a growing number of American corporations such as United Airlines and Dow Chemical [66]; this splits operations into routine and crisis conditions, with distinct expertise for each; the crisis team would also be alert for early warning signals such as minor incidents.

- O: Recognize that many governments do not have the resources to adequately monitor compliance with their own safety rules and controls; therefore, accept the burden of corporate responsibility to augment the level of local plant monitoring to fill this gap.
- O: Institutionalize the risk assessment and safety function in the company, clearly specify its responsibility and authority, and require this function to report directly to the local top management, short-circuiting the bureaucratic hierarchy.
- P: Give investigative journalists and "whistleblowers" more protection in exposing poor practices, thus anticipating potential catastrophes.

Recognizing the limits of the analytic or T view of the world, we call on the organizational and personal perspectives to enhance our understanding. Persons with certain backgrounds are likely to have a different balance (or imbalance) in perspectives than do scientists or engineers. We note, in particular, that lawyers, career bureaucrats, and journalists are likely to be attuned or sensitive to such factors as:

- O: Cultural differences relevant to technology transfer; proprietary nature of relevant information; stonewalling in the face of disaster ("circling the wagons"); governmental and corporate bureaucracy, such as ignorance, obsolete regulations and SOPs, nonenforcement, political pressure, suppression of uncertainties; and organizational linkages;
- P: Unintentional errors by workers and intentional failures.

The journalist can effect communication when the engineer/scientist is stymied; the lawyer can circumvent proprietary concerns. The bureaucrat can pinpoint other bureaucrats' maneuvers that escape analysts' detection and figure out how to make a safety audit group effective in a large, disinterested organization, for example, making it autonomous, reporting directly to top management.

Assiduous implementation of all these steps, difficult at best, still gives no guarantee of catastrophe prevention. There is another path.

• Level 2: Redesign the Existing System to Reduce Dangers

It is often possible to redesign the existing system to reduce dangers further. This suggests an altered design philosophy giving much greater weight to:

- T: Decoupling of subsystems as suggested, an easier task in the design phase than a posteriori;

- O: Creating a high-reliability organization with an entirely different outlook and culture than is normal in either U.S. or non-U.S. companies.

- O/P: Encompass the unique requirements of use in other cultural environments; this means system customization to the culture as needed to increase safety.

The approach calls for early introduction of multiple perspectives in the design phase. But this also cannot assure elimination of the possibility of catastrophic accidents. Redesign can respond to situations that can be anticipated, including some events previously thought inconceivable. But not all events can ever be anticipated, and new possibilities may arise from the redesign itself. This leaves us with the paradoxical situation that the human operator is most needed when a completely unanticipated situation is at hand, "the condition when he is least able to respond in a constructively creative way" [82].

• Level 3: Probe Conceptually Different System Solutions That Avoid Catastrophic Consequences Altogether

Common sense dictates that there be a search for alternative systems in which failure simply cannot lead to unacceptably catastrophic consequences. One example is a shift of transportation modes, in case of oil from sea to land (Canada). Another is a shift of production modes, in case of MIC as implemented by the Bayer facility in Dormagen, West Germany. It has produced MIC for 20 years using nonpoisonous raw materials [95].

- T: Alter the transportation or production process or use materials in such a way that the same need can be met in a technologically new way, one that excludes catastrophic accidents.

This constitutes a challenge to the technological community and an impetus for innovation. In the field of energy, we clearly have alternatives to nuclear energy. We expect that conceptually different system solutions will become available, for example, solar systems. But suppose we fail. Then . . .

• Level 4: Ask the Final Question

A societal decision is now unavoidable: can the consequence of a catastrophic accident be tolerated or not? History has shown that the human and ecological resilience to disaster is enormous, but there are limits! The evolution of technology drives the growth of system complexity inexorably and will raise even graver challenges than Bhopal and Chernobyl.

Consider the following three disturbing prospects:

Possible New Kinds of Catastrophic Occurrence

Forecasters envision the age of information technology giving way some time in the twenty-first century to the age of biotechnology. In 1976 ebola fever was observed in Zaire; in 1982 a new virulent strain of *E coli* emerged in the United States. In the same year the human immunodeficiency virus (leading to AIDS) was identified and by 1992 12.9 million were infected with it. By 2000 3.1 billion people will be crammed into urban "microbe heavens" while the rural poor will offer intimate contact with animals hosting viruses. Transportation has historically been an effective carrier of plagues: the Black Death in 1346 from Mongolia to Italy, the sixteenth century European explorers wiping out much of the vulnerable American Indian population. The advent of the twenty-first century will see technology creating the true global village, facilitating the rapid movement of huge populations and thus the transmission of new strains of viruses. We are engaged in a running battle with bacteria, the world's most successful form of life. They alter and adapt their genes to a changing environment, a process of mutation that is not random but suggests primitive learning operating at microbic levels [96].

A future bioengineering error creating a deadly virus that sweeps over the world with lightning speed is a possibility. So far, it is only a figment of the novelist's imagination, but it already seems far less remote than it did twenty years ago.

Risk Homeostasis

The Challenger launch explosion in 1986 was traced to faulty O ring design on the shuttle's rocket booster (in combination with low temperature). The Apollo 13 near-disaster was caused by the interaction of failures of the oxygen and hydrogen tanks in the spacecraft and the astronauts' attention diverted by an indicator light. At NASA deviations from the norm were calculated probabilistically and were assumed to be controllable. As a recent study of Challenger concluded, the launch decision was a rule-based decision, not a violation of rules [97]. Another study points out that changes made to make a system safer often lead to taking greater risks in another. Thus, an experiment has shown that antilock brake systems tended to make the driver speed up, turn faster, tailgate, and brake harder. This is now called "risk homeostasis" [98]. The same concept worked in the opposite way when Sweden changed from left-hand side to right-hand side driving. Instead of the expected rise in accidents, it was found that drivers compensated for their unfamiliarity with the new pattern by driving more carefully.

More Severe Demands on Management Capability

America's national strategic command and control capability is already seriously constrained by the lack of expertise, or illiteracy, in electronic technology on the part of responsible military commanders who must make critical decisions. According to a recent Undersecretary of Defense, the Pentagon has been quite unable to properly manage the command and control program. And there is even more concern regarding the ability of a president to manage a nuclear, biological, chemical, or electronic warfare crisis. He may well be a figurehead, an "honorary commander-in-chief" [93].

Debates on questions such as those posed here are likely to move center stage in other technology areas in the coming decades. Finally, we should resist the temptation of extremists at both ends of the spectrum:

- Those who discount possible adverse long-term consequences to humans and the environment and only see short-term costs to business;
- Those who discount the long-term resilience of humans and the ecosystem and see only the near-term adverse impacts of technology.

6.6 Conclusion

Risk analysts recognized in the 1980s that the understanding and management of risk requires what we term multiple perspectives. We could readily develop a table of distinct T, O, and P risk perspective characteristics (Table 6.1) analogous to the earlier general comparison (Table 3.1). We have taken a close look at the *Exxon Valdez* oil spill and the Bhopal chemical accident and shown how much O and P perspectives add to the traditional T perspective and make possible a fuller, more meaningful basis for decision and action.

Acknowledgments

Section 6.2 reprinted with permission from *The Challenge of the 21st Century* by Harold A. Linstone with Ian I. Mitroff by permission of the State University of New York Press, 1994, State University of New York. Part of section 6.3 reprinted by permission of Elsevier Science Inc., from "Notes on the Bhopal Accident: Risk Analysis and Multiple Perspectives," by B. Bowonder and H. A. Linstone, *Technological Forecasting and Social Change*, Vol. 32, 1987, pp. 183–202.

References

[1]   Starr, C., "Benefit-Cost Studies in Sociotechnical Systems," *Perspective on Benefit-Risk Decision Making*. Washington, D.C.: Committee on Public Engineering Policy, National Academy of Engineering, 1972.

[2]   Inhaber, H., *Energy Risk Assessment*, New York: Gordon & Breach Science Publishers, 1982.

[3]   Hohenemser, C., "Summary of Panel Discussion and Commentary," in *The Analysis of Actual Versus Perceived Risks*, V. Covello (ed.), New York: Plenum Press, 1983.

[4]   Litai, D., "The Public Perception of Risk," in *The Analysis of Actual Versus Perceived Risks*, V. Covello (ed.), New York: Plenum Press, 1983.

[5]   Seligman, D., "How Much Is Your Life Worth?" *Fortune*, March 3, 1986, pp. 25–27.

[6]   Tversky, A., and D. Kahneman, "Judgment Under Uncertainty: Heuristics and Biases," *Science*, Vol. 185, 1974, pp. 1124–1131.

[7]   Fischhoff, B., et al., *Acceptable Risk*, Cambridge, England: Cambridge University Press, 1981.

[8]   Fischhoff, B., et al., "Perceived vs. Actual Disagreements about Risk," in *The Analysis of Actual Versus Perceived Risks*, V. Covello (ed.), New York: Plenum Press, 1983.

[9]   Turner, B. A., "Organizational Responses to Hazard," in *Risk: A Seminar Series*, H. Kunreuther (ed.), Report CP-82-S2, Laxenburg, Austria: International Institute for Applied Systems Analysis, 1982.

[10] Covello, V., "The Perception of Technological Risks: An Overview," *Technological Forecasting and Social Change*, Vol. 23, 1983, pp. 285–297.

[11] Douglas, M., and A. Wildavsky, *Risk and Culture*, Berkeley, CA: University of California Press, 1982, p. 198.

[12] Thompson, M., "Political Culture: An Introduction," Working Paper WP-80-175, Laxenburg, Austria: International Institute for Applied Systems Analysis, 1980, p. 7.

[13] Thompson, M., "The Cultural Approach to Risk: The Case of Poverty," in *Risk: A Seminar Series*, H. Kunreuther (ed.), Report CP-82-S2, Laxenburg, Austria: International Institute for Applied Systems Analysis, 1982, p. 370.

[14] Kunreuther, H., et al., *Risk Analysis and Decision Processes*, Berlin: Springer-Verlag, 1983, p. 14.

[15] Ascher, W., and W. Overholt, *Strategic Planning and Forecasting*, New York: J. Wiley & Sons, 1983, p. 161.

[16] Perrow, C. E., *Normal Accidents*, New York: Basic Books, 1984.

[17] Lawless, E. W., *Technology and Social Shock,* New Brunswick, NJ: Rutgers University Press, p. 229.

[18] Holloway, M., "Sounding Out Science," *Scientific American,* Oct. 1996, pp. 106–112.

[19] Alaska Oil Spill Commission, *Spill: The Wreck of the Exxon Valdez.* Final Report, Feb. 1990.

[20] "The Future of Big Oil," *Fortune,* May 8, 1989, pp. 46–54.

[21] O'Leary, M. H., Testimony for Cordova District Fishermen United to the Alaska Oil Spill Commission, 1989.

[22] The Exxon Valdez Oil Spill: Report to the President, National Response Team, Department of Transportation, May 1989.

[23] *Wall Street Journal,* March 16, 1990; *Los Angeles Times,* March 17, 1990; *New York Times,* March 13, 1991.

[24] *Anchorage Daily News,* March 25, 1989; *Time,* March 26, 1990.

[25] Kemeny, J. et al., *Report of the President's Commission on the Accident at Three Mile Island,* New York: Pergamon Press, 1979.

[26] *Wall Street Journal,* March 16, 1990.

[27] "Anatomy of an Oil Spill," written and reported by John Tuttle, produced by Oregon Public Broadcasting System, *Frontline,* March 20, 1990.

[28] *Anchorage Daily News,* August 3, 1989.

[29] *Anchorage Daily News,* April 21, 1989.

[30] *New York Times,* Oct. 27, 1991.

[31] *Wall Street Journal,* July 6, 1989.

[32] *Anchorage Daily News,* May 14, 1989.

[33] *New York Times,* Aug. 5, 1991.

[34] *Los Angeles Times,* March 16, 1990.

[35] *Los Angeles Times,* March 18, 1990.

[36] *Los Angeles Times,* Feb. 28, 1990.

[37] *Los Angeles Times,* March 17, 1990.

[38] *New York Times Magazine,* Aug. 4, 1991.

[39] *New York Times,* April 25, 1991.

[40] *New York Times,* April 30, 1991.

[41] *Anchorage Daily News,* April 20, 1989.

[42] *New York Times,* March 24, 1991.

[43] *Wall Street Journal,* Feb. 12, 1993.

[44] *Time,* March 26, 1990.

[45] *Wall Street Journal,* March 16, 1990.

[46] *Los Angeles Times,* March 24, 1990.

[47] *Los Angeles Times,* March 25, 1990.

[48] *New York Times,* July 11, 1992.

[49] *New York Times,* March 21, 1991.

[50] *Los Angeles Times,* Feb. 7, 1992.

[51] *Money,* July 1989, pp. 77–83.

[52] *Los Angeles Times,* March 28, 1990.

[53] *New York Times,* Sept. 18, 1990; *New York Times,* March 14, 1991.

[54] Cousteau, J.-M., Interview, *CBS This Morning,* March 23, 1990.

[55] *Business Week,* April 2, 1990.

[56] Mitroff, I. I., and T. Pauchant, *We're So Big and Powerful That Nothing Can Happen to Us: An Investigation of America's Crisis Prone Organizations,* New York: Birch Lane Press, 1991.

[57] LaPorte, T., "High Reliability Organizations Project," unpublished memorandum, Berkeley: University of California, Dept. of Political Science, 1989.

[58] Bowonder, B., "The Bhopal Accident," *Technological Forecasting and Social Change,* Vol. 32, 1987, pp. 169–182.

[59] Bowonder, B., and H. A. Linstone, "Notes on the Bhopal Accident: Risk Analysis and Multiple Perspectives," *Technological Forecasting and Social Change,* Vol. 32, 1987, pp. 183–202.

[60] NIOSH/OSHA, Occupational Health Guidelines for Chemical Hazards, Report No. 81-123, Department of Health and Human Services, Washington, DC, 1981.

[61] ACGIH, Documentation of the American Conference of Governmental Industrial Hygienists, Pittsburgh, PA, 1984.

[62] Rameshesan, R., "Bhopal Gas Tragedy: Callousness Abounding," *Economic and Political Weekly,* Vol. 20, 1985, pp. 56–57.

[63] Morehouse, W., and A. Subramanian, *The Bhopal Tragedy,* New York: Council on International and Public Affairs, 1986.

[64] Union Carbide Corporation, Bhopal Methyl Isocyanate Incident: Investigation Team Report, Danbury, CT: Union Carbide Corporation, March 1985.

[65] Ascher, W., and W. Overholt, *Strategic Planning and Forecasting,* New York: John Wiley and Sons, 1983.

[66] "Coping With Catastrophe," *Time,* Feb. 24, 1986, p. 53.

[67] Lees, F. P., "The Hazard Warning Structure of Major Hazards," *Transactions of the Institute of Chemical Engineers,* Vol. 60, 1982, pp. 211–221.

[68] Bowonder, B., "The Bhopal Incident," *The Environmentalist,* Vol. 5, 1985, pp. 89–103.

[69] Bowonder, B., "Avoiding Future Bhopals," *Environment,* Vol. 27, 1985, pp. 6–16.

[70] Subramanian, A., and J. Gaya, "Toward Corporate Responsibility," *Business India,* Vol. 202, 1985, pp. 42–54.

[71] *Oregonian,* Jan. 30, 1985.

[72] Advertisement, *Newsweek,* May 26, 1986.

[73] Castleman, B. I., "The Double Standards in Industrial Hazards," in *The Export of Hazard,* J. Ives (ed.), Boston, MA: Routledge and Kegan Paul, 1985, pp. 60–89.

[74] Lanza, G. R., "Blind Technology Transfer: The Bhopal Example," *Environment, Science, and Technology,* Vol. 19, 1985, pp. 581–582.

[75] Gladwin, T. N., "The Bhopal Tragedy," *NYU Business,* Vol. 5, 1985, pp. 17–21.

[76] DeGrazia, A. A., "Cloud Over Bhopal," *Popular Prakhashan,* Bombay, 1985.

[77] *Oregonian,* Jan. 31, 1985.

[78] Kane, J., "A Primer for a New Cross-Impact Language—KSIM," *Technological Forecasting and Social Change,* Vol. 4, 1972, pp. 369–382.

[79] Hardin, G., "The Tragedy of the Commons," *Science,* Vol. 162, 1968, pp. 1243–1248.

[80] Bidwai, P., "Deadly Delay in Bhopal," *The Times of India,* Dec. 19, 1984, p. 6.

[81] Slovic, P., et al., "Facts and Fears: Understanding Perceived Risk," manuscript, Eugene, OR: Decision Research Inc., 1981.

[82] Otway, H. J., and R. Misenta, "Some Human Performance Paradoxes of Nuclear Operations," *Futures,* Vol. 12, 1980, pp. 340–357.

[83] *Washington Post,* Aug. 30, 1986.

[84] *New York Times,* Aug. 26, 1986.

[85] *Washington Post,* Aug. 22, 1986.

[86] *Nuclear Engineering,* Vol. 31/387, 1986, p. 3.

[87] Simon, J. C., "Complexity Concepts and the Limits of Computable Models," *Technological Forecasting and Social Change,* Vol. 13, 1979, pp. 1–11.

[88] Ausubel, J. H., "Political Fallout: What Fate Awaits Chernobyl in the New World Order?" *Sciences,* Vol. 31, Nov./Dec. 1991, pp. 16–21.

[89] Wahlström, B., "Avoiding Technological Risks," *Technological Forecasting and Social Change,* Vol. 42, 1992, pp. 359–360, 363.

[90] Shrivastava, P., "Technological and Organizational Roots of Industrial Crises: Lessons from *Exxon Valdez* and Bhopal," *Technological Forecasting and Social Change,* Vol. 45, 1994, pp. 237–254.

[91] Tuchman, B., *The Guns of August.* New York: Macmillan, 1962.

[92] Ball, G. W., *New York Review of Books,* Nov. 8, 1984, p. 5.

[93] Ford, D., *The Button,* New York: Simon & Schuster, 1985, pp. 88, 121, 186, 227.

[94] Clary, B. B., "The Enactment of the Nuclear Waste Policy Act of 1982: A Multiple Perspectives Explanation," *Policy Studies Review,* Vol. 10, No. 4, Winter 1991/92, pp. 90–102.

[95] Subramanian, S. K., "Die Bhopal-Katastrophe," *Echo,* April 1986, Carl Duisberg Gesellschaft, Köln, Germany.

[96] Garrett, L., *The Coming Plague: Newly Emerging Diseases in a World Out of Balance,* New York: Farrar, Straus & Giroux, 1994.

[97] Vaughan, D., *The Challenger Launch Decision: Risky Technology, Culture and Deviance at NASA,* Chicago, IL: University of Chicago Press, 1998.

[98] Wilde, G., *Target Risk: Dealing with the Danger of Death, Disease and Damage in Everyday Decisions,* Toronto: PDE Publications; Castor & Columba, 1994.

7

Technology: Forecasting and Planning

Die Zeit, die ist ein sonderbar Ding.
(Time is a strange thing.)
                    Hugo von Hoffmansthal, *Der Rosenkavalier*

The body travels more easily than the mind . . . We have not really budged
a step until we take up residence in someone else's point of view.
                    John Erskine, *The Complete Life*

Our comparison of the characteristics of T, O, and P (Table 3.1) noted the
striking difference in their planning horizons or discount rates. The significance
of this strongly affects the ability to integrate planning with action and explains
the frequent frustration of analysts as well as research and development staffs
with action-oriented corporate management and myopic politicians. We shall
therefore begin with a focus on this problem.

7.1 The Discounting Dilemma

Case studies such as the *Exxon Valdez* (Section 6.2) reveal how the short-term
and long-term views become the basis for conflict. For the oil company and
most Alaskans, the short-term view dominates. Environmental damage is seen
as requiring an intensive short-term clean-up effort. For the environmentalists
the major concern is the long-term impact. For the oil company high near-term
profits call for maximum oil sales and minimum regulatory requirements; for
the state's citizens, uninterrupted oil drilling means jobs, no state taxes, and an

215

annual check—all immediate benefits. The environmentalist is concerned with the adverse global impact of fossil fuel use (specifically carbon dioxide emission) and the long-term need for nonpolluting energy sources.

The *Exxon Valdez* is just a microcosm of the universal conflict between short-term and long-term concerns.[1] Over 2000 years ago, Aristotle already defined two distinct kinds of economics:

- *Chrematistics:* the manipulation of property and wealth to maximize the short-term return to the owner;
- *Oikonomia:* management of the household to increase its value to all its members over the long run [1].

The population and technology explosions amplify the effect of the chrematistic priority on the near term. The desire for immediate sexual gratification seems obvious to all; the long-term oikonomic impacts such as environmental degradation and megacity growth are not a vital concern for most Americans. There is heated debate on "the right to life," a near-term personal issue; while the population explosion, a huge long-term societal issue, is largely ignored. The same bias motivates many of our self-centered youth and senior citizens. A recent survey found that

> the typical young person doesn't want to hear about it "unless it's knocking on my door" . . . [a 22-year old entering law school] "people my age group are] only concerned about issues that affect them. When the drinking age went up, quite a few people were upset" [2].

Another example of the "fly now, pay later" philosophy among young people is the fact that about half of the 3.5 million unplanned pregnancies annually are attributed to the lack of any birth control. The immediate "benefit" of spontaneous pleasure outweighs the "cost" of pregnancy later [3]. A "buy now, pay later" philosophy is even promoted commercially at the high-school level. Mastercard International has proudly proclaimed that 10% of high-school juniors and seniors now use credit cards regularly. At the other end of the age spectrum, over 55% of doctors' patients over 65 fail to keep taking prescribed medicines vital to their long-term survival. A frequently cited reason is the disappearance of the immediate symptoms. Failure to follow doctors' preventive or therapeutic orders results in 125,000 preventable deaths annually at all ages [4].

---

1. Also see Section 2.8.

The pattern pervades the economy. Following the oil shock in 1973, a great interest developed in alternative energy sources (such as solar and synthetic fuels) and reducing America's dependence on foreign oil. More energy-efficient cars were produced and businesses became energy-efficient. However, as the oil crisis waned, the enthusiasm also faded. Gas guzzling cars are again popular and our oil imports have grown prodigiously. Funding for alternative energy sources has largely dried up. In a generation, the experience was largely forgotten.

Evidently, our horizon shrinks in both directions as we move away from the present—toward the past as well as toward the future. The experiments of Tversky and Kahneman clearly show how human beings distort the integration of their personal experience [5]. Recent events tend to be overstressed in comparison with more remote ones.

Belching smoke stacks mean work; protection of the forests means closure of lumber mills and stagnating mill towns. The U.S. government, bowing to business pressures, has been the principal stumbling block to a global treaty for effective reduction of carbon dioxide emissions, which constitute the foremost cause of atmospheric warming. As an old adage has it, "all politics is local." Utilities and automobile manufacturers cite the near-term costs to them and, like tobacco companies with cancer, dismiss or suppress the scientific evidence of long-term harm. In the case of Chernobyl, chronic monitoring will be needed for decades, not years.

In all these cases, the conflict seems rather one-sided, because (1) the seriousness of the long-term effects cannot be proven beyond a reasonable doubt, (2) corrective action will hurt those who exercise political power today, (3) effects may be harmful to a future generation that has no voting power today, and (4) human beings resist changing their habits.

Dow Corning knew in the early 1970s that some silicone gel could seep out of the breast implants' envelopes but saw no crisis in its short-term planning horizon. Its management downplayed the clear trouble signals it had, in the form of internal reports of leakage, until a full-blown crisis was at hand in 1992 [6]. This general myopia is also reflected in corporate leveraged buyouts and in the priority of near-term profits over research and development, which has a long-term pay-off.

Most Americans have moved light years away from Ben Franklin's long-term view that "a penny saved is a penny earned." In this respect, they are evidently unlike some of their economic competitors: capitalism does not make a short-term view inevitable. A 1992 study of 300 companies shows a stark contrast between long-term oriented European and Japanese companies and their short-term focused American counterparts. "Long-term" was defined as profits not expected in the first five years of an investment project. Japanese companies considered 47% of their projects long-term, European companies 61%, and

American companies 21%. The difference in attitude is related to the large, long-term institutional stakeholders of the overseas companies, the exception rather than the rule in America [7].

The lack of concern with the long-term is even reflected in the prospective Year 2000 studies dealing with state and local governments. A 1985 review of thirty such studies showed that they

> had a clear, sharp view of the trees, but proved weak in seeing either the leaves or the forest, that is, in seeing the micro or the long-term macro factors [8].

They shied away from the potential for long-term structural changes and radical changes in infrastructure technology such as the wired city and mass networking, focusing instead on near-term strategies that emphasized continuity and financing.

In discussing the differences among perspective types (Chapter 3), one parameter was the planning horizon (Table 3.1). It tends to be far for the T perspective, intermediate for O, and short for P. This at once explains a source of the difficulty of communication between the analyst and the lay person. Forrester's engineering perspective made it seem reasonable to run his world dynamics computer model out to the year 2100. The O and P perpectives are most unlikely to do so.

It is evident that this myopic philosophy is deeply imbedded in the American psyche and can ultimately prove exceedingly hazardous. It is analogous to driving at high speed at night on a dark, unfamiliar mountain road with low-beam headlights. The impacts of infrastructure decay and educational system deterioration become apparent only many years in the future. They do not enter the field of view of O and P until they become near-term crises and reach a catastrophic stage. We observed in Section 6.2 that the destruction of commercial fishing in the Great Lakes in 1939 could be traced to the construction of the Welland Canal in 1829 [9]. Today's carbon dioxide emissions may not increase global warming with any catastrophic effect until the middle of the twenty-first century. The population explosion, particularly in the world's tropical areas, may not be reflected in catastrophic effects due to deforestation and water pollution for decades.

Consider a comparison of two types of risk: (1) oil spills and waste dumps containing dangerous chemicals (Section 6.2) and (2) ozone layer depletion and the greenhouse effect. Many scientists view (2) as higher priority than (1); the public views (1) as higher priority than (2). The scientists see in the long term far more human lives endangered by (2) because of the global pervasiveness of the hazards. The public focuses on (1) because these hazards are "here and now."

A 1990 survey of 1000 Maryland households posed the following choice: Unless controlled, a certain kind of pollution will kill 100 people this year and Y people T years from now. The government has to choose between two control programs costing the same, but there is only money for one. Should it initiate program A, which will save 100 lives now, or program B, which will save Y lives T years from now? Y and T were varied, with T taken as 25 years and 100 years. The results showed a strong preference for the present. For example, 68% preferred to save 100 lives today over saving 200 lives in 25 years. If the saved future lives remain the same, but the time T is stretched to 100 years, the figure becomes 85%. Consistently, only 10% to 15% consider saving future lives at least as important as saving lives now [10].

We refer to this ingrained human habit as *discounting*. In a sense it is the enemy of forecasting! The word "discounting" is used because the tendency we have described is analogous to the practice in business and economics to discount future dollars relative to present dollars, that is, to determine the present value of future dollars. The discount is expressed in exponential form, $P = P_0 e^{-at}$, where P_0 is the undiscounted future value at time t, a the discount rate, and P the present value. Zero inflation will be assumed in this discussion. A contract giving us $1 million 10 years from now is worth less than a similar contract providing the $1 million up front. The reason is that we can work with the money received now to earn more with it for the next 10 years. Thus, a positive discount rate means that the present value of the future dollar is less than a dollar. Often the discount rate used is the cost of capital, that is, the rate of interest at which a company can borrow money.

Before proceeding, we should note that a negative discount rate signifies that the present value of the future dollar is more than a dollar. In this case, with no inflation, today's dollar buys less in the future. For example, this will occur if nonrenewable or slowly renewable natural resources are being depleted. Their cost will rise and future dollars will buy less and less. This is equivalent to a negative discount rate [11]. Instead of assuming zero inflation throughout this discussion, we can equally well interpret the same discount rate as "after inflation" (often labelled the "real discount rate").

There is obviously a close relationship between discounting and forecasting. The fact is that, as we move into the future, we move into a space of increasing uncertainty and ignorance. Thus, a positive discount rate is often justified as constituting a recognition of this state of affairs. If a discounting factor is imposed, as O and P perspectives are likely to do, the future crisis appears to shrink in significance compared to an equivalent near-term crisis. The higher the discount rate used, the greater is the shrinkage. We observe that the poor generally discount time more heavily than the affluent. They are concerned with the near-term crisis of their own survival, not with long-term problems such as environmental degradation. However, we also find among healthy and high-income individuals those who anticipate longer life and declining future income, hence a need to save and place increasing value on the long-term, that is, a negative discount rate.

A temporal discount rate can be applied to parameters other than money. Figure 7.1 illustrates the perception of the future global population problem in discounting terms, underscoring the analogy of looking at the world through the wrong end of the telescope. Using the global population in 1970 as a base, Forrester's world dynamics model calculated its behavior to 2100 [12]. The zero discount rate case shows a catastrophe in the middle of the twenty-first century. The population reaches three times the 1970 level and then plummets in an ecological system collapse. However, if a 5% annual discount rate is applied to the population increases, the crisis appears to shrink to total insignificance from our vantage point. No dramatic worsening of the current situation is perceived by today's observer.

The discount rate found in the Maryland survey is 7.4% for $T = 25$ years and 3.8% for $T = 100$ years. That means six lives would have to be saved in 25 years or 44 lives in 100 years to be equivalent to one life saved now. A commonly used real (after-inflation) "social discount rate" is 3%. That means a 3% economic growth rate per year, equivalent to a doubling of the economy in one generation or a tenfold growth in a human lifetime, is needed simply to assure no decline in the standard of living. Such considerations lead T-oriented analysts to question the entire discounting concept when intergenerational time spans are involved. They see in discounting no satisfactory way to protect the rights of future generations.[2]

In economic policy making, the discount rate can have a startling effect on decisions. Consider, for example, the choice between 20-year coal and solar energy programs that the Congress faced some years ago. If the after-inflation costs are compared using zero discounting, the programs appear as in Figure 7.2(a). The solar energy program has more expensive initial investments but very low later costs; the coal program has fairly constant costs over the same period. The solar program, measured by the area under the curve, appears

---

2. Rothenberg proposes that time discounting be restricted to a single generation at a time and that, beyond the present generation, the discount be considered as a very slowly decreasing step function so that costs and benefits beyond the present generation are not strongly diminished [13].

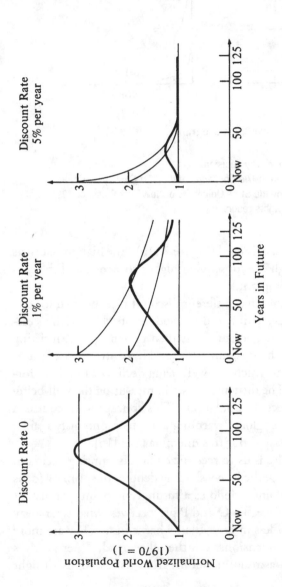

Figure 7.1 The discounting phenomenon: world population crisis (1970 = 1). Zero-discount rate is based on *The Limits to Growth* standard run [12]. Note that the application of a 5% discount rate to the population increase had the apparent effect of reducing a crisis 75 years in the future to insignificance.

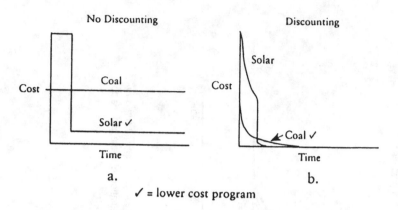

Figure 7.2 The effect of discounting on energy decision.
[Reprinted with permission from *The Challenge of the 21st Century* by Harold A. Linstone with Ian I. Mitroff by the State University of New York Press, © 1994, State University of New York. All rights reserved.]

cheaper. However, if a discount rate is used (Figure 7.2(b)), the high initial costs of the solar program far outweigh the subsequent higher coal costs and the economic decision favors the coal program.

Some analysts have suggested that different discount rates be used for different sectors of the economy, say, manufacturing and forestry [14]. Others dispute the focus on counting future goods for less than present goods, insisting that peoples' well-being should be discounted also. They introduce a "pure" discount rate, which is the rate at which the well-being declines as we look forward in time from the present. The difficulty arises in measuring the well-being and integrating it over large affected populations. This concept is, of course, a central concern in the debate over global warming and pits economists against ethicists. We shall have more to say about this dilemma later [15].

The preceding discussion leads us to recognize that discounting occurs in space as well as time. In Figure 7.3, the heavy shading denotes the primary focus of concern, the "me now" (a). Point x denotes a future time point, y a distant place, and z a distant time and place. To O and P perspectives, what is far away in time and space is normally of less interest than what is near. They are more comfortable with human-scale dimensions. On the other hand, T perspectives move easily from subatomic to astronomic levels, from nanoseconds to light years.

For O and P, an event that happens thousands of miles away is of less concern than the same event in our neighborhood. This is the famous NIMBY (Not In My Back Yard) syndrome and is central to environmental issues. Santa Barbara citizens become concerned about offshore oil drilling and its pollution

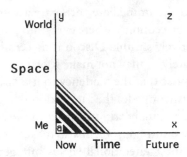

Figure 7.3 Discounting time and space.
[Reprinted with permission from *The Challenge of the 21st Century* by Harold A. Linstone with Ian I. Mitroff by the State University of New York Press, © 1994, State University of New York. All rights reserved.]

of the Santa Barbara Channel; they show little interest in the same problem in the Gulf of Mexico, thousands of miles away.

The space-time discounting tendency probably has its origin in human evolutionary development. It was undoubtedly vital for survival to concentrate on the "me now." In this constant struggle, there was not the luxury of ruminating about distant space and time (either past or future). We must remember that O and P perspectives evolved before T perspectives.

It is even today possible to make a potent argument for discounting. The farther we move from near space-time, the more uncertainties we encounter. Consider a current issue or problem P. We recall our discussion in Section 2.1 (Figure 2.2) in which we conceived of two alternative solutions, S_1 and S_2. Each of these is likely to create impacts or new problems, say S_1 leads to P_{11} and P_{12}. New problem P_{11} in turn will suggest new solution possibilities and so on. We see that P leads to an ever-growing sequence of problems and solutions.

A historic example of P is the problem of epidemic diseases such as bubonic plague, cholera, and polio. Public health measures solved the problem, cutting the death rate without affecting the birth rate. The solution helped to create an overpopulation crisis and massive starvation. The Green Revolution and other measures alleviate this problem but cause ecological imbalances and worsen environmental pollution. This reasoning may well lead to a Hamlet-like paralysis of action: why treat P when that only leads to unending new problems that may be even more difficult to solve? The answer: discount, so that the subsequent new problems can be ignored and action focused on dealing with the near term.[3] Many corporations also discount both space and time heavily. They

---

3. In mathematical terms, discounting is equivalent to converting a divergent infinite series to a convergent one.

ignore the world beyond the immediate corporate activities, a potentially fatal weakness in a global village economy where everything interacts with everything and space-time has effectively shrunk. Discounting certainly makes the decision process easier; unfortunately, it may not make it better.

It comes as no surprise that the tendency to use differing discount rates or planning horizons seriously impedes the interaction that is so vital among T, O, and P. This will be an increasingly critical matter in the coming decades.

The space-time discounting problem also makes us acutely aware of a profound ethical dilemma: intergenerational versus intragenerational equity (Figure 7.4). In an affluent society, how should we balance our concerns for our grandchildren (x) with those for the poor in our world today (y)? Which is more important, dealing with the inexorable carbonization of our grandchildren's atmosphere or dealing with today's water contamination that afflicts billions in poor areas? Will our grandchildren benefit more if we focus today on environmental protection at the expense of economic growth or on economic growth at the expense of environmental protection? Should we move along the diagonal, that is, toward z, keeping a balance between x and y?

In one view, a moral way for individuals, and a just way for institutions, is to act so as not to constrict the options of future generations. This idea is closely related to "sustainable growth." Churchman suggests that

> we should undertake to design our societies and their environments so that people of the future will be able to design their lives in ways that express their own humanity [16].

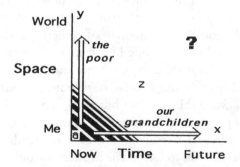

Figure 7.4   An ethical dilemma in extending our horizon.

In economic terms this means the use of a negative real (after inflation) discount rate, implying that our grandchildren are more important than we are. To some this defines a "strong culture."

7.2 Forecasting

Technological Forecasts

With World War II the military suddenly had to confront a technological revolution and, with the onset of the Cold War, a potential new enemy. Jet engines, radar, computers, supersonic flight, nuclear weapons, and guided missiles signified an order of magnitude increase in system complexity and unprecedentedly long lead times. It was evident that long-range planning was vital and this, in turn, galvanized the military to develop its technological forecasting capability. Much of the pioneering work in forecasting was done under its auspices, particularly by the U.S. Air Force. It set individuals like Ralph Lenz and Col. (Dr.) Joseph Martino as well as its think tank, the RAND Corporation, to work developing methodological approaches. Its aerospace contractors, such as Douglas and Lockheed, also became involved. Examples are trend extrapolation at Wright-Patterson Air Force Base, Delphi at the RAND Corporation (see Appendix A.4), and scenarios at Douglas Aircraft Company.

It is a common practice to divide technological forecasting into two complementary types: (1) exploratory forecasts and (2) normative or needs forecasts [17]. The former focus on what *can* be done in the future, based on the past and present technological capability; the latter focus on what *ought* to be done in the future. The former are strongly T-focused, the latter are influenced more by O and P.

Exploratory forecasts are expertly done by technologists in the field. For example, Moore's Law on the rate of increase of computer capability[4] proved to be a good guideline for many years. The pressure to increase the technological capability once the feasibility of the approach has been established clearly follows a familiar growth curve, facilitating forecasting.

Sometimes a requirement enunciated by a customer or government agency triggers an advance in technological capability. A recent example is *high-definition television* (HDTV). In 1987 the FCC, worried about Japanese advances, announced a competition for a new computer-age TV. A decade later the main problems were solved and introduction is anticipated in a few years. NetObjects is a company formed to solve the problem of how to create World

---

4. Microchips double in power and halve in price every 18 months.

Wide Web sites easily. They came up with a solution: software that writes the hypertext-markup language for the user.

T-Oriented Forecasts

As already noted, exploratory forecasts tend to have a dominant T orientation. In theory, the long planning horizon or low discount rate associated with the T perspective should be of direct benefit to such forecasts. While analysts do use a low discount rate for the future, we observe that they are sometimes inclined to apply a considerably higher discount rate to the past. For example, they may pay excessive attention to short-term trends, extrapolating on the basis of recent historical data only and thus missing the more meaningful, less distorted longer term trend, that is, the "envelope curve" (see, for example, [18]).

Besides direct trend extrapolation, T-type approaches in exploratory forecasting use analytical models, such as growth curves, causal models, and correlation methods. Growth curves have been particularly popular, beginning with the work of General Electric's Fisher and Pry on technological substitution [19, 20]. Such S-shaped logistic curves are similar to those developed by Pearl for demographic forecasting.[5] They have been widely applied and extended by Marchetti [21] and Modis [22]. Causal models attempt to take into account factors known to cause technological change, such as the growth of scientific knowledge. Correlation methods include the technological progress function and lead-lag relationships between technologies. Normative forecasting also has spawned some T-type approaches, including relevance trees and morphological models [17]. The latter maps out all possible combinations of technology theoretically able to achieve a certain system and then, in this large set of possibilities, rules out all but the few that appear technically feasible.

Perceived cycles have provided another basis for forecasting. It is evident that technological, as well as societal, advance exhibits both stable and unstable, regular and unique, phases. One might describe a sequence of S curves as a cyclic phenomenon, with stable growth followed by bounded randomness followed by stable growth, and so on. The cycles reflect significant systemic similarities but tell us nothing about the unique factors that conjoin to trigger the phase changes. For example, an examination of the worldwide use of various forms of energy—wood, coal, oil, gas—shows that the peaks in primary reliance have shifted with a periodicity that corresponds to that of the

---

5. The equation of this curve is $x = L / (1 + ae^{-bt})$, where L is the upper limit of growth of variable x, a and b are coefficients determined by fitting the curve to the data, and e is the base of natural logarithms. At time $t = -\infty$, $x = 0$; at $t = +\infty$, $x = L$. The inflection point is at $x = L / 2$.

Kondratiev long wave: 50 to 60 years [21]. But looking ahead, unique and unpredictable circumstances clearly enter in attempting to forecast the role of nuclear energy in impacting this pattern. The technologies that have spearheaded the U.S. economy since 1800—railroads, steel, oil, and information technologies—similarly match that periodicity, whereas the next overarching technology (biotechnology?) raises unique considerations that may galvanize the next technological era [23].

The work of Mensch, Graham, and Senge, and Marchetti on technological innovation is particularly interesting for forecasters. It strongly indicates that there is a connection between Kondratiev economic cycles and technological innovations [21, 24, 25]. A Kondratiev cycle comprises the sequence prosperity-recession-depression-recovery. Technological advances are classified as follows:

- *Basic invention:* discovery of a new idea or technical process;
- *Basic innovation:* the first practical application of the invention on a significant scale, creating a new type of human activity;
- *Improvement innovation:* incremental advances of an existing technology that do not alter its fundamental nature.

The interest here is in basic inventions and basic innovations. The most interesting findings are that (1) basic inventions and basic innovations cluster, the latter distribution showing much less dispersion than the former, and (2) the clustering correlates well with the Kondratiev cycles.

Basic innovations cannot be judged using conventional payback periods and discount rates. Their returns are slow at first and huge later [25]. Specifically, basic innovations come in spurts at the end of the depression phase of the cycle. When the economy is moving through recovery and prosperity, the emphasis is on "safe" improvement innovations rather than the more risky basic innovations. Toward the end of a depression, there appears to be greater willingness to move into more radical innovations. This pattern meshes with the preceding discussion of phases of high expectations/low risk/positive discount and low expectations/high risk/negative discount.

As an example of this behavior, the end of the Great Depression saw a bunching of major basic innovations. The period from 1930 to 1945 introduced atomic energy, jet engines, computers, radar, television, and nylon—each creating new industries. The "next" major depression predicted by the Kondratiev long wave (50 to 60 year) cycle has to date (mid-1998) been averted in the United States. However, there are signs that it is occurring in Southeast Asia. What does this mean for the clustering of basic innovations associated with this phase? We are uncertain. Possibly the global linkages and regulatory steps taken in the United States as a consequence of the 1930's depression have effectively dampened the waves.

The subject of cycles remains highly controversial, with orthodox T-oriented individuals, particularly economists and physicists, firmly opposed [26].

Biases

Not surprisingly, the dominance of T drives the forecaster inexorably to focus on greater technological sophistication in addressing future needs. Years of personal involvement in a narrow aspect of technology and communication with peers who think of the future in terms of the same descriptors of capability bias the forecaster (see [17, pp. 235–239]). Thus, O/P subtly influence T.

This bias is reflected in the adage that "the military are always planning to fight the last war over again with better weapons." The construction of the Maginot Line in France in the early-1930s assumed that a future war with Germany would be a war of firepower, like World War I, rather than a war of mobility. Yet the technology of tanks and aircraft was clearly advancing at the time. Nor were the slowly changing concepts and standard operating procedures confined to the French military planners. The German High Command also had little faith in highly mobile warfare and tended to see the future through a rear-view mirror. The Blitzkrieg of 1940 was the product of the planning of Hitler and three generals who were outsiders to the vaunted General Staff: von Manstein, von Rundstedt, and Guderian [27]. Hitler's charisma and personal power meant that a maverick P perspective overcame an entrenched O perspective.

"Assumption drag," that is, carrying along assumptions that were valid at the time the forecast was made but are not valid for the period being forecast, appears in many incarnations. Population forecasts for 1970 made during the 1930s depression assumed continuation of a low birth rate to 1970 and hence low estimates. Forecasts for 1970 made during the time of the post–World War II boom assumed continuation of the then-current high birth rate and resulted in high estimates for 1970 [28].

Needs analyses usually reflect the O perspective of the client organization or the P perspective of the forecaster far more strongly than do capability forecasts [29]. A case in point is the defense establishment. We already observed the importance of the O perspective in the case of the Navy's USS *Wampanoag* and the Army's M-16 rifle (Section 4.1).[6] In both cases, the contemporary analyst

---

6. More recently the pressure to produce an organizationally approved, but technically deficient new system, the Army's Armored Personnel Carrier, even led to tampering with field tests to make the system look good.

would have done poorly if he had ignored the O perspective and based his technological forecast strictly on a future capability estimate using the T perspective.

During my time in Corporate Planning, I directed four corporate planning "needs analyses" in the area of national defense and space programs. By the time of the fourth of these privately funded projects, our T perspective analysts had made an important discovery: "The gap between what is needed and what is marketable means that a 'needs analysis' is, in fact, a mirage" [30]. Our "need" is determined as much by what we like and are comfortable with as by the purely technical requirements. Pilots want aircraft to fly, so an all-missile force would be organizationally unpalatable, even if technically feasible. It would be a "destructive energy" in the Air Force society just as the USS *Wampanoag* was for the post–Civil War Navy (Section 4.1). Advancement in the Navy traditionally requires experience in commanding ships. Thus, the availability of an adequate number of ships must be given consideration in developing normative forecasts. Politicians want to keep military bases open that the Pentagon wants to close because they are no longer needed. The Congress has been spending nearly $4 billion annually on an antimissile defense system, pressuring the military to rush into production even though the technology is not ready and flight tests to date have been dismal failures.

A priority needs list based solely on a T perspective looks very different from one based on, say, T and O perspectives. The T perspective takes account of King Richard III's lament, "For the want of a nail the shoe was lost. . . ," so the list would include unglamorous items such as changes in training and maintenance procedures or in communications equipment. However, a list based on both T and O features the more prestigious items in the firepower and vehicle areas—glamorous aircraft, ships, and weaponry. As Representative J. P. Addabo (D., N.Y.) observed, "the Pentagon doesn't like anything that's small" [31].

The dialectic approach often seen in the O perspective is beautifully illustrated by the history of energy resource forecasts in the United States. As Wildavsky and Tenenbaum have shown, the deep division between industrial interests and conservationists on oil and gas resources was already apparent in the early 1900s [32]. Each side seized on the 1908 *U.S. Geological Survey* (USGS) estimates to confirm its policy stand. At that time USGS forecasted total U.S. resources to be between 10 and 24.5 billion barrels and indicated that we would run out of oil between 1935 and 1943. Many forecasts have been made since then. Except for the World War I and II periods, each faction habitually accuses the other of manipulating these forecasts for its own selfish purposes. Table 7.1 suggests the different views on resource forecasts. It becomes clear that the forecasts are the servants of policies already determined or preferred rather than being prerequisites for policy formulation. Today the oil re-

Table 7.1
O Perspectives on Oil Reserve Forecasts [32]

	When prices are high	When prices are low
Industrialists favor	high forecasts "major new supplies can be found if prices are high"	low forecasts "higher prices are needed to bring on more supplies"
Consumers favor	low forecasts "oil is no longer the solution"	high forecasts "no need to raise prices"
Conservationists favor	low forecasts "high prices encourage over-production"	low forecasts low prices encourage over-consumption"

[Reprinted by permission of Sage Publications, Inc., from *The Politics of Mistrust* by A. Wildavsky and E. Tenenbaum, p. 300, © 1981.]

serve picture through 2010 looks better than ever, with the Caspian Sea, South America, and West Africa recognized as new sources.

In cases where a forecast is done by organization A for client B and few constraints are imposed by B, the biases of A may be decisive for the forecast. If A is experienced in a certain forecasting technique, it is likely to prefer its use in responding to B, whether or not it is most suitable. A may also be subconsciously influenced by the possibility of future grants or contracts from B and avoid forecasts that may alarm B.

Thus, the organizational perspective explains constraints and core assumptions that strongly affect the forecasts [28]. Standard operating procedures, morale needs, as well as incrementalism and tradition determine the forecasts in important ways. And the personal perspective also merits recognition.

In a thoughtful essay on "Why Forecasters Flubbed the '70's," *Time* [33] recognized a paradox:

- Forecasters remain human beings and, as such, have optimistic or pessimistic biases.
- Forecasters are "triumphantly rationalistic," and exaggerate this aspect in human behavior.

One often wishes the forecasting community would exhibit such awareness of the "self."

One technique that openly admits O and P perspectives is Delphi [34]. This iterative questionnaire technique preserves the group members' anonymity and can preserve P-focused individuality. It will not suppress the maverick because no consensus is forced. However, the tendency for the individual to align his views with those of the group, that is, the Asch effect, may influence the results (see Section 3.3). In its early stages of development, Delphi was viewed primarily as a forecasting technique, and this remains a major area of application. In the past two decades it has been the principal tool in national "foresight projects" in Japan, Germany, Korea, and elsewhere [35]. For more details on Delphi, see Appendix A.4.

Scenarios

Roy Amara [36] and Uno Svedin [37] have suggested that scenarios may be usefully classified into three types as shown in Table 7.2. It is striking that these three types can be related to our three perspectives as shown.

It is reasonable to expect a T perspective scenario to be analytic and judged on its reproducibility. The O scenario is the product of organizational planning, hence participatory and prescriptive. The P scenario is significant only if it is imaginative or visionary, for example, More's *Utopia* and Toffler's *Power Shift*. It contrasts with corporate planners' projections (O) and technologists' computer-produced scenarios (T). In the latter category we find Forrester's system dynamics models (see Section 2.4) and the business scenario models of the Nixdorf Institute [38]. Forrester's efforts, culminating in his *World Dynamics,* spawned a cottage industry of global modellers. Such models ignore crucial aspects of human behavior, such as adaptability, creativity, willingness to defy odds, indomitable faith and hope, greed, and aggressiveness. They fatally oversimplify complex system realities, as we shall point out in Chapter 8. The parallel

Table 7.2
Scenario Typology

	Probable	Preferable	Possible
Criterion	Analytical (reproducible)	Value (explicative)	Image (plausible)
Orientation	Exploratory (extrapolative)	Normative (prescriptive)	Visionary
Mode	Structural	Participatory	Perceptual
Creator	Think-tank teams	Stakeholders	Individuals
Perspective Type	Technical (T)	Organizational (O)	Personal (P)

and interactive use of T, O, and P generated scenarios minimizes the constraints inherent in any single-perspective scenario development.

7.3 Planning

In Section 7.1 we noted that American industry characteristically favors short-term planning over long-term planning. T-based corporate planning generally has had its ups and downs. Periods of intensive formal planning seem to alternate with periods of minimal formal planning.[7] At times consulting groups "sell" their favored models, such as econometric models, only to see them scorned a few years later.

There are many planning models, and much has been written about various analytical aspects, such as top-down and retrogressive planning, cybernetic modeling of the corporation, and environmental scanning. These reflect the T perspective of the analyst.

We have discussed discounting and forecasting; planning must deal with their interaction. Consider a company with products that have life cycles. Technological obsolescence must always concern the planner. If new products are not introduced, sales will begin to decline as the present products age. If there is a corporate sales objective, a gap will appear and grow, as shown in Figure 7.5 [39]. If a significant discount rate is in place, the future threat will not be evident early and the management will at some point suddenly realize that it is being passed by its competitors who have new products on the market.

New products may require a long gestation period with major investments years before their fruition. Thus, the key question for management should be the balancing of funds and effort spent on short-term, low-risk improvements of current products and long-term, high-risk investments in new products. Increasing expectations reflect a period when the current product is seen to have a great future and a positive discount rate is the norm. Decreasing expectations reflect a period when the current product is declining and a negative discount rate is appropriate.

As Ayres points out, this situation is not properly reflected in the single discount rate used in cost-benefit analysis and economics [40]. It basically inhibits long-term investments. He recommends that the usual exponential function used to express discounting be replaced by a hyperbolic function, which, in

---

7. The pattern suggests the speculation that it may be related to the Kondratiev long waves, that is, planning is in vogue during the strong, stable growth phase and out of favor during the downturn phase (see Sections 8.2 and 8.5).

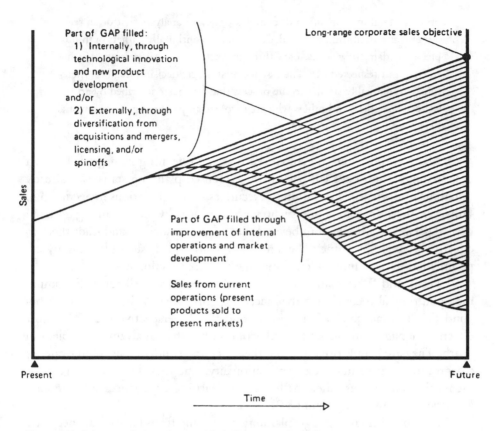

Figure 7.5 Sales gap diagram for a multi-product enterprise [39].
[*Source:* Reprinted by permission of Elsevier Science Inc, © 1973.]

practice, increases the discount in the short-term and reduces it in the long-term. Thus, it gives somewhat more weight to the long-term investment.

The discussion of discounting (Section 7.1) has alerted us to the fundamental dilemma encountered if we move beyond near-term planning: the O and P perspectives tend to have a much shorter planning horizon than the T perspective. Yet the executive rightly feels that he needs the multiple perspectives. Halal in his survey of strategic management in 25 major U.S. corporations found that:

> skillful executives do not rely primarily upon the outcome of formal planning. They base their decisions on heuristically derived knowledge that is internally tested and found to be intuitively true and senseful rather than

upon a literal interpretation of complex data and analyses that often seem esoteric and doubtful . . . The decision maker continually gathers opinions, pieces of data, new ideas, etc., through exchanges with persons that are trusted and respected . . . The essence of strategic decision making, therefore, is remarkably similar to the process that has been described by artists, writers, scientists, and others who are involved in producing creative works [41].

Many corporations are convinced that "an operating manager is his own best strategist" and have cut back their T-focused planning staffs. We already noted the importance of intuition to executives in the quotations in Section 3.4. However, there are some leaders who have an unusually long planning horizon; their P perspective reaches out beyond that of their associates and leads them to effective strategic planning. The alternative is to replace such planning by experimentation or training in crisis management (see Section 8.4).

Peters and Waterman have studied 43 particularly well-run U.S. companies, and they also concluded that success is correlated to the ability to go beyond the "rational model," that is, beyond the T perspective [42]. The most effective managers are biased toward action rather than analyzing a problem to death. They are people oriented, and they encourage individuals to innovate, to a degree that may seem to verge on irrationality. And they don't penalize experiments that fail but use them as important learning experiences (see the City Manager's comment in Section 3.3).

Not surprisingly, strategic planning consulting firms have broadened their thinking beyond strategy to include staff, style, skills, systems (of communication), structure, and shared values—the inevitable acronym: "The Seven S's." The interaction among these is seen as the basis for incremental forward movement of the company [43]. It should be obvious that this shift signifies a de facto shift to multiple perspectives.

The CEO may indeed see the role of strategic planning as one of raising the awareness of his people of the future, extending their usual horizon, and reducing their parochialism. This role may be far more valuable than the generation of formal plans. Too often a division adopts a defensive attitude due to fear of the future (for example, new business line development seen by a department as a threat to its own integrity) or inbreeding leads to fatal misjudgment of the environment. Typically, ritualistic trend extrapolations are made using obsolete core assumptions.

The complacency-inducing effect of shared values and an era of success led the American automobile industry into a period of serious difficulties. In the words of a former G.M. executive, Detroit's auto executives "live together, they work together, they drink together, they play golf together, they think together." The result is executive myopia in planning. The top executives are yearly given cream-of-the-crop cars that are maintained free of charge for them, washed daily, and filled with gas in the company garage. Thus, they do not sense the aggravations of the common, garden variety car owner. The executives are concerned that their cars ride comfortably on Michigan's flat highways, start and stay warm in the cold winters, keep cool in the hot summers, and carry a family and its gear to and from their Upper Peninsula summer homes. This they accomplish beautifully [44]. In fairness, it should be pointed out that the Mercedes and BMW, built within 100 miles of the Alps, analogously reflect their executives' concern with mountain driving, for example, precise steering.

Success from 1910 to 1970 lulled the industry into the perpetuation of assumptions long after they ceased being valid, that is, assumption drag (see Section 7.2). Examples of these assumptions include: styling is more important than quality, efficiency in production is more important than good labor relations, and workers have interest only in money but not in participatory decision making [45]. It is increasingly evident that many other American corporations have suffered severely from similar handicaps—one only needs to point to the shipbuilding and steel sectors [46].

An encouraging counter-example to the G.M. case is that of the Gillette Corporation. Like G.M.'s cars, its product, razor blades, is hardly perceived as high-tech. Nevertheless it has consistently focused on R&D to drive innovation. Whenever it launches a new product, its follow-on is already being developed. The corporate (O) culture stresses technological supremacy, forming a strong O-T linkage. This is demonstrated by its successive products, the Sensor-Excel, the Manx, and the Mach 3 razor, each involving a significant technological advance. The result is an enviable combination of product superiority and popularity: the company currently has two-thirds of the male shaving market and is very profitable [47]. It is an excellent example of the recognition of, and response to, the process displayed in Figure 7.5.

In Japan, the government long ago recognized the limitations of its industrial long-range planning. It created the *Ministry of International Trade and Industry* (MITI) before World War II to formulate and facilitate implementation of "industrial policy." Thus, a focal point for long-range planning is provided, and it becomes action-directed. The dominant perspectives are: (1) the technical T and (2) the national O. Such planning is designed to mesh a corporation's O perspective with that of the country, a situation often characterized as "Japan, Inc." But it does not mean that intraindustry competition is stifled. For example, Japan has more automobile manufacturers than does the United States. Neither does it imply that corporate leadership is forced to accept MITI's recommendations. The national foresight efforts noted in the preceding section are another indication of Japan's continuing interest in facilitating corporate long-term planning.

In a flexible and pragmatic manner, MITI has served as a catalyst to assist Japanese industry to:

- Reconstruct key sectors after the almost total destruction of World War II, for example, electric power, coal, iron, steel, and fertilizer companies in the 1945–1952 period;

- Pursue a "dynamic comparative advantage strategy" in capital-intensive sectors with high-growth potential and higher added value, for example, synthetic textiles, petrochemicals, and machinery in the 1952–1960 period;

- Follow a "trade liberalization strategy" in the 1960–1973 period;

- Initialize a "positive or active industrial policy" to support promising sectors for the 1980s and an "adjustive industrial policy" to deal with declining sectors in the 1973–1983 period [48].

The Japanese are imbued at an early age, at the elementary school level, with the importance of cooperation and collective values. Subsequently their concept of management melds the people in the organization in the sense that (1) each person is exposed to the others' P perspective (for example, through discussions and job rotation) and (2) the resulting polyocular vision of each person facilitates mutual accommodation and formation of an O perspective. Superficially it would appear that the organization and its people are "synonymous" [42]. It is more accurate to say that this flexible process reinforces societal cohesion.

Knowledge-intensive, high-technology industries have been nurtured through subsidies (for example, for super large-scale integration research involving several firms), and alternative energy sources are given strong R&D assistance. On the other hand, the high-cost coal mining, textile, and basic material industries have been declining. Long-range planning in such cases has focused on "adjustment" (for example, disposing of obsolete excess capacity, joint ventures in developing countries) or phase-out, while protectionism was eschewed. MITI helped the ship-building industry to scrap over 40% of its capacity when it became less competitive in the 1970s. By contrast, the federal government in the United States has at various times given extensive support to ailing and obsolescing sectors, such as ship-building and tobacco.

The foremost negative aspect of Japan's approach is the conservative, seniority-based governing bureaucracy that controls financial policy and inhibits badly needed structural and regulatory reform, particularly of capital flow. Mismatched to the needs of a twenty-first-century information society, the obsolete governance system is increasingly neutralizing Japan's industrial strength and weakening its global competitive position. (The crisis has infected the other, more vulnerable, economies of Southeast Asia as well.)

France also has a tradition of national strategic planning in support of the private sector. Its administrative elite developed a sophisticated planning process under General de Gaulle. Corporations are encouraged to participate by means of government subsidies, orders, and favors. The 1967 Plan Calcul in the information technology area, for example, provided 1906 million French francs in assistance to French computer manufacturers [49]. Germany balances priorities of wealth, welfare, and well-being in a unique long-term ecological socio-capitalism [50].

Americans tend to prize individualism and self-interest over collective interest, except in time of all-out war. While its national industrial planning may be weak, America is pre-eminent where individualism plays a vital part, that is, in research. This dominance is reflected in the Nobel prize awards in science (1901–1997): United States 199, Japan 5.

In the United States, older organizations have more political power than budding ones, hence more influence in governmental decisions. Labor unions are strong in obsolete industries, and large old enterprises have had a long time to develop political ties. By contrast, young companies are naive politically and ineffective. (Microsoft's recent problems are the consequence of such naiveté.) Hence, the obsolescent companies obtain government assistance much more readily. The one major exception in the United States is the military/industrial complex. Its success during the Cold War may be in no small part due to the unique and fortuitous bond between politically potent old components, the Army and Navy, and young high-tech components, the Air Force and aerospace companies.

As already suggested in Section 7.2, the most effective U.S. governmental involvement in strategic planning has been in the aerospace sector. Industry followed the lead of its prime customer, the military, and undertook its own long-range planning efforts. The author's MIRAGE projects at Hughes Aircraft Company and Lockheed Corporation exemplify these efforts [30]. Thus, MIRAGE 70 (Military Requirements Analysis—Generation 1970) was undertaken in 1959–1960.

Another instance of effective U.S. government involvement was cited in Section 7.2, specifically, the action by the FCC to move the development of HDTV forward. Historically, we can trace constructive federal government involvement with technology back to the nineteenth century and its support for land grant colleges and county agents to help farmers use new techniques.

The benefit to American agriculture has been enormous. Computer development was advanced by U.S. Army projects in World War II and the commercial jet aircraft development by the U.S. Air Force KC-135 aerial tanker project, while the internet is an outgrowth of the Department of Defense's ARPA activity.

Still, there has been a strong current of discomfort abroad in the land, with any governmental involvement seen as socialistic or worse. The recent financial difficulties have given the "Asian model" a black eye and strengthened the hand of those who oppose governmental coordination or other participation, such as nonmilitary research support and development planning.

The history of *technology assessment* (TA) illustrates the point. The origin of TA was concern over the impacts of technology, for example, the potential damage done on ground structures by aircraft flying at supersonic speed over land. At the instigation of individuals like Charles Lindbergh, Senator Edward Kennedy, and Representative Emilio Daddario, Congress created the *Office of Technology Assessment* (OTA) in 1972. By its very nature this subject could not confine itself to technical aspects of systems and was forced to confront sociotechnical systems in all their complexity.

As an example of the subtleties of TA, consider the first modern information technology revolution that was galvanized by the invention of Gutenberg's interchangeable type and printing press in 1457.[8] One prerequisite was cheap paper, which was facilitated by the success of the spinning wheel in Europe that made linen rags, an essential ingredient of good paper, plentiful and inexpensive [51]. A major impact of the remarkably rapid spread of the printing press—within 23 years printing presses were established in 110 towns—was a rise in literacy; this in turn played a major role in the Protestant Reformation [52]. It is inconceivable that a technology assessor at the time of Gutenberg could have envisioned the pervasive and awesome impact of this technology.

In light of the difficulty of TA, it is all the more impressive that OTA became an effective analysis arm of the legislative branch. However, its excellent quality of work never enjoyed the support of industry. In 1995 its lack of any political clout made it an ideal candidate for passionate budget cutters and it was abolished with minimal debate. Today TA is being more actively pursued in Europe [53].

As the O perspective points to possible U.S. disadvantages in global industrial competition, the P perspective indicates this country's unique strengths. Consider the following examples.

---

8. It was actually not the first information technology revolution. That distinction belongs to the invention of Egyptian writing and the Mesopotamian/Phoenician alphabet.

James B. Hunt, Jr, Governor of North Carolina, was instrumental in obtaining a $24.4 million grant from his state legislature for construction, equipment, and initial operating costs of the Microelectronics Center of North Carolina. Hunt is unfazed by state bureaucracy and feels that

> only the governor can bring it all together. I doubt you'll ever get maximum effort without a strong governor. You need the leader who will go out and take the initiative to get more resources [49].

Erich Bloch, an IBM executive, was the mover in creating a consortium of some 20 corporations to eventually channel $50 million annually into pure research in semiconductors and computers.

John Young, the Chief Executive of Hewlett-Packard, took the lead in inducing 17 companies to contribute $13 million for the creation of a Center for Integrated Systems at Stanford University to do research in computer science and electrical engineering.

As a final observation, America can be viewed in terms of a structure resting on a strong triadic foundation: science/technology (T), democracy/capitalism (O), and individualism (P). It is their balance and integration that has made its society successful. But today it faces a widening gap between the realities being created by the pace of technological innovation (T) and the lagging conceptual models of governance (O). It is an issue already raised in Section 3.7 in conjunction with our discussion of information technology and societal organization. This gap is the reverse of that at the time of the French Revolution, when the reality lagged the new ideal conceptual model of society [54]. The situation underscores the urgency of experimentation (Section 8.4) and research (Section 8.5) on the governance-technology linkage.

Acknowledgments

Portions of Section 7.1 reprinted with permission from *The Challenge of the 21st Century* by Harold A. Linstone with Ian I. Mitroff by permission of the State University of New York Press, 1984, State University of New York.

References

[1]   Burnett, M. S., "Valuing the Future As If It Mattered: The Negative Discount Rate and Sustainable Development," in *Proceedings of the Annual Meeting of the International Society for the Systems Sciences,* Denver, July 12–17, 1992.

[2]   *New York Times,* June 28, 1990, pp. A-1, A-12.

[3]   *Los Angeles Times,* Jan. 6, 1993.

[4]   *New York Times,* Sept. 5, 1992; Sept. 16, 1992.

[5]   Tversky, A., and D. Kahneman, "Judgment Under Uncertainty: Heuristics and Biases," *Science,* Vol. 185, Sept. 27, 1974, pp. 1124–1131.

[6]   *Los Angeles Times,* Feb. 12, 1992.

[7]   *New York Times,* Sept. 2, 1992.

[8]   Coates, J. F., "Preparing for the Urban Future," *Technological Forecasting and Social Change,* Vol. 42, 1992, pp. 309–316.

[9]   Lawless, E. W., *Technology and Social Shock,* New Brunswick, NJ: Rutgers University Press, 1977, pp. 208–216.

[10] Cropper, M. L., and P. R. Portney, *Resources,* Resources for the Future, Summer 1992, No. 108.

[11] Odum, H. T., "Simulating Ecological Economic Parameters," in *Proceedings of the International Society for the Systems Sciences,* Denver, July 12–17, 1992.

[12] Meadows, D., et al., *The Limits to Growth,* New York: Universe Books, 1972, p. 124.

[13] Rothenberg, J., "Time Comparisons in Public Policy Analysis of Global Change: an Economic Exploration," manuscript, communicated by H. Brooks, 1992.

[14] Livingstone, I., and M. Tribe, "Projects with Long Time Horizons: Their Economic Appraisal and the Discount Rate," *Project Appraisal,* Vol. 10, 1995, pp. 66–76.

[15] Broome, J., "Discounting the Future," *Philosophy and Public Affairs,* Vol. 23, Spring 1994, pp. 128–156.

[16] Churchman, C. W., *Thought and Wisdom,* Seaside, CA: Intersystems Publications, 1982, p. 21.

[17] Martino, J., *Technological Forecasting for Decision Making,* second edition, New York: North-Holland, 1983.

[18] Ayres, R. U., *Technological Forecasting and Long Range Planning,* New York: McGraw-Hill Book Company, 1969.

[19] Fisher, J. C., and R. H. Pry, "A Simple Substitution Model of Technological Change," *Technological Forecasting and Social Change,* Vol. 3, 1971–1972, pp. 75–88.

[20] Linstone, H. A., and D. Sahal, *Technological Substitution,* New York: Elsevier, 1976.

[21] Marchetti, C., "Society as a Learning System: Discovery, Invention, and Innovation Cycles Revisited," *Technological Forecasting and Social Change,* Vol. 18, 1980, pp. 267–282.

[22] Modis, T., *Predictions,* New York: Simon & Schuster, 1992.

[23] Linstone, H. A., with I. I. Mitroff, *The Challenge of the 21st Century,* Albany, NY: State University of New York Press, 1994.

[24] Mensch, G., *Stalemate in Technology: Innovations Overcome the Depression,* Cambridge, MA: Ballinger, 1979.

[25] Graham, A. K., and P. M. Senge, "A Long-Wave Hypothesis of Innovation," *Technological Forecasting and Social Change,* Vol. 17, 1980, pp. 283–312.

[26] Modis, T., "Limits to Cycles and Harmony in Revolutions," *Technological Forecasting and Social Change,* Vol. 59, 1998, pp. 33–38. See also articles by Mallmann and Lemarchand, Berry, and Modelski on cycles in the same issue.

[27] Rowe, V., *The Great Wall of France,* London: Putnam Press, 1959.

[28] Ascher, W., *Forecasting: an Appraisal for Policy-Makers and Planners,* Baltimore, MD: The Johns Hopkins University Press, 1978, p. 53.

[29] Linstone, H. A., "When Is a Need a Need?" *Technological Forecasting and Social Change,* Vol. 1, 1969, pp. 55–71.

[30] Project MIRAGE 85, Vol. III (DPR-87), Corporate Development Planning Dept., Lockheed Aircraft Corporation, April 1970.

[31] *Sunday Oregonian,* April 10, 1983, p. A14.

[32] Wildavsky, A., and E. Tenenbaum, *The Politics of Mistrust,* Beverly Hills, CA: Sage Publications, 1981, p. 300.

[33] *Time,* "Why the Forecasters Flubbed the 70s," Jan. 21, 1980.

[34] Linstone, H. A., and M. Turoff, *The Delphi Method: Techniques and Applications,* Reading, MA: Addison-Wesley Publishing Company, 1975.

[35] *Technological Forecasting and Social Change,* Special Issue on National Foresight Projects, Vol. 60, No. 1, 1999.

[36] Amara, R., "The Futures Field," Report P-95. Palo Alto, CA: Institute of the Future, Sept. 1980.

[37] Svedin, U., "Scenarios, Technology, and Development," presented at the Conference on Natural Resources and Regional Development, Cocoyoc, Mexico, Oct. 8. 1980.

[38] Gausemeier, J., A. Fink, and O. Schlake, "Scenario Management: An Approach to Develop Future Potentials," *Technological Forecasting and Social Change,* Vol. 59, 1998, pp. 111–130.

[39] Blackman, A. W., "New Venture Planning: The Role of Technological Forecasting," *Technological Forecasting and Social Change,* Vol. 5, 1973, p. 28.

[40] Ayres, R. U., and R. Axtell, "Foresight as a Survival Characteristic: When (If Ever) Does the Long View Pay?" *Technological Forecasting and Social Change,* Vol. 51, 1996, pp. 209–235.

[41] Halal, W., "Strategic Planning in Major U.S. Corporations," study prepared for General Motors Corporation at George Washington University, Washington, D.C., 1980. See also Halal, W., "Strategic Management: The State of the Art," *Technological Forecasting and Social Change,* Vol. 25, 1984, pp. 239–264.

[42] Peters, T. J., and R. H. Waterman, Jr., *In Search of Excellence,* New York,: Harper & Row, 1982, p. 39.

[43] Kiechel, W., III, "Corporate Strategists Under Fire," *Fortune,* Vol. 106, Dec. 1982, pp. 34–39.

[44] Yates, B., *The Decline and Fall of the American Automobile Industry,* New York: Harper & Row, 1983.

[45] Mitroff, I. I., and H. A. Linstone, *The Unbounded Mind: Breaking the Chains of Traditional Business Thinking,* New York: Oxford University Press, 1993, Chap. 5.

[46] Hayes, R. H., and W. J. Abernathy, "Managing Our Way to Economic Decline," *Harvard Business Review,* Vol. 58, No. 4, July–Aug. 1980, pp. 67–77.

[47] Surowiecki, J., "The Billion-Dollar Blade," *New Yorker,* June 15, 1998, pp. 43–49.

[48] Sawada, J., "Government Industrial Policy for a Healthy World Economy," *Technological Forecasting and Social Change*, Vol. 24, 1983, pp. 95–105.

[49] Botkin, J., D. Dimancescu, and R. Stata, *Global Stakes: The Future of High Technology in America*, Cambridge, MA: Ballinger Publishing Co., 1982.

[50] Gazdar, K., *Germany's Balanced Development: The Real Wealth of a Nation*, Westport, CT: Quorum Books, 1998.

[51] White, Lynn, Jr., "Technology Assessment from the Stance of a Medieval Historian," *Technological Forecasting and Social Change*, Vol. 6, 1974, pp. 359–370.

[52] Durant, W., *The Reformation*, New York: Simon & Schuster, 1957, p. 159.

[53] Bimber, B., and D. H. Guston (eds.), "Technology Assessment: The End of OTA," *Technological Forecasting and Social Change*, Vol. 54, 1997, pp. 125–286.

[54] Kash, D. E., and R. W. Rycroft, "Synthetic Technology—Analytic Governance: The 21st Century Challenge," *Technological Forecasting and Social Change*, Vol. 54, 1997, pp. 18–19.

8

Looking Ahead: Complexity Science, Chaos, and Multiple Perspectives

> The whole purpose of science is to find meaningful simplicity in the midst of disorderly complexity.
>
> Herbert A. Simon, *Models of My Life*

> Through reason and the methods of science alone we are inadequately equipped to deal with the present problems of metabiological evolution.
>
> Jonas Salk, *Anatomy of Reality*

The most exciting development in the systems area in recent years is that of complexity science, focusing on nonlinear, dynamic, adaptive systems. Galvanized by recent biology-based work on complex living systems, it is continuing to advance the frontiers of the T perspective and expanding its realm to develop insights on sociotechnical systems. At the same time it makes transparent the limitations of traditional T-based analysis. Even so, this progress does not close the gap between models and the real world: the need for O and P perspectives persists.

8.1 Complex Adaptive Systems

The Santa Fe Institute's John Casti observes that twentieth-century science has demonstrated the limits of scientific knowledge [1, pp. 196–198]. Gödel's Incompleteness Theorem, Turing's Halting Theorem, and Heisenberg's Uncertainty Principle all underscore the fact that knowledge of the real world cannot be satisfactorily attained by means of the world of mathematics as it exists today. But it does not mean that the human mind and its creative capability are necessarily subject to these constraints.

Nonlinear systems may be (1) stable, that is, converging to an equilibrium; (2) oscillating stably; (3) chaotic within predictable boundaries; or (4) diverging unstably. In the chaotic state the system appears to exhibit paradoxical behavior: it is deterministic because it is fixed by equations and yet incorporates randomness. It may be orderly and suddenly become chaotic or vice versa. The system is exceedingly sensitive to initial conditions, making the use of historical data as a basis for forecasting seem futile [2]. Neither the rigid order of stability nor the randomness of chaos is as interesting to researchers of complex systems as the border between them, that is, "the edge of chaos." That is where novel behavior emerges.

Casti sees complex systems as either nonadaptive or adaptive. The former are characterized by the ability to see the whole picture. They permit no rule changes and can be described effectively by available predictive mathematical models. An example is astronomy. *Complex adaptive systems* (CAS) cannot see the whole picture, do permit rule creation or change, and are *adaptive*. They tend to be medium-sized, that is, not describable either by a few variables or by a very large number (in which case they would be amenable to statistical approaches as, for example, the particles in a gas). As Casti admits, there is no theory yet for such systems—"we're not even close" [1, p. ix]. He suggests that we are at a stage reminiscent of gamblers in 1600 before Pascal and Fermat developed the theory of probability. Complexity still evokes much perplexity.

We have already noted the counterintuitive behavior of complex systems with regard to deterministically engendered randomness. A second source of such surprising behavior is uncomputability that results in the transcendence of rules, that is, there may be no deductive rule governing a system's activity. For example, in economics, the rule of price adjustment arising from a given set of agent preferences and endowments can be any rule desired, not necessarily a rule leading to Adam Smith's invisible-hand equilibria [1, p. 112]. The specter of uncomputability has also been raised by physicist Roger Penrose in his insistence that cognition involves activities that transcend simple rule following.

A third source is instability that results in large effects from small changes (the "butterfly" effect). A fourth is connectivity, resulting in behavior that cannot be decomposed into parts. A fifth source of counterintuitive behavior is emergence, resulting in self-organizing patterns.

It is evident that the challenge for the forecaster is an awesome one. Better understanding of the internal dynamics of nonlinear systems is vital for more effective forecasting and it will require unprecedented insight and ingenuity.

8.2 Limits on Forecasting

We discussed the logistic or Pearl or S curve in Section 7.2. It is fascinating to note that the logistic equation describing this curve as a continuous function of time becomes, in its discrete recursive form, the foundation of chaos theory:

$$dx \, / \, dt = Kx(L - x) \longrightarrow x_{n+1} = Kx_n(1 - x_n)$$

where L is the growth limit and K is a constant. The latter equation can exhibit all the four behaviors mentioned previously, that is, stability, oscillation, chaos, and unstable divergence [3]. Plotted as a function of K, it becomes the bifurcation diagram that displays another characteristic of nonlinear dynamic systems: fractal self-similarity. This means that the bifurcation pattern is repeated at different levels of magnification. The S curve itself leads to a fractal pattern: the envelope of a series or cascade of S curves is itself an S curve [4].

If we put the solution of the logistic differential equation into discrete form (instead of the equation itself), we find that chaotic behavior appears at both ends of the familiar S curve; Figure 8.1 illustrates the behavior [5]. The start of the chaotic phase can be increasingly anticipated when logistic growth fades, but its precise timing remains elusive. Increasing obsolescence or inadequacy of an established pattern leads to a critical situation where a minor event can suddenly push the system into chaos. The timing of the end of the chaotic phase and emergence of a new configuration is similarly uncertain. However, as it becomes increasingly stable with growing success, predictability improves dramatically.

Shermer cites the technology of the typewriter development as an example of the chaotic period preceding an S curve. Between 1714 and the 1860s at least 112 typewriters were developed, exhibiting wide diversity in design, before Stoles produced the one that led to the Remington. It would have been impossible to forecast the successful innovation and its S curve during the chaotic phase [6]. The instances of accidental discovery are legion. The nuclear age unexpectedly produced nuclear fallout, neutron radiation, magnetic field disturbances, electromagnetic pulses creating component burnout, and radio isotopes for medical diagnosis and treatment [7].

The existence of chaotic phases at the beginning and end of the S curve, together with the cascading series of such curves typical of technological evolution, clearly points up the constraints or "walls of unpredictability." The chaotic behavior at the start prevents us from pinpointing the take-off timing of the successful innovation. Consider the competition between Betamax and VHS formats for video cassette recorders. Initially both systems became available at

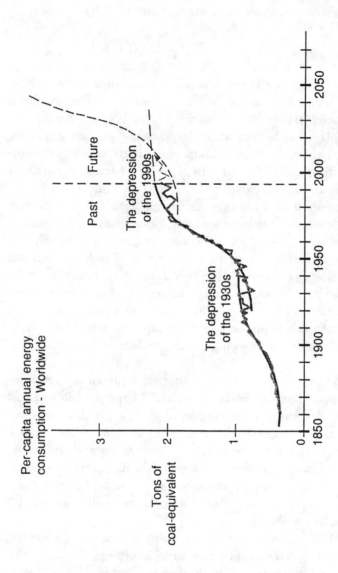

Figure 8.1 S-shaped growth curves showing chaotic behavior at beginning and end [5].

the same time and sold at similar prices, leading to comparable, albeit fluctuating, market shares. This unstable situation was decided by the positive (amplifying) feedback triggered by a small gain in VHS market share, a seemingly chance event that could not have been forecast [1, p. 88]. Although in some ways inferior to Betamax, VHS offered a more attractive selection of movies. Brian Arthur of the Santa Fe Institute recognized over a decade ago that a technologically inferior product can beat a superior one by its ability to exploit "network externalities," for example, the fact that a slight edge in marketing can lead to positive feedback: the value of the product increases as its use spreads [8]. Another example is the announcement by the dominant firm of nonexistent future products ("vaporware"), thereby discouraging smaller competitors, who may actually be ahead in the technology, from pushing forward with their product development.

Once the new technology is on its way, forecasting becomes quite feasible. Usually the S curve can be estimated well once 5% to 10% of the potential market has been attained. As the asymptote (L) is approached and technological stagnation sets in, the forecaster is frustrated once more because the trigger that sets off the chaotic phase is elusive. Even so, the examination of the envelope curve, that is, the S curve at the next fractal level, gives significant insight for forecasting. It follows from this discussion that it is generally, but not always, true that short-term forecasting is more feasible than long-term forecasting. It all depends on the system phase(s) that pertain over the forecast time span.

The existence of stable and chaotic phases may also illuminate a relationship between the Kondratiev long wave cycles and the historic development of forecasting and planning (Chapter 7). Once a depression with its chaotic aspects passes and renewed growth replaces it, the increasingly stable environment becomes favorable for forecasting and planning. This was the situation when the Great Depression of the 1930s was followed by the economic growth of the 1950s and 1960s. It was during this period that new methodologies were developed. The results are evident in the spate of books on technological forecasting that appeared between 1967 and 1972 (Jantsch, Bright, Ayres, and Martino) as well as the professional journal *Technological Forecasting and Social Change* (1969) and various technological forecasting and planning workshops for industry.

Stability seems to have peaked by 1972; the subsequent downturn phase is reflected in forecasting and planning falling out of favor. We recall that the perceived weaknesses of the analytic approaches gave rise in the 1970s to the multiple perspective concept, based on the 1971 work of Allison and Churchman (Chapters 2 and 3). In the 1980s chaos theory clearly demonstrated the inherent limits of forecasting. In the fluid systems environment of the 1990s, complexity science is strongly hinting that new approaches to forecasting and planning may be in the offing, to be exploited in the next economic growth period.

8.3 Modeling

Modeling constitutes a primary tool in forecasting. We recall that Forrester's system dynamics model was the basis for the well-known *Limits to Growth* and the many subsequent global modeling projects undertaken in the 1970s (Section 2.4). Complexity science underscores the weakness of these models. They can suggest basic megatrends. But, as Herbert Simon has pointed out:

> The fundamental conclusion drawn from the model—that exponential growth cannot be sustained indefinitely—is entirely true, has enormous impact for public policy, and could have been inferred from textbook treatments of linear dynamic systems without any computation . . . There may even be actual harm in carrying out such a modeling exercise . . . It may give skeptics entirely too much ammunition for questioning even those conclusions that can be validly drawn from the model [9].

These models ignore the unstable, chaotic phases that accompany the catastrophes that they project and consequently their inherent unpredictability. Two successive runs of such a nonlinear model may have quite different outcomes. This means that a sudden change in system behavior may not be the result of an external change but may be entirely due to the internal dynamics of the system. We recall that this reflects precisely one of the differences cited previously between the T and O/P perspectives (see Chapter 3). The science-based T assumes replicability of experiments, but that is not meaningful for O and P. A retrial or a replay of a game with the same participants may produce quite different outcomes.

The use of the computer as a laboratory tool to study complex, nonlinear dynamic systems is now opening up new paths for the forecaster. In particular, it may well become a most effective methodology to deepen our understanding of systems whose elements are adaptive, such as sociotechnical systems [10].

One of the most promising approaches is the use of computer simulation to "grow" complex nonlinear dynamic systems from the bottom up [1, 11]. New worlds are created that are miniatures of the real world or true silicon worlds. The system elements, or agents, are intelligent and adaptive in the sense that they can make decisions on the basis of simple rules, modify the rules, or create new ones. No single agent has access to what all the other agents are doing; that is, he/she has local, but not global, information.

The creation of such electronic worlds can provide remarkable insights, such as emergent behaviors resulting from the interaction of these agents. Microlevel interactions between individual agents and global, aggregate-level patterns and behaviors mutually reinforce each other. This bottom-up simulation approach has already been used successfully to model a variety of systems:

- The traffic in Albuquerque, encompassing 200,000 households, 400,000 daily travelers, and 30,000 road segments—showing the appearance and disappearance of traffic jams;
- Genetic regulatory networks, involving a network of the 100,000 genes in a human body cell that switch each other on and off—exhibiting a powerful tendency to self-organization and indicating that a cell type is a stable recurrent pattern of gene expression;
- Biological systems, starting with a simple stick figure that mutates in accordance with a simple set of rules, creating a set of offspring each determined by a single mutation; the striking result is that highly complex forms evolve, including look-alikes of real primitive plants;
- Social systems involving primitive exchange-type economies that can test the efficient market hypothesis—with the surprising result that if the agents are at least a little bit human in their behavior, there is no reason to assume markets will perform the way economic textbooks tell us they should [1].

The last of these models, *Sugarscape,* should be of particular interest to forecasters. It offers a means to sweep in various disciplines and examine their interactions, such as demography and economics.

> A wide range of important . . . phenomena can be made to emerge from the spatio-temporal interaction of autonomous agents operating on landscapes under simple local rules [11, p. 153].

An example is the distribution of wealth in a simple sugar-consuming society. The agents are endowed with uniformly distributed vision acuity and metabolic rates. The sugar resource is distributed on the landscape in two "mountain" sites. Two results become apparent as the computer model is run: (1) self-organization is at least as efficient as top-down planning; and (2) there is a widening gap between rich and poor, that is, the bell-shaped initial wealth distribution turns into a highly skewed one [11, p. 34]. A few agents accumulate much wealth and an increasing number of agents become poorer.

A relevant question, raised by the developers of this model, is the effect of foresight on the agents. Trading sugar and spice, they initially make their decisions based on their current holdings of these resources. If agent behavior is modified so that they can look ahead a certain number of time intervals, one finds that

> clearly, some foresight is better than none in this society since the long-run average foresight becomes approximately stable at a nonzero level. However, large amounts of foresight . . are less "fit" than modest amounts [11, p. 129].

In other words, too much foresight may be as bad as too little foresight.

Another potential capability is the introduction of technological innovations into *Sugarscape* as substitutes for diminishing resources and determining how they affect the economies of the traders.

Taking off from the simulation approach to biological system evolution, Kauffman raises the question whether artificial technological worlds can be created in this manner. He suspects that the variants of an innovation—many tried with one successful and the others becoming extinct—mirror biological (co)evolution [12]. In other words, technological (co)evolution may be guided by the same laws as biological (co)evolution.[1] This suggests the possibility of viewing the technological web as driving its own transformation by continual creation of new niches. Using Lisp programming language logic, "symbol string" models with simple "grammar" rules provide a means of dealing with "tools," "raw materials," and "products." The initial strings represent, say, certain renewable physical resources that produce certain goods and services. At each period thereafter, the goods and services previously invented create new opportunities to create still more goods and services and the technological frontier expands [12]. Thus, one can consider, for a preset planning horizon and discount rate, the possible sequences of technological goods and services that might be created and choose the one with the highest value added. After imple-

---

1. However, there are distinct differences as well. Unlike technological evolution, biological evolution is non-directional, that is, it has no vector. *Homo sapiens* notwithstanding, bacteria are still the most successful life form. Also, biological evolution is very slow (Darwinian), whereas cultural and technological evolution is rapid (Lamarckian). Technological information is transmitted extremely fast compared with the glacial pace of natural genetic change.

mentation in the first year, the process is repeated each year with a "rolling horizon."

Although the grammar model is highly simplified, it may well provide a useful tool in studying the pattern of technological evolution and coevolution of a web of technologies. Just as in the coevolution of organisms, the processes of niche creation and combinatorial optimization seem to occur with technologies. In a similar fashion the web structure itself plays an essential role in the way the web evolves and the artifact system is transformed. Kauffman believes that this approach will show that, as the complexity of the grammar rules increases, technological diversity begets diversity and it, in turn, begets growth.

Lane [13] derives four principles from such electronic worlds:

- Chance may be decisive in the evolution of a market where two products compete (recall the VHS-Betamax case);

- Coevolution occurs in an evolutionary system, be it organism or artifact: successful strategies shift over time as relationships range from complete cooperation to complete competition; such shifts correspond to unstable periods;

- It is useful to think of organizations not merely as structures but as processors that generate structures;

- Intelligent behaviors and decisions are not necessarily rational ones; the electronic worlds echo Simon's "bounded rationality" (see Chapter 1) and underscore the relevance of the O and P perspectives, which are not tied to scientific logic, cause-and-effect, and rationality.

8.4 Perspectives on Business Organizations

Lumley [14] has addressed teamwork in business organizations and observes that the traditional view of organizational management is characterized by linear thinking, as exemplified by clear causal models and simplistic, readily quantifiable measures of effectiveness. Frederick Taylor with his "scientific management" was the archetype of this analytic approach (see Chapter 1). But effective business teams employ dual modes of thinking and working that equate well to the notions of equilibrium (stable periodic) and nonequilibrium (aperiodic or chaotic). Lumley depicts the value V arising from the team process as a complex variable $V = F + iC$, where F is the "fabricative" linear, tangible, reductionist component and C the "creative" nonlinear, interactive, learning component. In the complex environment of the information technology age, there is an increasing emphasis on C. High-performance teams are "learning organizations," where V is a synthesis of F and C, where team performance cannot be measured by piecewise mechanical assembly of components and must be viewed in a larger space-time setting. Note the reference to reductionism (T), learning (P), and team performance (O); see also Figure 3.7 on the T-O-P view of creativity.

Using computer modeling, Huberman has addressed the problem of cooperation in problem solving [15]. Among the insights drawn forth:

- Beginning with few agents and increasing their number quickly raises the probability of solving a problem; the same happens when the diversity of the agents is increased.

- As the organization size increases, some agents will far outperform others and some get a "free ride." Just as the *Sugarscape* model runs showed the skewing of wealth distribution, the performance distribution of the agents is skewed here.

- Informal groupings tend to emerge almost unconsciously through self-organization, based on the ability to interact effectively and frequently. As the overall group size increases, the number of component clusters also increases, but their size decreases.

The whole is more than the sum of its parts, but we can neither linguistically describe nor practically quantify it—a frustrating situation for management. Stephen Gould has used baseball to illustrate the point. The disappearance of .400 hitters is not due to declining performance but to improved overall team play. In other words, the usual quantitative data neglect the context of the whole [16]. It is thus hardly surprising that most managers discount C in determining rewards and investments. The high-reliability organization proposal elicited by the application of multiple perspectives to the *Exxon Valdez* case (Section 6.2), as well as the behavior-oriented reward approaches fostered by Herb Kelleher at Southwest Airlines and Bob Galvin at Motorola show an appreciation of the dual modes of thinking.

Having recognized the limitations of forecasting, the increasing system complexity, and the work-in-progress nature of complexity science, the frustration of executives with long-range planning is understandable. At the most fundamental level, complexity science implies the evolution of a significantly different approach to corporate planning, "growing strategies" to fit a rapidly changing environment, facilitating self-organization and maximizing adaptability.

Of more immediate practical value may be the following options:

Crisis Management

One lesson the business planner can draw from military planning concerns training to deal with unanticipated situations. The business planner tradition-ally begins with the "most likely" scenario for the future. Even when of-fered—say, high, medium, and low-economic growth scenarios—he or she will usually proceed on the basis of the medium one. In contrast, military officers train by extensive war gaming, confronting many alternative scenarios, none of which they expect to face in the real world. The point is to train the decision maker to react effectively regardless of which actual situation materializes. This training enhances the ability to manage crises by focusing on robustness. In the words of a Southern California Edison Co. planner,

> How much confidence do we have that the future will be as depicted under the [single] "reference" scenario? Very little . . . How much confidence do we have that we will be prepared to deal with whatever happens? A great deal [17].

In light of the experience with industrial accidents and their growing sig-nificance in a crowded world (see Chapter 6) *crisis management* (CM) has be-come a distinct field of study in recent years. Some corporations, such as United Airlines, have set up disaster teams to deal with accidents. Others have imple-mented concepts drawn from the high-reliability organization discussed in Sec-tion 6.2 (see Table 6.5). Kovoor-Misra uses multiple perspectives to develop an approach to crisis management [18]. For further insights the reader is referred to the work of Mitroff [19].

Experimentation

Once again the military provide an interesting example of dealing with complex sociotechnical systems. It is the "lessons learned" process, which focuses on try-ing out systems operationally in a realistic setting, rapidly gathering the lessons of success or failure, and disseminating that information to all relevant units. Thus, misconceptions are corrected and learning is much more efficient. The *Center for Army Lessons Learned* (CALL) has been created specifically for this function [20].

Planners can learn one lesson from the Founding Fathers who produced the U.S. Constitution. They clearly recognized the complexity of the system they were formulating. James Madison carefully studied the Greek city-states and confederations for "experimental instruction" about the balance between local and federal governments (the systemic balance between centralization and decentralization we discussed in Section 3.7) [21]. The writers created a framework that is perceived by the physicist and Nobel laureate Richard Feynman two hundred years later as:

> The result [was] to invent a system to govern when you don't know how. And the way to arrange it is to permit a system, like we have, wherein new ideas can be developed and tried out and thrown away. The writers of the Constitution knew of the value of doubt. In the age where they lived, for instance, science had already developed far enough to show the possibilities and potentialities that are the result of having uncertainty, the value of having the openness of possibility . . . To solve any problem that has never been solved before, you have to leave the door to the unknown ajar. You have to permit the possibility that you do not have it exactly right [22].

Experimentation implies an acknowledgment that the decision maker does not know the "right" answer. This is distasteful to most modern politicians and CEOs. After all they are chosen by an electorate or Board of Directors with the expectation that they have answers to the problems confronting the state or organization [23]. The pressure for certainty is characteristic of the individual's P perspective (see Table 3.1) and constitutes a potent force, as is well understood by ideologues as an effective, albeit simplistic, path to garnering strong support.

The one time that experimentation is acceptable is in time of crisis, such as a depression or organizational collapse. We already noted in Section 7.2 the willingness to take greater risk with radical innovations during times of depression than in times of prosperous growth. President Franklin Roosevelt developed the New Deal domestic reform in the Great Depression, clearly recognizing its experimental character. Some of its programs failed, such as the *National Recovery Administration* (NRA) and the *Agricultural Adjustment Administration* (AAA). Others were highly successful, such as the *Tennessee Valley Authority* (TVA) and the Social Security System.

Jefferson expected that there would be a Constitutional Convention every generation to apply the lessons learned through feedback and periodically adjust the framework of this grand unfolding experiment. It is good advice for dealing with complex systems today.

Exploiting Stability-Instability Boundaries

Recognition of the distinct regimes in complex systems opens up the opportunity to use that knowledge. The planner who seeks system stability in the nonlinear system can take steps to steer it away from the limits or develop policies that are effective at the limits. Chaos or wide oscillation can be avoided by slowing the system down, reducing feedback in the system or decoupling elements in the system (see Table 6.2) [24]. Alternatively, a system suffering decline due to excessive stability can be pushed toward chaos. We note the connection between chaos and creativity. At times an organization must be shaken up and rejuvenated; stability can turn into death, which is, after all, the most stable state. The Kondratiev long wave cycle pattern was noted in Section 7.2. Stable economic growth leads to a peak that is followed by an unstable period of sharp decline. The historic clustering of innovations observed toward the end of depressions can be readily seen as a reflection of the chaotic aspect of the downturn. Risk-taking is far more acceptable at that time; when times are good "safe" improvements are preferred. The pattern has been observable for two centuries. No one knows whether such cycles will persist in the twenty-first century as information technology spurs simultaneous decentralization and globalization.

8.5 Areas of Research

Forecasting and Planning (Sections 7.2 and 7.3)

There is a distinct difference between explanation and forecast and both can yield useful insights for planning. Consider the following examples [25]:

- Excellent forecast and excellent explanation: Newton's theory;
- Excellent forecast and poor explanation: quantum mechanics;
- Poor forecast and excellent explanation: Darwin's theory.

Rather than merely confirm the inherent limits to forecasting, complexity science should be seen as opening up new paths to reveal important insights to assist decision making. The study of the evolution of complex dynamic systems shows that the conjunction of order and chaos, stability and instability, self-organization and chance is decisive for progress. Thus, complexity science presents the technological planner and manager with challenging new tasks.

- Develop a theory of system coevolution; it should apply to both biological and technological coevolution. Such a concept would constitute a breakthrough in understanding complex adaptive system behavior and should give rise to a whole new approach to technological forecasting. In particular, it would clarify the boundaries between forecasting and surprise. Biological and technological evolution may have similar patterns.

- Try to understand and map the domains of system stability, stable oscillation, chaos, and instability. What triggers the shifts from one regime to another? What can we learn from the chaotic interval? It is vital that the system state be correctly diagnosed, that is, the stability-chaos pattern be recognized. This is not always an easy task; what appears to be chaos may simply be noise.

- Recognize that random-appearing data may not be random and, conversely, a perceived pattern may actually be produced by chance [2, 24]. Misinterpetations may thus be avoided. For example, the shift from chaotic to stable behavior suggested by the recursive data may be illusory, signifying a brief interlude of apparent order. Or a shift from stable to chaotic behavior is erroneously assumed to be due to disturbances external to the system. The role of randomness in innovation is significant: it creates fluctuations that act as natural seeds from which new patterns and structures grow [26].

- Find ways to circumvent the limitations to provide improved insights. One example is the use of a metatrend such as an envelope curve to anticipate the next S curve. Another is the recognition that insights and explanations can evoke means of substituting for forecast limitations. The creation of high-reliability organizations can respond to unpredicted crises (Section 6.2). Examples are the *Federal Emergency Management Agency* (FEMA), airline crisis management teams, and the US Air Force Strategic Air Command's airborne readiness system.

- Explore means to stimulate a phase change. Creativity and technological change can be triggered by creating chaos in a stagnant, stable system. Alternatively, new stable growth can be instituted by determining and supporting a promising technological approach during the chaotic phase. In other words, learn to manipulate the order/chaos phases by nudges at the right time and place [24].

- Recognize how to delay or forestall a phase change. Inappropriate timing of the onset of chaos can be averted by cutting feedback loops in the system and/or applying external "kicks." For example, it may be dangerous to speed up information flow when there is the potential of inducing chaos that management cannot handle [2, 24]. Slowing down short-term international capital flows by introducing circuit breakers in the feedback loops may prevent or mitigate worldwide financial chaos.

- Work with models such as *Sugarscape* to develop insight on critical questions raised by the impact of technology on society. A prime example is the question raised earlier with regard to information technology: what is the desirable balance between organizational centralization and decentralization (Section 3.7)? How is the balance maintained as the organization evolves? Such computer simulation can be used to develop relevant insights and examine other technological changes as they affect the agents and their interactions. Valuable comparisons among emergent self-organizational patterns are then possible.

Recent events (see, for example, Chapter 6) have shown that the consequences of mismanagement of the evolving sociotechnical systems are causing increasingly serious concerns. These complex systems inevitably involve human beings and are nonlinear, dynamic, adaptive, and emergent. It is now quite clear that such systems face inherent bounds on their mathematical describability, computability, and predictability. But it is also becoming clear that we are at the frontier of exploration in drawing on complexity science to advance our understanding of these systems in entirely new ways for the benefit of the planner and decision maker. In our context this means that the T perspective is cognizant of its limitations and is striving to deepen its approaches to encompass aspects for which we must now rely on O and P to gain vital insights. The examples cited in Section 8.3, such as an economic behavior in the *Sugarscape* model not in accord with classical economic theories and the finding that in electronic worlds the most intelligent behaviors and decisions (not necessarily rational ones) make the point.

Discounting (Sections 7.1 and 7.3)

The T, O, and P perspectives usually have different discount rates, hence different planning horizons. This mismatch inhibits important tasks, such as strategic planning. As we noted earlier (Section 7.3), Ayres's recent work has underscored the inadequacy of the economists' traditional discounting approaches and suggested consideration of hyperbolic functions to replace the usual exponential function [27]. Rothenberg (Section 7.1) has proposed restricting discounting to a single generation and using a very slowly decreasing step function beyond the present generation [28]. The use of negative discount rates also needs to be more fully probed.

Two means to reduce the gap in time horizons among perspectives have been suggested by the author and are schematically shown in Figure 8.2 [29]:

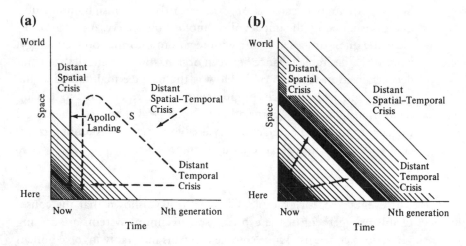

Figure 8.2 Space-time perception: (a) moving crisis or opportunity closer and (b) extending perception out [29].

1. Moving the distant crisis or opportunity well within the organization's or individual's current planning horizon;

2. Extending the present planning horizon farther out.

As noted earlier, we discount in physical space as well as time (Figure 8.2(a)). Telecommunications have been successful in drastically foreshortening the space dimension, for example, bringing the distant Apollo manned lunar landing and Kennedy assassination events vividly into our living room. Technology has been far less effective in foreshortening the time dimension. Orson Wells's famous broadcast of H. G. Wells's *War of the Worlds* is a rare successful example. In some instances it may be possible to substitute space for time and then compress the space dimension by telecommunications (arrow S in Figure 8.2(a)). Distant space/near time is used as a surrogate for distant time/near space. A future situation of concern to us will be more readily comprehensible if we can find a current analog somewhere else in the world. An example is the insights obtainable on future U.S. social legislation by examining and communicating (via television) the current impacts observable in Sweden that has long been a precursor in this area by about fifteen years. Similarly some possible U.S. urban transportation options are already at hand in Europe and can thus be communicated into American living rooms. Option 2 (Figure 8.2(b)) may be achievable by the slower process of education, particularly at the elementary and high-school levels. Computer simulation games such as *Simearth* and *Simcity* may be helpful in this endeavor.

Identification of T-O-P Balance in Individuals (Section 3.6)

It is important in any application of the multiple perspective concept to draw in diverse perspectives and simultaneously to avoid mistaking one perspective for another. Does a specific O perspective put forward in an interview really represent the designated organization, or is it actually a personal perspective? It would be desirable to develop means to facilitate the identification of a perspective type or dominance of one perspective in a mix. The problem is related to that of determining psychological profiles. It is quite similar to that addressed by consultants for opposing sides in a courtroom trial, namely, the determination of desirable and undesirable jury candidates from the roster of available citizens. Another aspect of considerable interest is the stability or instability of perspectives and mixes held by individuals.

Cross-Cuing and Integration of Perspectives (Sections 3.6 and 3.7)

A decision maker frequently is presented with a series of perspectives that are then "processed" in his mind and lead to a decision. Similarly, a jury hears witnesses and summations by the attorneys, "processes" such input, and reaches a decision. In each case, the "process" may well be a mysterious one, difficult to predict or even to analyze a posteriori. How does one perspective support or neutralize another? Why is one perspective weighted heavily and another ignored? There exists no neat formula for integrating perspectives. If there were, the analyst or the computer could do the integration for the decision maker and possibly even replace high-level executives altogether! The subtleties and complexities of this "process" are such that we do not anticipate a "solution." However, research may begin to illuminate some aspects of the process and inform the analyst about the number and variety of perspectives to use.

Communication Techniques for O and P Perspectives (Sections 3.3 and 3.4)

Means to obtain input and transmit output for the O and P perspectives differ significantly from those familiar to T perspective analysts (see Chapter 9). Interviews clearly play an important role, but other methods, such as participant observation and guided group dialogue, require closer examination in connection with the multiple perspective concept.

8.6 Closing Comments

This brief list gives ample evidence that, with this book, we have only taken a few steps on a very challenging and fascinating path. We close this chapter with two thoughts.

A Nagging Worry

The Singerian inquiring system, implied by the use of multiple perspectives, understandably jars those—scientists and technologists—accustomed to Lockean (data-based), Leibnizian (model-based), and Kantian (data plus model or multimodel) inquiring systems (Section 2.4). It also leaves us with the residual fear that the O and P perspectives may be unconsciously transformed into T perspectives. This concern is best alleviated in practice by (1) creating an interparadigmatic, rather than interdisciplinary, team at the beginning of a project (see Chapter 9, guideline 3) and (2) discouraging academic efforts to create formal, T perspective, theories for the application of multiple perspectives.

A Different Perspective on the Perspectives

Our present limitations in dealing with complex adaptive systems, including the lack of a theory (Section 8.1), leave large voids; multiple perspectives may help to fill them. Evolution of life from the "primeval soup" to an information society has not relied solely on man's creation of science and technology. The process began, and proceeded admirably, long before the output of science and technology could have an impact. Replicating molecules were striving for negentropy (higher organization), range (expansion in space), and control through collaboration and Darwinian competition. The process has been stunningly successful [30]. One can argue that much of this heritage (accumulated genetic knowledge?) resides in human beings (individually and collectively as a species) although not yet encapsulated in formal science and technology. "Humanness" may even reflect emergent properties that cannot be so systematized. Thus, O and P perspectives may automatically sweep in "knowledge," augmenting that which is consciously developed by T perspective analysis.

References

[1]   Casti, J., *Would-Be Worlds,* New York: John Wiley & Sons, Inc., 1997.

[2]   Gordon, T. J., and D. Greenspan, "Chaos and Fractals: New Tools for Technological and Social Forecasting," *Technological Forecasting and Social Change,* Vol. 34, 1988, pp. 1–25.

[3]   Modis, T., *Predictions,* New York: Simon & Schuster, 1992.

[4]   Modis, T., "Fractal Aspects of Natural Growth," *Technological Forecasting and Social Change*, Vol. 47, 1994, pp. 63–74.

[5]   Modis, T., and A. Debecker, "Chaoslike States Can Be Expected Before and After Logistic Growth," *Technological Forecasting and Social Change*, Vol. 41, 1992, pp. 111–120.

[6]   Shermer, M., "Exorcising Laplace's Demon: Chaos and Antichaos, History and Metahistory," *History and Theory*, Vol. 34, 1995, pp. 59–83.

[7]   Schelling, T. C., "Research by Accident," *Technological Forecasting and Social Change*, Vol. 53, 1996, pp. 15–20.

[8]   Arthur, W. B., "Positive Feedbacks in the Economy," *Scientific American*, Feb. 1990.

[9]   Simon, H., "Prediction and Prescription in Systems Modeling," speech at the IIASA Conference on Perspectives and Futures, Laxenburg, Austria, June 14–15, 1988. Edited version in *Operations Research*, Vol. 38, 1990, pp. 7–14.

[10] Axelrod, R., "Advancing the Art of Simulation in the Social Sciences," *Complexity*, Vol. 3, No. 2, 1997, pp. 16–22.

[11] Epstein, J. M., and R. Axtell, *Growing Artificial Societies*, Washington, DC: The Brookings Institution; Cambridge, MA: The MIT Press, 1996.

[12] Kauffman, S., *At Home in the Universe*, New York: Oxford University Press, 1995.

[13] Lane, D., "Models and Aphorisms," *Complexity*, Vol. 1, No. 2, 1995, pp. 9–13.

[14] Lumley, T., "Complexity and the 'Learning Organization,'" *Complexity*, Vol. 2, No. 5, 1997, pp. 14–22.

[15] Huberman, B. A. (ed.), *The Ecology of Computation*, New York: North-Holland, 1988.

[16] Gould, S. J., *Full House: The Spread of Excellence from Plato to Darwin*, New York: Harmony Books, 1996.

[17] Southern California Edison Co., "Planning for Uncertainty: A Case Study," *Technological Forecasting and Social Change*, Vol. 33, 1988, pp. 119–148.

[18] Kovoor-Misra, S., "A Multidimensional Approach to Crisis Preparation for Technical Organizations," *Technological Forecasting and Social Change*, Vol. 48, 1995, pp. 143–160.

[19] Mitroff, I. I., "Crisis Management: Cutting Through the Confusion," *Sloan Management Review*, Vol. 15, 1988.

[20] *Wall Street Journal*, May 23, 1997.

[21] *The Federalist Papers: A Collection of Essays Written in Support of the Constitution of the United States (1787)*. 2nd edition, Garden City, NY: Anchor Books, 1966. Essays No. 10, 14, and 45 by James Madison; Essays No. 18 and 20 by Alexander Hamilton and James Madison.

[22] Feynman, R. P., *The Meaning of It All: Thoughts of a Citizen Scientist*, Reading, MA: Addison-Wesley Publishing Co., 1998.

[23] Coates, J., "What to Do When You Don't Know What You Are Doing," *Technological Forecasting and Social Change*, Vol. 50, 1995, pp. 249–252.

[24] Gordon, T., and D. Greenspan, "The Management of Chaotic Systems," *Technological Forecasting and Social Change*, Vol. 47, 1994, pp. 49–62.

[25] Casti, J. L., *Searching for Certainty*, New York: W. Morrow and Co., Inc., 1990, p. 407.

[26] Resnick, M., "Unblocking the Traffic Jams in Corporate Thinking," *Complexity*, Vol. 3, No. 4, March–April 1998, p. 29.

[27] Ayres, R. U., "Foresight as a Survival Tactic," *Technological Forecasting and Social Change*, Vol. 51, 1996, pp. 209–236.

[28] Rothenberg, J., "Time Comparisons in Public Policy Analysis of Global Change: an Economic Exploration," manuscript, communicated by H. Brooks, 1992.

[29] Linstone, H. A., "On Discounting the Future," *Technological Forecasting and Social Change*, Vol. 4, 1973, pp. 335–338.

[30] Marchetti, C., "On the Role of Science in the Post-Industrial Society: 'Logos'—The Empire Builder," Keynote Address, St. Paul de Vence Conference, May 19–21, 1981; reprinted in *Technological Forecasting and Social Change*, Vol. 24, 1983, pp. 197–206.

9

Guidelines for the User

The man who neglects the real to study the ideal will learn how to accomplish his ruin.

Niccolò Machiavelli

The test of a first-rate intelligence is the ability to hold two opposed ideas in the mind at the same time . . . and still retain the ability to function.

F. Scott Fitzgerald

We begin with a brief review of the kinds of insight gained in our case studies in Chapters 4 to 6 (Table 9.1). Our experience over the past 20 years has included lectures, workshops, seminars, and application projects in North and South America, Europe, the Near East, and Asia. It is encapsulated in the following guidelines for the user.

9.1 Seven Guidelines (Linstone and Meltsner)

1. Strive for a Balance Among T, O, and P Perspectives

An individual steeped throughout his working life in one set of paradigms and trained to suppress the others will find it difficult to apply another in developing a new perspective. Thus, the scientist or technologist is accustomed to T and may be unable to do justice to O or P. We find that a T-trained person will see, or assume, a world populated by rational actors and afflicted with problems to be "solved" by data- and model-based techniques. Such an individual often views the O perspective as mere detail and the P perspective as dirty politics.

Table 9.1
Examples of Insights Derived from T, O, and P Perspectives

T	O	P
MILITARY TECHNOLOGY (Section 4.1)		
USS Wampanoag		
New ship superior to ships in other navies. Sea trials very successful, performance exceeds specs.	Ship is a destructive energy in Navy society. Adverse effect on morale. Not a school of seamanship.	Isherwood is a brilliant designer.
M-16 Rifle		
AR-15 (later M-16) superior in tests and Vietnam; more lethal (faster, smaller bullet); lighter weight permits carrying more ammo.	Marksmanship tradition(accuracy, long range) strong in Ordnance Corps. Ordnance developed M-14.	Stoner develops and pushes AR-15. Col. Neilsen, Gen. LeMay, SecDef McNamara want it.
Atom Bomb Use		
Dropping bomb on Japan without warning most cost-effective alternative; ends war with fewest U.S. and Japanese casualties.	Anticipates threat of Soviet expansion; fear Manhattan Project is seen as boondoggle if bomb is not used.	Truman as new President cannot challenge policies in place, must appear decisive and bold.
LOCAL DECISIONS (Sections 4.2 and 4.3)		
Mount St. Helens Eruption		
Watershed management an important long-term problem. Traditional flood control: Corps of Engineers builds levees, dredges channels.	Predictions ignored. Resistance to change even after eruption. Exception: Cowlitz County control of land use. Multiple flood control measures raise interorganizational problems.	Individual perceives only immediate flood risk.
Denver International Airport		
FAA has developed a master planning process. Initially Denver was the hub of three airlines. A superior baggage system was designed.	The power of the airlines has greatly increased with deregulation, reflected in their leverage and demands (e.g., United's baggage system)	The negotiating skills of the Denver mayors, Gov. Romer, Sec. Skinner, the Denver Chamber of Commerce head, and Adams Co. heads were key

Table 9.1 (continued)

T	O	P
CORPORATE DECISIONS (Chapter 5)		
Hydroelectric Facility		
Building 60-MW facility is most cost effective.		New president brings in outsiders and changes corporate decision process.
Corporate Acquisition		
Venture analysis showed candidate to be an excellent choice for purchase.	Corporate culture favors in-house, develops rather than buys, is very conservative.	The corporate secretary exercised decisive power.
Commercial Aircraft		
Risk analysis shows a disastrous outcome if Big 4 airlines split orders between DC-10 and L-1011. DC-10 cargo door/cabin floor failure seen in early tests.	Bribery is an SOP in foreign sales. Animosity between FAA and NTSB. Engineers overriden by Marketing considerations.	Haughton's leadership, charisma, and negotiating skills saved Lockheed during Rolls-Royce crisis. Mr. Mac's inexperience with airlines hurt DC-10 marketing.
INDUSTRIAL ACCIDENTS (Chapter 6)		
The Alaska Oil Spill		
Spill clean-up technology is primitive. Marine transport is an error-inducing rather than a safety-reinforcing system.	Exxon could quickly mount a major operation. Alyeska had let its contingency capability decay to save costs. Blame placed solely on individuals.	Individual perceptions of probability tend to mislead. Exxon top management has image of arrogance.
The Bhopal Chemical Accident		
Corporate safety manuals clearly indicate precautions and safety measures for MIC.	Corporate audit found poor local safety practices, but UCIL management inertia prevailed. Initial reaction usually stonewalling.	Individual workers at scene inexperienced. No senior supervisory personnel at site. Local doctors and officials unfamiliar with MIC.

The O and P perspectives similarly have preconceptions about the T perspective, usually viewing it as naive. The mutual misperceptions are shown in Figure 9.1.

Individuals with a strong bias toward analysis, such as engineers and scientists, are likely to devote an excessive, if not obsessive, proportion of their time on T, with which they are comfortable, and treat O and P as superficial addenda, if indeed they are even willing to consider them at all. As a general rule, one should partition the effort into four roughly equal parts on T, O, P, and their integration. This may seem a crude rule, but it is far better than the 90% effort devoted to T that we have observed so often.

With experience the practitioner will develop a sense for the appropriate balance in any given case. A newly emerging technology may call for more emphasis on the T and O perspectives, while a current technology is likely to produce richer O and P perspectives.

2. Use Good Judgment in Selecting Perspectives

There are as many O perspectives as there are "organizations within an organization." Within a company or agency, each separate department or division has its own unique perspective. One cannot include them all. In addition, many O perspectives are often in conflict. The analyst is well advised to construct a dialectic between different internal O perspectives to draw out differing insights into the complexity of the organization. The same cautions apply to the P perspectives. The hierarchy of the organization is not always a good guide to follow; key persons may not appear on the organizational chart. Individuals who act outside of an institution may be as important and affect its outcomes significantly. Remember that there are formal and informal organizations.

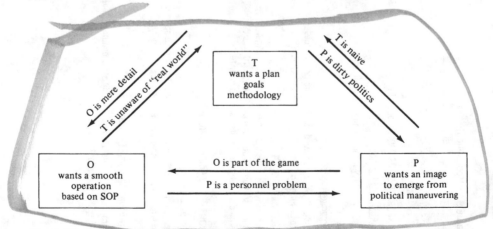

Figure 9.1 A basis of miscommunications [1].

In dealing with an emerging technology, one should recognize the practical difficulty of using multiple perspectives when the technology is mainly in the hands of a coterie of scientists and engineers, and the rest of the potentially interested participants have only latent and inchoate opinions about it. Such situations call for an aggregative effort to determine the locus of decision and assess the possibilities of coalition formation. In addition, for these technically dominated situations, it is also important to use the P perspective to bring out differences and similarities with respect to beliefs and orientations about the physical reality and the consequences of the technology. Such an approach will complement the technical aspects of the analysis by indicating potential conflicts and possible lines of technical development. Of course, as the technology matures, in the sense of developing a more textured political and social environment, the emphasis on the P perspective would probably lead to an appreciation of the value of a wider circle of potential participants. No longer would it make sense to apply the P perspective just to technical participants when nontechnical ones would be equally or more relevant.

In using the P perspective, the number of individuals to which the perspective is applied has to be severely limited. One should particularly look for individuals who are likely to act outside of an organizational or institutional role and who would affect outcomes (because they will not be included in O perspectives). It is also vital to determine whether a perspective presented by an individual is his own (P) or his organization's perspective (O).

3. In Obtaining Input, Recognize That O and P Require Distinctly Different Methods Than Does T

Each of the three perspective types sees the world through different lenses, that is, using different paradigms. Stated another way, the distinction between perspectives is *how* we are looking rather than at *what* we are looking. The T perspective relies on data and models and their analysis. However, O and P have proven crucial in revealing what makes an organization and individual actors "tick." Conventional documentation will not do because these perspectives are often politically sensitive. Structured interviews or Delphis are no substitute for direct one-on-one interviews. Talented interviewers must be good listeners, sensitive to nuances and nonverbal communication. What is not said is often as important as what is said. Volunteered asides may be as significant as direct responses to formal questions. Academics with their generally pronounced T bias tend to make poor interviewers in soliciting O and P perspectives. O and P become especially critical in understanding corporate as well as foreign cultures.

For instance, the author's research in China revealed that the Chinese generally understood well what was being probed for with O-type questions.

Chinese culture is bureaucratic and hierarchical, so O games and strategies are widely known. Power relationships are enshrined in all kinds of slogans such as "two down, one up" for the planning process and "the pyramid of power" in an organization. P perspectives present more of a hurdle. Often the answers to such questions are sparse, so one must push for concrete examples and anecdotes to flush out and flesh out critical insights. All translation becomes interpretive and thus requires sophisticated knowledge of the local culture.

In all O and P efforts skilled interviewers are highly desirable. We would like the interview subject to speak for himself or herself without our providing some clue as to what we want to hear. We want to understand and see things from the other person's point of view. Ethnographers and other skilled field investigators are quite sensitive to this problem and have taken steps to reduce, control, or at least identify the sources of bias. Regardless of whether we conduct several independent analyses, corroborate our findings with participant observation, do repetitive intensive interviewing with the same informant, or extensive interviewing with a variety of participants, there is bound to be some mixing of the observer and the observed. The interviewer at least has to be clear about which perspective he or she is using in the field, in the subsequent analysis, and in the write-up.

We always deal with individuals to obtain the necessary information. In employing the T perspective, for example, we may be interested only in rational cause-and-effect linkages or the relation between physical components, but have to elicit the information from an individual who reflects both organizational and technical concerns. Trying to use the O perspective we may see that a particular organization will be central to the outcome. We would then take that organization as an empirical referent and proceed to work on describing roles. But in interviewing a number of individuals, we would soon discover that these individuals are not necessarily confined by their organizational roles in their responses. Indeed, the same informant may provide information for understanding several perspectives. An actor could also behave in idiosyncratic ways that may be outside his institutional role. The consequences of the idiosyncratic behavior are essential for specifying the P perspective; the institutional role is essential for specifying the O perspective. Consider Admiral Rickover's pursuit of nuclear submarines. Some of what he did reflected the U.S. Navy; while the maverick in him reflected his own propensities, independent of the organizational context.

What we think we have learned about an individual's behavior via the P perspective may not be what that individual feels or thinks at all. Yet, what we observe or infer may be quite acceptable and important. Suppose that the total thrust of what we have learned from a variety of sources indicates that an organization is dragging its feet in implementing a decision about a new technology. Then it will be of only slight significance that a civil service informant feels that he is protecting some interest instead of creating red tape. True, one person's regulation is another's red tape; but this is a difference of perception that can usually be assumed away. Similarly, in the analysis using the O perspective, we are likely to assume that certain organizations will operate, for our purposes, as monoliths. Obviously, organizations are composed of many individuals with differing values, goals, and beliefs, but this fact should not prevent us from assuming the organization, as a coalition, can act in concert. Distortions that do not affect major findings should be ignored.

The Italian journalist Oriana Fallaci, in some ways a model interviewer, has elicited these views (the second from an interviewee, Henry Kissinger):

> Hers is a mind of intuitions. It is a very bright mind, as one quickly finds on reading her interviews [2].
>
> Fallaci caught that mood . . . She wrote history in the Roman style; she sought psychological, not factual truth [3].

In our experience recording has usually been done in one of two ways: summarization immediately after the interview or taping of the interview. The latter is superior to the extent that it constitutes a more accurate memory and minimizes distortion or bias by the interviewer. But it may also inhibit the interviewee. Care must be taken to preserve anonymity (that is, no attribution) or other constraints imposed by the interviewee, and ethical questions may arise to confound the interviewer. He or she may be subject to manipulation, being "used" to plant ideas, or becoming brainwashed, slowly turning into an advocate or apologist. Finally, Hannah Arendt reminds us that "truthfulness has never been counted among the political virtues, and lies have always been regarded as justifiable tools in political dealings" [4].

To design a field strategy for using multiple perspectives, the first question to ask is: Who cares about this system or problem? Individuals and organizations who care and are concerned about it are more likely to come into the political arena than those who are indifferent. In the early stages of the investigation, we do not have to worry about whether that concern is supportive or hostile, only that it is a likely indicator of future activity and behavior.

We do not start trying to create a scientific random sample but more of a snowball sample, going from one key informant to another on the basis of leads. One must be alert that successive recommendations do not simply reinforce one point of view. For future technology, we are likely to go to the scientists or the designers or the technology and then proceed from producers to likely policy makers, consumers, and other groups who may act on, or be affected by, the technology. With an existing or near-term technology, it is possible to start with any concerned informant, and the more knowledgeable, the better. Within the resource constraints of the effort, it is preferable to be expansive in choosing people to interview or otherwise observe. Some people from analogous fields may have useful perspectives, and others may represent views that will become relevant in the future.

We should have an interview schedule with which to start, but as the investigation proceeds, we should be prepared to be opportunistic and adapt it to emerging issues. The initial schedule can be based on a literature review. Generally, we should not expect policy makers and individuals who are distant in time and concerns from the technology to have specific knowledge and preferences; the aim of such interviews is to get at underlying predispositions that later on in the analysis phase of the investigation we can use to make appropriate inferences. For a newly emerging technology, it may be desirable to use short scenarios or hypothetical questions to get at these predispositions, but we should be very careful not to put words into the mouth of the informant. In any team effort it is strongly urged that the team be chosen to reflect an interparadigmatic mix rather than merely an intraparadigmatic, albeit multidisciplinary, mix. An example of an interparadigmatic team is an engineer, journalist, lawyer, and businessman. An example of a multidisciplinary, intraparadigmatic team is a systems analyst, an electrical engineer, an economist, and an environmental scientist.

For more on interviewing, see Appendix A.5.

4. Address the Cross-Cuing, Interdependencies, and Prototype Integration of the Perspectives

There is no formula or procedure that guarantees that all interactions are considered or that the perspectives are weighted in integrating them. We are dealing with complex adaptive systems with phases of stability and instability. It is impossible to methodically consider all possible interactions. We recall from our discussion in Section 2.3 that even a stable system of only 10 elements potentially can have over a million pairwise subset relationships, assuming only one relationship between any two subsets. The judgment that is critical in this effort is readily recognized as a basic trait of effective decision makers. They rely heavily on their intuition in cross-cuing and integrating perspectives.

The analyst or planning staff should provide the decision maker with the T, O, and P perspectives and one or more prototype integrations. But the final integration must be the task of the decision maker (as is the final integration of testimonies the task of the jury in a trial).

Cross-cuing recognizes that a technology is always embedded in a social context. The cases mentioned in Table 9.1 all exhibit interactions among perspectives. For example, individuals like Secretary of Transportation Sam Skinner and Governor Roy Romer had to maneuver disparate organizations to get agreement on the Denver Airport (P → O) and organizations like Alyeska and Union Carbide of India failed to deal properly with technical problems (O → T). The use of digraphs (Appendix A.1) may facilitate the cross-cuing process. In particular, it may help bring to the surface feedback loops that are commonly ignored.

Institutions are not isolated in their behavior resulting from technology. They are not closed systems but are open to influences from their environment. What one organization does affects the behavior of another. The various organizations and individuals that make up the social context are bound together by a process of social exchange: states accept federal money for airport development, which then must satisfy certain constraints.

One perspective may shed light on another. For example, the individual's search and need for personal security is reflected in the organization's resistance to change. An organization may, in fact, be organized to maximize the exercise of P perspectives in formulating an O perspective. Corporations that emphasize decentralization (say, autonomy of product teams) and decision making by consensus (say, participative management) consciously strive to create an O perspective that is in harmony with the P perspectives of the employees. The assumption is that such an approach is more attuned to the role of the corporation in the coming decades and, specifically, to deal with complex sociotechnical systems.

There are other facets as well. Under normal conditions, an organizational network has a high degree of stability. However, the network may be confronted with severe external pressures that endanger that stability. Individuals and their P perspectives may assume a critical role when the network breaks down. Max Weber pointed out long ago that charismatic leaders emerge at a time when social organization is undergoing basic change. This is not to say that P perspectives are only important at such junctures, but they may have a profound impact under such conditions. The Great Depression endangered the United States and Germany: one produced Franklin Roosevelt and the other Adolf Hitler. Their P perspectives were exceedingly influential in generating the New Deal and the Third Reich, respectively. Each drastically altered not only the nature of the countries as organizations, but completely changed their O perspectives.

Let us consider the case of the wide-body trijets (L-1011 and DC-10) discussed in Section 5.3. The organizational network included the airlines, aircraft manufacturers, subcontractors, and FAA, for example. Dan Haughton maneuvered his corporation through a crisis only by restabilizing a network of organizations (that is, Rolls-Royce, the airline customers, and the British and U.S. governments) that were ready to break an established set of relations.

In the case of Acousticon (Chapter 5.2), the founders' P perspective had permeated the organization for a long period, shaping an O perspective that made other perspectives favoring an acquisition appear alien or intrusive to the corporate culture.

One of the key tasks in a technology assessment is to identify the combination of external circumstances and internal vulnerabilities that would make a P perspective prevail over an established O perspective, for example, to facilitate implementation of a change and to predict the characteristics of the individual(s) who could effect it.

One practical advantage of the multiple perspective concept not previously stressed is its potential to compress the time for the decision-making process. The simultaneous attention to several perspectives not only facilitates cross-cuing (Section 3.6) but shortens the need for serial consideration of different perspectives. The executive saves considerable time if he can short-circuit the more conventional procedure, that is, ordering a lengthy T perspective analysis, recognizing its limitations, then seeking organizational perspective input, and finally soliciting various individual perspectives. Furthermore, he can thereby reduce the total cost because the T analyst knows that he may concentrate on those aspects that lend themselves to a T perspective and need not worry about the others being pursued in parallel. Thus, none of the perspectives waste time searching for the Holy Grail of comprehensiveness.

5. Beware of Thinking Statically in a Dynamic Environment

In its ideal form, the multiple perspective approach is nonterminating. It recognizes the dynamic and ongoing nature of systems in the real world. Actors, both individual and organizational, come and go. If a decision process is analyzed, we often find that it is sequential, moving through several rounds, and that the actors change from one round to the next (see Appendix A.2). Even if they do not change, their perspective may well change over time. Even traditional operations analysts, such as RAND's Charles Hitch, recognized that every significant problem they tackled had to be redefined once their analysis was under way.

Real-life sequential decision processes can also lead to weaknesses. By changing actors and definitions of the problem across rounds, important feedback and opportunities for cross-cuing may be missed. For instance, a multiple perspective study of the 1980 California Medfly Eradication Program found this to be a serious handicap in the decision process [5].

6. Fit the Medium to the Message, That Is, Fit the Mode of Communication to the Perspective

We have already noted that the means of gathering input for O and P differ strongly from those appropriate for T. Technical reports and group meetings may be routine in technical communications, but they are seriously deficient for O and P. Different perspectives invite different modes of communication.

To communicate the O and P perspectives, consider the use of excerpts or summaries of interviews, oral briefings, scenarios, and vignettes. A talented communicator can also use the P perspective to get all of the perspectives (T, O, and P) across to a wide audience. However, only rarely is this a practical option; outstanding writers are seldom available, and use of media is usually constrained by the project budget. A recent example is Jonathan Harr's bestseller *A Civil Action* on a New England industrial pollution case.

7. Recognize the Political Sensitivity of O and P

Only the T perspective has the luxury of being neutral and politically harmless, but the price is high. It may, by itself, also prove rather useless. The O and P perspectives reflect the realities of human beings, encompassing both the "original sins" of greed, crime, and selfishness, and the "divine touch" of creativity, leadership, and concerted action pro bono publico. Political sensitivity may not arise as a problem in purely technological activities such as systems design, but it is inescapable in strategic planning, decision analysis, issues management, risk analysis, and technology assessment. There are no simple answers; each case has unique aspects. The following are some alternatives that a multiple perspective effort should consider:

- Provide the final output in two (or even three) parts, reflecting different levels or areas of sensitivity (for example, one part the client can distribute widely, another to be held in-house);
- Present each part of the output in two forms: one written, the other oral;
- Use sensitive material implicitly rather than explicitly;
- Substitute quotable references, statements, and examples that communicate the same idea as unquotable ones;
- Transform unquotable material into fictional format, as in the case of George Orwell's *Animal Farm.*

Options such as these may be anathema to the T perspective purist, but they are recognized by every executive and bureaucrat. The naive or careless analyst could conceivably find himself or herself in a difficult position, so legal advice may have to be sought in certain cases.

9.2 Sample Work Plan

The following plan should be clearly understood as an illustrative example, not as a prescription or formal methodology. It must in every case be adapted to specific needs.

1. *Initial problem statement:* Begin with a preliminary problem definition. This will usually be based on a decision that needs to be made or a problem discerned that requires action. The definition will also include preliminary problem boundaries.

2. *Perspective identification:* Identify what appear to be important T, O, and P perspectives. This requires determination of the stakeholder organizations and key individuals who appear to be affected by, or who will affect, the decision or problem.

3. *Initial assessment:* Examine the problem from the point of view of each T, O, and P perspective. This requires technical expertise for T and in-depth interviewing for O and P. Each perspective may see, and thus define, the problem or system differently and may use different assumptions (including assumptions about the other parties at interest) and system boundaries (important factors to include and exclude). Each perspective may favor a means of resolving the problem or prefer a certain decision. Each may have significant input concerning implementation.

4. *Interactions:* Probe the interactions among the perspectives. The procedures outlined in Appendix A.1 may prove useful. It will become apparent what commonalities and conflicts there are in definitions, boundaries, assumptions, preferred decisions, and means of implementation. Search for potential impacts.

5. *Iteration of steps* (1) *to* (4): Retrace the sequence of steps (1) to (4) on the basis of the insights drawn so far. For example, there may be additions or subtractions of stakeholders, changes in definitions, boundaries, and assumptions. It will usually not be possible to resolve major conflicts at this stage. Therefore, this should not be an attempt to develop "final" versions of disputed aspects.

6. *Prototype integration:* Perform a prototype integration and indicate the expected consequences. This is the user's subjective summation and proposed decision or problem resolution and implementation plan. It is analogous to a prosecutor's or defense attorney's summation of a trial to the jury. Also explain the uncertainties and possible subsequent actions to deal with anticipated and unanticipated impacts.

7. *Conference—phase A:* Bring together in a conference representatives of each perspective and review the perpectives and prototype integration to initiate the discussion. If possible, the decision maker should participate in this session. Aim for a new integration based on the discussion.

8. *Conference—phase B:* Develop a base scenario using the new integrated version and reasonable assumptions for its evolution or implementation. Impose possible shocks or surprises on the base scenario and discuss their impacts.

9. *Action proposal:* Construct an action proposal based on the conference evaluations. The proposal should include: what is to be done, when, and by whom. Should there be a test or experimental program? How should progress be monitored? What are milestones for subsequent decisions? How should unanticipated crises be managed?

10. *Communication:* Communicate the output of steps (7) to (9) in a format designed specifically for the decision maker or other client. Keep in mind guideline 6 (Section 9.1) on communication.

Further helpful suggestions are provided in Appendix A.5.

9.3 Coda

We conclude our look at the multiple perspective concept with these thoughts. Paul Feyerabend insists that "the only principle that does not inhibit progress is: anything goes" [6]. Thus he echoes Singer's pragmatism in the use of inquiring systems [7]. He adds that only by going outside the circle of an accepted corpus of theory will its limitations become clear. Hence, a pluralistic approach is seen as essential for the expansion of knowledge. This line of argument suggests that multiple perspectives—specifically T, O, and P—make us see the limitations of any one type. In effect, multiple perspectives offer just that: the advantages of polyocular vision, a perception of the complex system as an integrated whole not possible with any one way of viewing it.

Finally, the reader might recall the "Catch 22" noted in the introduction (Chapter 1): one cannot deal with an interparadigmatic concept using intra-paradigmatic procedures. In concrete terms, we cannot hope to validate hypotheses" such as the correctness of a set of perspectives. After presenting the multiple perspectives, we cautioned ourselves and subsequent researchers not to build a "theory" of multiple perspectives or attempt a "rigorous formalization" of the concept (Section 8.5). It is an appropriate note on which to end. When we see the first set of equations involving perspectives $x_1, \ldots, x_n$ and the first computerized model for weighting or integrating perspectives, we will have come paradoxically full circle—right back to the T perspective.

Acknowledgments

Portions of Section 9.1 reprinted with permission from *The Unbounded Mind: Breaking the Chain of Traditional Business Thinking* by Ian I. Mitroff and Harold A. Linstone by permission of Oxford University Press Inc., 1993; portions of Section 9.2 reprinted with permission from *The Challenge of the 21st Century* by Harold A. Linstone with Ian I. Mitroff by permission of the State University of New York Press, 1994, State University of New York.

References

[1] Umbdenstock, L., "The Perinatal Regionalization Project: A Study in Form and Development," Systems Science Ph.D. Dissertation, Portland State University, Portland, OR, 1981.

[2] Howard, J., "A Woman," *Quest/81,* April 1981, pp. 14–18, 86–87.

[3] Kissinger, H., *The White House Years,* Waltham, MA: Little Brown & Co., 1979.

[4] Meltsner, A. J., *Policy Analysts in the Bureaucracy,* Berkeley, CA: University of California Press, 1976, p. 284.

[5] Lorraine, H., "The California Medfly Eradication Program: An Analysis of Decision Making Under Non-Routine Conditions," *Technological Forecasting and Social Change,* Vol. 40, 1991, pp. 1–32.

[6] Feyerabend, P., *Against Method,* London: Verso Editions, 1978.

[7] Churchman, C. W., *The Design of Inquiring Systems,* New York: Basic Books, 1971.

Appendix

A.1 Interaction Mapping: Digraphs

It is useful to adapt a T-oriented system structuring procedure, directed graphs or "digraphs," to exhibit the relationships among perspectives. The general rules for working with digraphs are as follows.

1. System elements are represented by points or nodes and the relations between them are shown by arrows:

    (a) If an increase in A causes an increase in B and a decrease in A causes a decrease in B, the arrow from A to B carries a plus sign.

    (b) If an increase in A causes a decrease in B and a decrease in A causes an increase in B, the arrow from A to B carries a minus sign.

2. A causal loop denotes a sequence of arrow relationships that ends at the starting node, that is, $A \rightarrow B \rightarrow \ldots \rightarrow A$.

    (a) A loop is positive or impact-amplifying if it has zero or an even number of minus signs.

    (b) A loop is negative or impact-counteracting or damping if it has an odd number of minus signs.

We now consider an application to the interaction among perspectives. An arrow marked plus from T to O_1 means that the T perspective is supportive of O_1; that is, the T analysis presented to the organization favors implementation of the organization's preferred strategy. An arrow marked minus from O_1 to T may signify that it is in the organization's interest to scuttle or discredit the

277

T analysis. An illustration, drawn from the case of the evolution of the M-16 rifle in the U.S. Army (Section 4.1), is shown in Figure A.1. The perspectives are Springfield Arsenal designs (T_1), outsider designs (T_2), Army Ordnance Corps (O_1), Army Caliber Board (O_2), the rifleman/sharpshooter myth (P_1), maverick inventor Spencer (P_2), and President Theodore Roosevelt (P_3).

Army Ordnance created the Springfield Arsenal, and the mutual support relationship is shown by the two arrows connecting O_1 and T_1. The Western rifleman myth strongly influenced O_1 as shown by the plus arrow P_1 to O_1. Outsider Spencer evolved a different technical approach (P_2 to T_2). However, Army Ordnance opposes the outsider (O_1 to T_2). Teddy Roosevelt and the Caliber Board subsequently also supported an outside design (P_2 to T_2, P_3 to T_2). The relation O_1 to O_2 signifies the Chief of Staff's disapproval of the Caliber Board recommendation.

We note that there are four loops in the directed graph:

1. $T_1 + O_1 + T_1$, positive or reinforcing;
2. $T_2 + O_2 + T_2$, positive or reinforcing;
3. $T_2 + O_1 - T_2$, negative or countering;
4. $T_2 + O_1 - O_2 + T_2$, negative or countering.

Because O_1 was far more powerful than O_2, the reinforcing loop $T_1 O_1 T_1$ was the dominant positive effect and T_1, part of one strong positive loop, triumphed over T_2, part of two negative loops and one weak positive loop.

Maruyama offers another application involving multiple perspectives, the role of bribery in socialist or post-socialist countries such as Poland, Russia, Romania, and China. Available goods and services are of poor quality and scarce, so one uses bribery to obtain basic necessities. Bribes may not only be in money but also in goods and services, such as apartments, telephones, university entry,

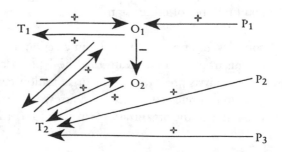

Figure A.1 Example of a digraph of perspectives.

a passport, or information. The system is one of mutual reciprocity and trust, serving as a stabilizing factor in the society [1]. The elements are:

- *Technical:* productivity (P), quality and quantity of products and services (Q), low value of money (L);
- *Organizational/institutional:* planned economy (E), authority to control flow of materials and services (A), shortcut of cumbersome official procedure by bribe (S);
- *Personal/individual:* willingness to work hard (W), bribing by giving things or services (B).

Figure A.2 presents the causal loop diagram. The causal loops are:

1. $W + P + Q - A + B - W$, positive or reinforcing;
2. $E - W - E$, positive or reinforcing;
3. $E + A + B - W - E$, positive or reinforcing;
4. $A + S - P + Q - A$, positive or reinforcing;
5. $W + Q - L + B - W$, positive or reinforcing;
6. $E - P + Q - L + B - W - E$, positive or reinforcing;
7. $W + P + Q - L + B - W$, positive or reinforcing;

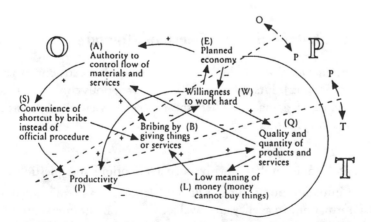

Figure A.2 Interactive causal loop diagram of bribery in Poland, Russia, Romania, and China. [Adapted with permission from "Overcoming the Socialist Aftereffects in East Europe" by Magoroh Maruyama, *Technological Forecasting and Social Change*, Vol. 40, pp. 299, © 1991.]

All loops are reinforcing or "vicious circles." However, changes in any element can begin to turn things around. For example, the shift from a planned economy (E) to a market economy (E*) changes $E - P$ to $E^* + P$ after some time has elapsed. The time lag is due to the need to replace obsolete machines and outmoded management systems.

Similarly, the effect of E* on A and W will face delay. The market economy provides incentives to work hard (W), that is, $E^* + W$, but many workers will initially be unwilling to change their ways and therefore oppose E*, that is, $W - E^*$. Thus, for some time, the new loop (2) will be damping, $E^* + W - E^*$. Later, we expect $E^* + W + E^*$ as the workers see the benefit to them of working hard (more pay) and the reinforcing effect takes hold. It becomes evident that the transition to a free market system must proceed with an appreciation of the dynamics of relationships that derive from different perspectives. Thus, the unique presocialist cultural traditions (O) prove as important as economic theory (T) in effecting a successful transition.

The digraph technique itself reflects the advantages and limitations of the T perspective. The structuring helps to identify, and often uncover, significant neglected feedback relationships. The situation is usually quite complex, and the digraph can serve as a roadmap to the interactions. It can test the effect of policy changes by tracing through the linkages of the roadmap. The disadvantage is that it abstracts and simplifies the interactions. The T-oriented procedure may therefore give a false sense of comprehensiveness and fail to represent the way O and P perspectives "see" the problem.

A.2 Multiattribute/Multiparty Decision Structure

The *multiattribute/multiparty* (MAMP) framework creates a structure to analyze the decision process [2]. First, the parties and their various concerns are identified and depicted in a matrix. Then the process is viewed as consisting of rounds, each having four facets.

1. A problem formulation with stated assumptions and questions;
2. An initiation point, such as an application for a permit, a request for information, an agency approval, or a government intervention;
3. Interaction among the parties, represented by the positions and arguments of the parties;
4. A conclusion, which may be a decision, a stalemate, a change in the focus of the debate, or an exogenous event.

To illustrate the framework, the first round in the LNG facility siting process in West Germany is summarized in Tables A.1 and A.2. In this siting process the parties include the applicant, government agencies (federal, state, local), and a local citizens' group. The concerns: national (need, import policy), regional (for example, industrial development), local (for example, economic benefits, risks to population), and applicant-specific (profit, image, control over sources).

There were four rounds in all, extending to July 1979. The problem formulation, initiation, interactions, and conclusions changed in each round.

The structuring of the decision process clearly helps to understand the perspectives of the actors and their interactions. But it has its limitations. Any structure has the advantage of creating order and the disadvantage of forcing everything into one mold. As one reviewer put it,

Table A.1
First round (of four) in the MAMP framework for LNG facility siting in the
Federal Republic of Germany [1972–July 1976]

I. Problem Formulation

- Assumptions

  (1) Natural gas is an important source of energy and its benefits are generally accepted.

  (2) The possibility exists to import Algerian LNG.

  (3) The site at Wilhelmshaven is an area created to encourage industrial development.

- Question

  Given its feasibility, is the proposed LNG project suitable and desirable for Wilhelmshaven?

II. Initiation

Two companies, Ruhrgas and Gelsenberg announce to Lower Saxony (the state in which Wilhelmshaven is located) their intention to build an LNG terminal (1972). The companies form a subsidiary, DFTG. Wilhelmshaven is considered to be the most appropriate harbor by DFTG and the Lower Saxony Ministry of Economic Affairs and Transportation (ME&T).

III. Interaction

See Table A.2.

IV. Conclusions (1976)

Lower Saxony and Wilhelmshaven commit themselves to support the project at the selected site; the gas companies and DFTG agree on certain conditions (settlement contract).

Table A.2
Interaction

Party	Position	Arguments
DFTG, gas companies	For site at Wilhelmshaven	Need for natural gas, fits regional development plans, technology is safe
Wilhelmshaven	For site at Wilhelmshaven, subject to environmental impact conditions	Contributes to industrial development, safety and high degree of environmental protection have to be ensured
ME&T	For site at Wilhelmshaven subject to conditions on business structure	Beneficial to regional economy, support of gas supply companies in Lower Saxony

you seem to be imprisoned by the notion that all the various partisan participants in problem solving agree, during any one round, on a definition of the problem . . . But it is a common characteristic of interactive problem solving that many, perhaps most, of the participants carry a distinct version of what "the problem" is in their minds . . . They are not working on any one given problem, nor do they think they are [2].

In our terms, MAMP is itself a T-type representation. The implication is that such a structure cannot help but be repressive; it buys structure at a price. One should really seek multiple MAMP versions that reflect the different perspective types.

A.3 Assumptional Analysis

A major source of difficulty in integrating perspectives can be traced to the fact that the different parties make different assumptions about the system or "the real nature of the problem." Then each collects input that confirms its view of the problem and accentuates the differences in the assumptions. We stress that assumptions are the property of the stakeholder, not the property of the problem.

A most helpful step in the integration process is the clarification of the assumptions made by all the parties, in particular, the degree of certainty and the importance attributed to them. We shall use an actual case study undertaken by I. I. Mitroff and and J. Emshoff for a drug company [3].

The problem is as follows. Drug manufacturer McNeil, a subsidiary of Johnson and Johnson, produces a well-known, narcotic-based prescription pain-killer under its brand label. It has suddenly learned that a generic substitute version has appeared on the market at a much lower price.[1] The situation portends a potential catastrophe for McNeil because much of its profit comes from this brand-label drug. Twelve key McNeil executives have been brought together to advise the CEO. The twelve have coalesced into three groups, each favoring a different alternative in pricing the brand-label drug: group A, lower the price; group B, raise the price; group C, no price change.

Group A wants to out-generic the generic version. Group B wants to communicate to the marketplace that it is of far superior quality. It assumes that many people equate price with quality. While groups A and B are oriented to the marketplace, group C presents a different argument: keeping the price unchanged, profits can be raised by cutting internal costs, that is, eliminating the R&D arm of the company.

Each group collects data, reinterpreting data it has in common with the others to back up its case and procuring new data to further strengthen it. The process unconsciously becomes a circular one: each alternative is used to direct its believers to gather data that confirms the validity of that alternative.

Here is where assumptional analysis comes in. There are at least ten parties that have an interest in this problem: Johnson and Johnson, McNeil's management, McNeil's sales force, suppliers, stockholders, customers or patients, the competition, the federal government, pharmacists, and physicians. For example, the government is involved through the Federal Drug Administration and the regulations concerning imports of opiates from foreign countries.

The assumptions with regard to the physician prove to be the most critical. Consider groups A and B. Group A assumes that skyrocketing health care costs are making physicians price-sensitive. They will prescribe the generic drug if it is significantly cheaper. Group B is assuming that physicians are motivated by the traditional model of health care, that is, the well-being of the patient irrespective of cost. Thus, they are assumed to be price-insensitive. Another assumption by group B is that the patient will rely on the doctor and ignore the pharmacist's countersuggestion.

We now determine how the three groups view the stakeholder assumptions along two axes: (x) their importance or criticality and (y) the confidence in their validity. Figure A.3 maps these views and tells us that the assumptions about the physician are both the most important and most uncertain. For group B this means the assumption that the physician is insensitive to price is

---

1. In some states the pharmacist is required to tell the patient coming in to fill a brand-label prescription that there is an available generic version.

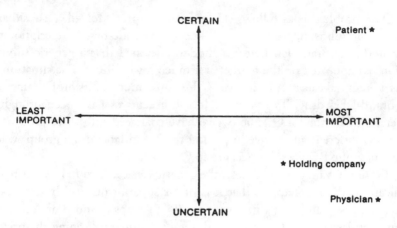

Figure A.3 Assumptions associated with stakeholders.
[Reprinted with permission from *The Unbounded Mind: Breaking the Chains of Traditional Business Thinking* by Ian I. Mitroff and Harold A. Linstone, Oxford University Press, Inc., © 1993, p. 144.]

not only critical but also highly questionable. It now becomes apparent that the data available to the group does not provide any enlightenment about this assumption.

Another party regarding which assumptions are important but uncertain is Johnson and Johnson. Is it more interested in maximizing profits or market share, more profit per drug sold or more volume? Why has McNeil not tried to find out the parent company's goal if it is important to the decision? Possibly the McNeil corporate culture has so far precluded such a step. Figure A.3 also shows that there is little uncertainty about the patient: a low-cost, quality product is desired.

The procedure actually helped the McNeil executives to agree as a whole to try alternative B in selected areas. The price of the drug was raised in test locations, and the results were monitored. It could then be quickly determined whether the market will tolerate the price increase.

A.4 Delphi

The Delphi Method was developed at The RAND Corporation in the 1950s under the auspices of the U.S. Air Force as a technique to apply expert input in a systematic manner using a series of questionnaires with controlled opinion feedback. Its first application to technological forecasting was a 1964 RAND report (Figure A.4) [4].

Delphi is defined by Linstone and Turoff as "a method for structuring a group communication process" [5]. Elsewhere, it is described as a remote structured conferencing procedure. The key features are use of a panel of participants, iteration, feedback, and anonymity. Many variations are possible. The method has become popular in Asia and Europe as well as America, with the largest scale forecasting undertaken by Delphi in Japan. It has become the preferred technique in national foresight projects [6].

Typically, a panel of experts is selected and a first round questionnaire is prepared. If the subject is biotechnology forecasts, the panel might consist of researchers in academe, government, and industry. The first round questionnaire might be transmitted to each participant essentially blank, asking each to list the biotechnology achievements he or she anticipates in, say, the next fifty years. The results are combined into a single new list that is circulated to the panelists as the second round.

Each panelist is now asked to indicate for every item the 50% likelihood year, that is, the year for which the occurrence is as probable to be earlier or later. The results are combined into a new list (the third round) with the group's quartile and median "50% years" indicated for the second round responses, but without participant name identification. For example, achievement A might have been forecast by one-quarter of the participants to have 50% likelihood of occurring by 2005, by half to occur by 2015, and by three quarters to occur by 2030.[2] Each panelist now sees how his first estimate compares with the others', but without knowing who gave which date. If a panelist's second-round response differed markedly from that of the other panelists, he might be asked in the third round to briefly explain the reason for his previous response.

Next, each panelist is asked to re-estimate the 50% year for each item (which may or may not be the same as the estimate given in the previous round). The total number of rounds depends on the variations between rounds. The process should stop when stability is attained, that is, there are no more significant changes. A consensus may or may not develop. The process could, for example, lead to a bell curve distribution or a bipolar distribution. A common misconception is that the process is designed to produce consensus.

---

2. In the case shown in Figure A.4, there were 4 rounds, with 15 responses in the first round, 11 in the second, 18 in the third, and 23 in the fourth. The first round requested each panelist to list "major inventions and scientific breakthroughs in areas of special concern to you that you regard as both urgently needed and feasible within the next 50 years." Collation and paring of responses led to a list of 49 items that were presented to the panel in the second round. Figure A.4 shows for each item the "50% year" response distribution in terms of the quartiles and the median. For example, "chemical control over heredity—molecular biology" produced a median of 1993 and quartiles of 1982 and 2033. Note that "never" is a permissible response year.

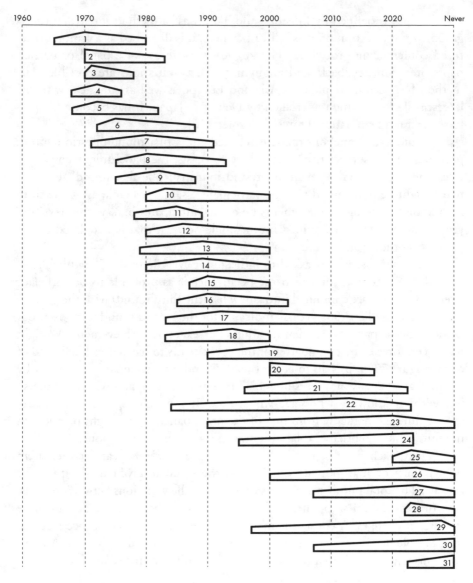

Figure A.4 The RAND Delphi Panel on Scientific Breakthroughs.
[Reprinted with permission from RAND Report P-2982, Report on a Long-Range
Forecasting Study by Ted Gordon and Olaf Helmer, Sept. 1964, © The RAND
Corporation, 1964.]

1. Economically useful desalination of sea water

2. Effective fertility control by oral contraceptive or other simple and inexpensive means

3. Development of new synthetic materials for ultra-light construction

4. Automated language translators

5. New organs through transplanting or prothesis

6. Reliable weather forecasts

7. Operation of a central data storage facility with wide access for general or specialized retrieval

8. Reformation of physical theory, eliminating confusion in quantum-relativity and simplify particle theory

9. Implanted artificial organs made of plastic and electronic components

10. Widespread and socially widely accepted use of nonnarcotic drugs (other than alcohol) for the purpose of producing specific changes in personality characteristics

11. Stimulated emission ("lasers") in X and Gamma ray region of the spectrum

12. Controlled thermo-nuclear power

13. Creation of a primitive form of artificial life (at least in the form of self-replicating molecules)

14. Economically useful exploitation of the ocean bottom through mining (rather than off-shore oil drilling)

15. Feasibility of limited weather control, in the sense of substantially affecting regional weather at acceptable cost

16. Economic feasibility of commercial generation of synthetic protein for food

17. Increase by an order of magnitude in the relative number of psychotic cases amenable to physical or chemical therapy

18. Biochemical general immunization against bacterial and viral diseases

19. Feasibility (not necessarily acceptance) of chemical control over some hereditary defects by modification of genes

20. Economically useful exploitation of the ocean through farming, with the effect of producing at least 20% of the world's food through molecular engineering

21. Biochemicals to stimulate growth of new organs and limbs

22. Feasibility of using drugs to raise level of intelligence (other than as dietary supplements and not in the sense of just temporarily raising the level of apperception)

23. Man-machine symbiosis, enabling man to extend his intelligence by direct electromechanical interaction between his brain and a computing machine

24. Chemical control of the aging process, permitting extension of life span by 50 years

25. Breeding of intelligent animals (apes, cetaceans, etc.) for low-grade labor

26. Two-way communication with extra-terrestrials

27. Economic feasibility of commercial manufacture of many chemical elements from subatomic building blocks

28. Control of gravity through some form of modification of the gravitational field

29. Feasibility of education by direct information recording on the brain

30. Long-duration coma to permit a form of time travel

31. Use of telepathy and ESP in communications

Figure A.4 Continued

The panelists' responses are not constrained to the T perspective.[3] In fact, Delphi can serve as the means to construct a shared reality and thus help to develop a group O perspective [7]. Delphi also proves useful in cross-cuing and

---

3. This accounts for the strident opposition to Delphi by Sackman and some other T-oriented analysts.

integrating multiple perspectives. In this role it complements the digraph approach described previously.

The popularity of Delphi, viewed by some analysts as "a method of last resort," is indicated by the fact that more papers have been devoted to it in the professional journal *Technological Forecasting and Social Change* over the past 30 years than to any other forecasting tool. However, other uses for this communication tool should also be recognized. In the form of a *policy* Delphi, it can bring to the fore the various perspectives and facilitate their circulation among the participants, provided they are selected to sweep in the appropriate T, O, and P perspectives [8]. The Delphi exercise should

- Clarify the perspectives themselves;
- Indicate the most significant conflicts or differences;
- Minimize discrimination in favor of any one view;
- Suggest the rigidity or flexibility of each perspective (by the change or lack of change in later rounds).

In the form of a *decision* Delphi, this procedure can assist in integrating the diverse perspectives into a decision [9]. It is more action oriented than the policy Delphi and may serve as

- A prototype integration of perspectives;
- A means to examine the dynamics of the integration process.

The following example pertains to a multiple perspective study done by Linda Umbdenstock of Perinatal Regionalization in Los Angeles County hospitals. It involved the coordination of institutions giving perinatal care services [10]. This Delphi was initiated following the development of the T, O, and P perspectives; and its aim was to design a regional network organization based on the different perspectives through participative action. The steps in this process follow.

Step 1: Selection of the Delphi participants. The choices were based on (1) criticality of individuals as determined by the O and P perspectives analyses and (2) need for representation from the principal organizational and professional decision-making components. There were doctors, nurses, administrators, and nurse educators; these represented private doctors, public hospitals, private non-profit hospitals, private proprietary hospitals, and Regionalization Project staff. Of 57 invited, 44 actually participated.

Step 2: Introduction to decision Delphi.   A letter from the Regionalization Project Director and personal discussions with the prospective participants introduced the Delphi to them and put everyone "in the same game."

Step 3: The first round.   Four 1985 scenarios were provided to the participants; each described a form of organization for attaining regional perinatal goals. The four are the regional consortium model, Board of Directors model, pyramid model, and free enterprise at work model. A series of questions on specific mechanisms accompanied each scenario. Each participant was asked to choose the one scenario that would suit him most and would constitute a good system. The questions corresponding to that scenario were then to be answered. (Sample: Each hospital or doctor sets its [his] own protocols. Would this mechanism contribute greatly to a good regional organization? [yes, no]; Would this mechanism work very well for you? [yes, no].) Telephone calls reminded the participants to mail back their responses.

Step 4: The second round.   Summaries of the first-round responses were presented. An opportunity for reaffirmation of the participant's round-one choice or a change of mind was provided in the second round. Next, positive and negative factors were to be listed for the preferred scenarios together with tasks for implementation. The results were picked up in person to speed the process.

Step 5: The third round.   Each packet was delivered personally and a pick-up time arranged. Controversial issues drawn from the responses were listed. (Samples: Smaller hospitals have little expertise to offer; a loss of doctor-patient relationship would result from the Board of Directors model.) In each case, the participant checked one of the following: I support greatly, I support some, I don't care, I oppose some, I oppose strongly.

The result of the Delphi was a strong preference for the Board of Directors model. All respondents were willing to participate in some future organization. The process itself confirmed the importance of participatory decision making (even if system resources are hierarchical). However, the transition of an organization to a new form requires leadership for take-off. The lack of this element meant that more interest than energy was generated. Thus, a conclusion focused on the importance of timing of the Delphi. The need to enlarge the imaging power of Delphi as a design process was also recognized.

With regard to anonymity, Rauch finds that it is not desirable in a decision Delphi [9]. A participant is only motivated to take the task seriously if he knows who the other participants are. However, Rauch recommends "quasi-anonymity": the names are known but the statements or responses are still anonymous, that is, not attributable to an individual.

A.5 Additional Guidelines for O and P Development

The following recommendations have been developed by A. J. Meltsner and should be of particular help to T-trained persons not accustomed to dealing with O and P.

A.5.1 Basic Procedure

These guidelines are intended to provide a schematic outline of the activities that are necessary to implement organizational and personal perspectives for the analysis of sociotechnical systems. They are not intended to take the place of the numerous books on qualitative research and elite interviewing.

Prefieldwork

- Read relevant material on the proposed technology, on past but similar technologies, and on the policy processes associated with these past and present technologies.
- Develop a preliminary list or map of the key actors (both individuals and collective or organizational) who have been or might be involved with the proposed technology. One basis for selection is who cares or who has something to gain or lose by the introduction of the technology, and one clue to possible involvement is past involvement.
- Delimit the site or area or scope of investigation on the basis of an issue paper. The point is to have a representative sample of informants but also to recognize the limits of research resources. If need be, delimit the subject technology.

Fieldwork

For the interview process the reader is referred to Section A.5.2.

Analysis

From the typed interviews and other written material analyze the feasibility of the proposed technology. From the organizational perspective determine whether the technology is congruent with the way the present organization functions. Does the technology have to change or does the organization have to alter its tasks and structure? Similarly, for the personal perspective, look to see whether the technology is likely to be adopted by private and public policy makers. If so, which type of individual will push for such adoption and which type of individual will oppose it? Who are enthusiasts? Who has leverage and exercises it? Can alternative implementation paths be defined? Suppose each path is followed to fruition, what then? A typical check list of questions, designed for a technology assessment (TA), is presented in the next section. The material from each perspective should be examined to elicit insights.

A.5.2 On Interviewing

The actual interview can be characterized by the personality and motivation of both the interviewer and the respondent, the physical setting of the interview, and the topic being discussed. Some people are pleasant and helpful as a matter of course; others are just as naturally grumpy and obstructive. One setting can be quiet and conducive to an engaging dialogue, while another can be like being on a rush-hour bus. Some topics are controversial, others barely able to generate a yawn. The analyst must be able to determine quickly the kind of interview it will be and adopt an appropriate strategy. Here is a brief description of some of the types of people you can run into in an interview and some suggestions about how to get the most out of them.

Interviewee Types[4]

The technician. This is the man or woman concerned with details, precision, and accuracy to the point that it borders on being anal compulsive. The stereotype of an engineer is an example of this role. If you are interviewing this person, your major problem is that he spends so much time talking about irrelevant (to you) details that you have a difficult time getting to the larger issues. This is the person who not only cannot see the forest for the trees, he can't see the trees because he's too busy looking at an insect crawling around the bark of one of the trees. If you find yourself, as an interviewer, stuck with this kind of person, you can either cut the interview off as soon as possible or, more usefully, take advantage of the situation to ask him about some issue about which you really do need details, such as the inner workings of a processing plant or the methodology a laboratory assistant follows when he gets a sample of water he has to analyze.

The pretender. This is the person who does not belong where he is. He is pretending to be competent, but it soon becomes obvious to you that he does not know the first thing about the topics you're studying, even though he should know. You have made a mistake interviewing this person. If there's no way to

---

4. Appreciation is expressed to C. Bellavita, who suggested some of these types and developed the images.

use this person, the best thing to do is have a pleasant conversation for a reasonable amount of time and then leave. Don't forget to review the process you used to reach the conclusion that this was a person you ought to interview; you might be able to learn from that.

The busy executive.   This person makes it very clear through his behavior that he has a great deal of work to do, most of it is important, and you're lucky you got an appointment at all. The telephone rings and people walk in and out asking for decisions or audiences. The best thing here is to know what you want to talk about in specifics; don't go on fishing expeditions. Work between the spaces or interruptions. Be prepared to summarize the last answer he gave you, or the last partial answer, when he asks, "Now, where was I?"

The teacher or helper.   This kind of person realizes that you are a "student" in the general sense of the word and enjoys being in the position of someone with superior knowledge. He honestly goes out of his way to be helpful to you by rephrasing your questions or guiding you in certain directions. It is easy to get seduced by this kind of person. He is so helpful and informative that you sometimes leave the interview knowing a lot that you did not know before but knowing little about what you came to get. Because he considered himself a "teacher," he gave you what he thought was "best" for you instead of listening to what it was that you really wanted. On the other hand, he can also point you in a new, unanticipated direction you may find useful.

The protector.   This person is interested in protecting what he has. You have come with a request for information, and he is not sure why you want it. He can be afraid of what you will do with the information, of what your hidden agendas are, or of who put you up to this. He can resent the fact that you are butting your nose into his affairs, that you are questioning his ability to do his job—in a word, he is afraid of you for one or several of many reasons. You can see the signs of this tendency when you arrive at his office; he may be nervous, brusque, quiet, or recalcitrant. He views you as a potential threat. If you do nothing to put him at ease, you are not likely to get much out of the interview. If you can overcome that initial fear, you may end up with some useful information. Most of the time there is little that you can do to overcome the fear that is inside him, whatever manifestation it takes. You need to be extremely tactful.

The boaster.   This person's world revolves around himself. He sees all things in terms of a stage on which he is the true center. He is good for getting negative information about others. It is usually heavily biased, but once you make the proper allowances he may provide some inside information you are not likely to get elsewhere. Frequently this person will also be dissatisfied with the organization, and he is a good source for gossip about other organizations.

The weathervane. This individual's stories change each time you see him. You will get a feeling for today's climate of opinion. The information reflects the individual's high discount rate. The current information may be useful, but interpretation is not.

The counterpuncher. This individual tries to turn the relationship interviewer-interviewee around; that is, he would like to ask, rather than answer, questions. Possible reasons are a wish to cover up, an interest in the interviewer's project, or the desire to find out what others have told the interviewer. Try to determine quickly whether you can get the interview back on track.

The patient on the couch. This interviewee uses the opportunity to unburden himself. You are the psychiatrist/priest and he is the patient/confessor. His own problems may indeed reflect organizational problems; at the other extreme you may only become enlightened about his unhappy family life.

The angel. This person is not common to this planet, at least not that we have discovered. Essentially, this person knows just what you want to find out, gives you the information in such a way that you cannot help but understand it, and can also use it to make pithy and profound empirical generalizations. He also tells you what you did not ask but should have. He is a pleasant conversationalist and devotes the time you ask for directly to you.

Preparation for the Interview

- Read exhaustively but critically whatever field you are exploring. Immerse yourself in the subject matter so that in an interview you can isolate a statement that does not fit and begin to wonder why it does not fit. This is where the pay-offs come, that is, comparing the mismatches and then trying to discover why they exist.

- Get to know roughly as much about the important facts as the people you're talking to and be able to turn those facts this way and that way without the constraints of people who are actually in the institution. By reading and interviewing, eventually you should be able to think like someone actually dealing with the technology and make little fantasy decisions to see how those decisions might change outcomes. It is not only useful but fun to get to that stage.

- Avoid being sponsored by an organizational "has-been" or known troublemaker. However, the has-been himself may be a valuable subject. Often a vice-president is "kicked upstairs" into, say, corporate planning, as a decompression chamber before retirement. Such a person may be relaxed and provide a highly perceptive long-range view of the organization. He can be objective since he is out of the rat race.

- When someone refuses, have a sponsor or friend of interviewee help set up the meeting.

- Avoid complex, detailed explanations about the project; say just enough to get the interview.

- Try to schedule an interview so as to avoid interruption and distraction.

- When asked, state that the length of the interview depends on the interviewee. If pushed, understate the time requirements slightly. Do not give the feeling that the interview will take a great deal of time.

- Do not schedule interviews too closely to try to save time. You need to think and have some unscheduled time as well as travel time.

The Interview—General

- Be punctual.

- Consider using two people to interview a person, either together or separately. This may be important where questions of race, insider-outsider positions, style and personality differences, complementarity, or orientation for the study might prove significant.

- Consider the advantages and limitations of tape recorders carefully. What is very effective with one person can turn another person off. An alternative is to use a tape recorder immediately after the interview while your impressions are fresh.

- Interview all actors in an unstructured manner. Try to get an understanding of what is being said from the actor's own frame of reference. Under no circumstances use the proposed technology as a directing device or as a way of focusing the responses. In the case of the O perspective, try to find out what the particular person does and how that affects the functioning of the organization. In the case of the P perspective, try to elicit the propensity of the actor to support or oppose the proposed technology by ascertaining basic beliefs, values, worldviews, and motivations.

- Follow up clashes of information for interpretation and refinement. Use questions like "On whom do you rely to get _____ done? To get word through?" "Someone mentioned _____: do you agree?"

- Look for phrases like "off the record" or "what you don't understand is _____."

- Play "what if?" This can make the interview particularly useful. The worst that can happen is that the person interviewed will not know how to play this game. He may be so rigid that nothing beyond SOP or business-as-usual has ever come to mind. The best that can happen is that the interviewee will know how to play and will turn up all sorts of impact and policy-related points.

- Always ask a few more questions than you have on the list when an interview starts. During World War II, a CBS correspondent talked with an injured Marine pilot in a hospital for an hour about the details of the pilot's being shot down and parachuting into the water, and as he was leaving he remarked that the pilot seemed rather badly hurt for having been dropped gently into the water by the parachute. It was only then that the pilot thought to mention that his parachute had not opened.

- Do not assume anything and particularly do not worry about asking silly questions. Stop the interview if the person to whom you're talking says something you do not understand. Most people really enjoy talking about things they do and think and, while you will run into someone occasionally who will claim that he thinks the question is foolish or ignorant, most of the time people really want to make things clear and will be patient until they are.

- Do not hesitate to interview someone from whom you anticipate little additional information because an atmosphere of trust can boomerang if certain people feel left out. If someone recommends a number of sources he is sure will be of use, at least one should be contacted to show you do take the whole interview seriously. If a group perceives certain people as key or "important," the credibility of your approach is at stake.

- Be observant to "test" situations. Sensitivity to information that must not be traced may be tried before other information is given to the interviewer. You can get better information only to the extent you have already gotten some good information. Catching on to inside humor is a good test also; it shows what one knows.

- Circulate bits of information that are interesting but will not betray confidences in order to trace communication patterns.

- Select your "targets of interest" carefully. Start with someone with whom you have an "in" with or feel comfortable. Add to or drop from the list as you go along, being sure to maintain a cross section.

- To the degree that interviewing is investigative reporting, it is nothing more than old-fashioned detective work. Put together little scraps of information one piece at a time until things fit together. If one scrap is wrong, nothing will fit. Investigative reporting is commonly seen these days to involve efforts to discover what's wrong, as in "Watergate," but it is as easily applied to discovering what went right or simply what went on.

The O Perspective Interview

- When you're exploring an institution always start at the bottom but keep going until you get to the top. Any situation looks very different to people at all levels of an organization. If you settle for the view from middle management, you will miss even more. Often it is very useful to talk first to someone who has a good overview of the area, a terrain specialist who likes to talk and knows everybody. From this interview refine a list of actors.

- Be sure to get to "front line people" (that is, the workers doing the task) as well as top and middle management in an organization. The comparison allows tracing lags, SOPs, and relationships.

- Be able to recognize "middle level information" and distinguish it from vague generalities, trivia, and petty office intrigues without particular value.

- Try to allow sufficient time for a second pass through the organization and with the informants. One purpose of the second pass is to fill in gaps in understanding, but it is also possible at that time to ask more directed questions dealing with the proposed technology.

- Try to find out what the particular person does and how that affects the functioning of the organization.

- Find the "gatekeepers"—to get in, to know how to get in, and to learn the view of the world from that office. Often those easiest to talk to are now power holders, so the entrance must be achieved step by step.

Sample Starter Question List for a Technology Assessment Using T, O, and P Perspectives

Technology:

- Do *you* really understand the subject technology well?
- How do the technologists see its advantages and disadvantages?
- Read relevant material on the proposed technology, on past but similar technologies, and on the policy process associated with these past and present technologies.
- From typed interviews and other written material analyze the feasibility of the proposed technology.
- Would problems with the subject technology implicate a group or class of technologies?
- What might happen if the technology became very widespread or was vastly scaled up?
- Which seemingly unrelated technologies could have a major impact on the one under assessment?

Physical and environmental settings:

- What are the anticipated beneficial and adverse effects on the environmental and physical environment?
- Are there low probability impacts that would be of large magnitude?
- Are there high-likelihood impacts that are currently assumed to have low magnitude?
- Are there impacts that are difficult or impossible to detect with current sensing or monitoring systems?
- What impacts might be caused by synergism with other technologies?

Sociotechnical setting:

- Who are the likely beneficiaries and victims?
- Develop a preliminary list or map of the key actors (both individuals and collective or organizational) who have been or might be involved with the proposed technology. One basis for selection is who cares or who has something to gain or lose by the introduction of the technology; one clue to possible involvement is past involvement.

- What organizations are "responsible" for monitoring and for regulating the technology?
- What are the appropriate SOPs for each organization?
- How does information flow through each organization?
- How centralized or decentralized is each organization?
- What organizations might become involved if serious problems or alarm developed?
- What are appropriate policies to deal with the technology from a cost-benefit point of view?

Technopersonal:

- What individuals have a strong personal stake in setting the technology and possess power?
- Are there impacts that may galvanize specific individuals to action and, if so, what kind of action?
- How will this technology help or hurt progress toward the career objectives of the key actors?
- Does organization X have to hire or fire people (as a result of the new technology)?
- Whose task is made more difficult or easier by the technology? How?
- Which type of individual is likely to push for adoption and which type of individual will be opposed to it?
- How does the technology change the way you make decisions?
- Which individuals have taken strong public stands regarding the technology?

Organization actors:

- What are the official aims of the organization/group?
- What are the unstated aims of the organization/group?
- Is there a difference in perception between the technologists and organization X regarding the meaning and significance of the technology (for example, due to the technologists confusing peers with clients)?
- How does the technology impact the official aims and the unstated aims?

- Which organizations/groups compete most directly for financial resources with organization/group X?
- What is the most effective way to change SOPs in organization X?
- What does the organization chart look like? How does it differ from the real power structure? Who controls policy?
- What does organization X consider to be the most serious misconception on the part of the technologists?
- What are the organization's vulnerabilities to influence?
- Will or should the SOPs of the organization/group change as a consequence of the new technology?
- Who are this organization's strongest friends and strongest enemies?
- Are there conflicting jurisdictions among regulatory/control agencies?
- What plans do regulatory/control agencies have for monitoring the new technology—continuous, one-shot, periodic?
- When and how are SOPs circumvented in organizations?
- What links exist among research organizations and commercial interests?
- What kind of legal actions have been taken involving the technology?

Individual actors:

- What does the psychological profile of each key actor look like?
- What are the career objectives of each key actor?
- What links exist between "experts" in the field and manufacturers/promoters of new technology—research funding, consulting, and prior jobs, for example?
- What links are there between regulatory actors and manufacturers/promoters?
- What type of individual is likely to support/oppose the technology?
- Who are the "strong" individuals?
- Who is a risk taker? Who is a risk avoider?
- Who is a maverick? How is he faring?
- Who is a long-range thinker (or low discounter)?
- Who is vulnerable to influence?

Political action:

- What strategies and tactics are likely to be tried?
- What coalitions are feasible?
- How do the styles of play of the key actors compare?
- Are issues regarding this technology linked to other political/technological issues?
- How can money be used most effectively to influence policy relating to this technology?
- What tradeoffs are possible to help achieve agreements?

Decisions:

- What are likely/desirable/unlikely/undesirable decisions? Why?
- Are decisions part of organizational politics or ad hoc?
- What decisions have been avoided or neglected and by whom?

Acknowledgments

Appendices A.1 to A.3 reprnited with permission from *The Challenge of the 21st Century* by Harold A. Linstone with Ian I. Mitroff by permission of the State university of New York Press, © 1994, State University of New York.

References

[1] Maruyama, M., "Overcoming the Socialist Aftereffects in East Europe," *Technological Forecasting and Social Change*, Vol. 40, 1991, pp. 297–302.

[2] Kunreuther, H.C., J. Linnerooth, et al., *Risk Analysis and Decision Processes*, Berlin: Springer-Verlag, 1983, pp. 25–30.

[3] Mitroff, I. I., and H. A. Linstone, *The Unbounded Mind: Breaking the Chains of Traditional Business Thinking*, New York: Oxford University Press, 1993, pp. 140–150.

[4] Gordon, T. J., and O. Helmer, "Report on a Long-Range Forecasting Study," RAND Paper P-2982, Santa Monica, CA: The RAND Corporation, 1964.

[5] Linstone, H. A., and M. Turoff, *The Delphi Method*, Reading, MA: Addison-Wesley Publishing Company, 1975.

[6] Grupp, H., and H. A. Linstone, "National Technology Foresight Activities Around the Globe," *Technological Forecasting and Social Change*, Vol. 60, No.1, 1999.

[7] Scheele, D. S., "Reality Construction as a Product of Delphi Iteration," in *The Delphi Method*, H. A. Linstone and M. Turoff, Reading, MA: Addison-Wesley Publishing Company, 1975.

[8] Turoff, M., "The Policy Delphi," in *The Delphi Method*, H. A. Linstone and M. Turoff, Reading, MA: Addison-Wesley Publishing Company, 1975.

[9] Rauch, W., "The Decision Delphi," *Technological Forecasting and Social Change*, Vol. 15, 1979, pp. 159–169.

[10] Umbdenstock, L., "The Perinatal Regionalization Project: A Study in Form and Development," Doctoral Dissertation, Systems Science Doctoral Program, Portland State University, Portland, Oregon, 1981.

About the Author

HAROLD A. LINSTONE is University Professor Emeritus of Systems Science at Portland State University and editor-in-chief of the professional journal *Technological Forecasting and Social Change* since its founding in 1969. He is the author of *Multiple Perspectives for Decision Making* (the first edition of this volume), co-author of *The Unbounded Mind* and *The Challenge of the 21st Century*, as well as co-editor of *The Delphi Method, Technological Substitution,* and *Futures Research: New Directions*. He has 20 years' industrial experience at Hughes Aircraft Company and Lockheed Aircraft Corporation (with the latter as Associate Director of Corporate Development Planning). He has also served as Visiting Scientist at the International Institute for Applied Systems Analysis in Austria and Visiting Professor at the Universities of Rome, Washington, and Kiel. His doctorate is in Mathematics from the University of Southern California.

Index

For further information on these and other Artech House titles, including previously considered out-of-print books now available through our In-Print-Forever® (IPF®) program, contact:

Artech House
685 Canton Street
Norwood, MA 02062
Phone: 781-769-9750
Fax: 781-769-6334
e-mail: artech@artechhouse.com

Artech House
46 Gillingham Street
London SW1V 1AH UK
Phone: +44 (0)171-973-8077
Fax: +44 (0)171-630-0166
e-mail: artech-uk@artechhouse.com

Find us on the World Wide Web at:
www.artechhouse.com